MW01097109

Copyright © 2021-All rights reserved.

No part of this publication may be reproduced, distributed, or transmitted in any form or by any means, including photocopying, recording, or other electronic or mechanical methods, without the prior written permission of the publisher, except in the case of brief quotations embodied in reviews and certain other non-commercial uses permitted by copyright law.

This Book is provided with the sole purpose of providing relevant information on a specific topic for which every reasonable effort has been made to ensure that it is both accurate and reasonable. Nevertheless, by purchasing this Book you consent to the fact that the author, as well as the publisher, are in no way experts on the topics contained herein, regardless of any claims as such that may be made within. It is recommended that you always consult a professional prior to undertaking any of the advice or techniques discussed within.This is a legally binding declaration that is considered both valid and fair by both the Committee of Publishers Association and the American Bar Association and should be considered as legally binding within the United States.

CONTENTS

INTRODUCTION

Imagine your family sitting around a big picnic table, talking and laughing, and enjoying a feast of pulled pork, smoked turkey, twice baked potatoes, grilled fish and chocolate brownies. Now imagine you're not on vacation at a 5-star restaurant, but you're in your own backyard and you've cooked everything on one great appliance.

The Traeger Grill is the one-stop-shop you've been waiting for. Known as the premier wood pellet grill, the Traeger is also of the best smokers and barbeques on the market. It can be used as a smoker, grill and oven, and will quickly become your ultimate favourite appliance.

Barbeque is said to be one of the first methods of cooking – and although the principals of cooking meat over a fire are still the same, the game of barbeque has changed a lot. Traeger entered the scene to take the guesswork out of grilling and smoking, and provide a healthy way for you to enjoy all your favourite meals while using less oil and packing in more flavour.

In this book, we will show you how to not only make your favourite smoked classics – pork shoulder, steaks, fish and vegetables, but we'll also guide you through how to find the best model for you, how to maintain it and how to get the most out of your Traeger. You'll discover how to make a whole smoked turkey, perfect breakfast bacon, cold smoked salmon and yes, even cinnamon buns.

Firstly, we'll tell you all about the art of barbequing, the history of the Traeger and provide you with all kinds of tips on how to make the most of this incredible appliance!

CHAPTER 1 THE BASICS OF TRAEGER GRILL

The History of The Traeger Grill

Joe Traeger invented the first wood pellet grill in Mt. Angel, Oregon, in the early 1980's after becoming increasingly unsatisfied with the grill options on the market. He wasn't a world champion pit master... he was just a regular guy cooking for his family, fed up with the cheap barbeque options that were available to him. The barbeques he was used to had so many flaws. The direct heat directly under the food created 'hot spots' which meant food was often burnt or were left with a chemical taste. He also found that once the barbeque was lit and came up to temperature, there was no way to regulate it. He grew increasingly frustrated and decided he wanted to make something better. The Traeger was born and he never looked back!

By adding wood pellets to the Traeger grill system, he was able to turn his new invention into not only a grill, but a smoker as well. This also eliminated unwanted flames and hot spots, reducing food waste because his dinner was never burnt anymore!

The Traeger Grill has continued to improve since that original version. Often imitated, never duplicated – the original principals of the Traeger still ring true today. Promising to help keep your grilled meats and fish moist and tender, while imparting subtle smoke flavour, the Traeger will deliver! We won't bore you with all the improvements made through a more advanced control system or a state of the art drain system... basically all you need to know is that the current model of the Traeger Grill is as good as it gets on the market. The newest design includes Wi-Fi controls and enables you to see exactly where your grill is hottest to further avoid burning your food. It also includes "Set It And Forget It" features which allow you to monitor your food via an app (WIFIRE technology) so you can add large pieces of meat to your barbeque and let it cook low and slow overnight and wake up to some of the best food you've ever had. We're not saying the Traeger is magic... but it comes pretty darn close!!

We are grateful for all that food that Joe Traeger burned over the years – because without the cheap grills creating hot spots and making him feel fed up, we may not have this amazing appliance today. If you're in the market for a new grill – one that does it all – and you also want to become a master chef in the eyes of your family and friends, the Traeger Grill is right for you. Now that we've told you about the history of the Traeger, we're going to walk you through what makes the Traeger Grill so special, and why you should be so excited to make it your next home appliance!

Why Are Wood Pellets So Great

For a long time, having a barbeque at home meant you had a stainless steel box connected to either your gas line or a propane tank, that works similar to your oven at home – it heats stainless steel rods via a fire in the bottom and then your food cooks on those rods. This is okay for basic cooking, but it doesn't impart any flavour and makes it incredibly easy to burn your food. It is also true than when cooking this way, you need to add lots of oil to your food to prevent it from sticking, thus making what was a healthy dinner of grilled fish and vegetables, less healthy.

In addition, with a traditional grill, there is very little control over what parts of your grill will get the hottest, and virtually impossible to control flare ups of hot spots caused by fat dripping down from the surface to the fire raging below. Even on the lowest setting, it is possible (and even likely) to dry out lean meats using this traditional grill.

If you're someone who had desired real barbeque flavour from your outdoor cooking experience, you may have switched from this outdated model to a charcoal grill... which is one step better but you will still run into the same problems with hot spots and having very little control over the heat distribution within your grill. A charcoal grill does indeed impart the smoky flavour you are craving if you're a barbeque enthusiast but is fairly high maintenance – they take a long time to heat up and then it is very difficult to maintain the same temperature over the course of a few hours. They take constant attention to keep the embers burning and then you have to deal with ash and dirty coals.

If you're someone who doesn't like to create a massive mess to clean up every time you cook, a charcoal barbeque is definitely not for you. But, you might have considered an electric smoker. These are great for keeping mess to a minimum but the flavour you'll achieve with these machines in nothing compared to the real thing. Most electric smokers on the market reach a maximum temperature of 225F which is not nearly enough heat to penetrate past the surface of a large cut of meat. The flavour can also become artificial or even chemical, which will miss the mark if you're trying to achieve true barbeque flavour.

Barbeque purists may take it one step further than coal and decide to burn their own hardwood in these grills. You'll run into similar problems here with making an absolute mess of your outdoor space, but you will also have to deal with fire hazards! It is very hard to control the level of smoke when using raw hardwood and you may end up with a product that is so smoky, it's inedible. You will have to make sure the wood you are using is completely dry (but not too dry,) and that it's not too green. Basically, it's a lot of guesswork. Even if you do get a great log of hardwood, it is difficult or near impossible to maintain the temperature once you hit it, or to control the rate of burning on the wood. You will end up opening the grill a lot, making the temperature fluctuate even more and wasting valuable time and heat.

When wood pellets entered the scene, everything changed for the home grilling enthusiast! A by-product of sawmills, these wood pellets are made from material that would otherwise go to waste (another reason to love Traeger!) The by-product is ground up finely and then sends into a die that forms it into a small puck. There is no need to use glues or chemicals in the manufacturing process, making wood pellets completely natural and chemical free. This is part of the reason they make food taste so good! The only added ingredient in Traeger wood pellets is a food-grade soybean oil, which is used to help form the ground up wood into a puck shape.

These tiny wood pellets burn just like a real log of hardwood but are much cleaner, more predictable and easier to maintain. You will find a variety of wood pellets at your local hardware store or you can order them in bulk online, but basically once you have your bag, you will just empty it into the hopper on the side of your Traeger Grill and away you go! There is no need to soak, stir or mix. The pellets provided by Traeger come in a variety of flavours which we will outline later, but just know that they are specifically designed to work with Traeger grills. They are developed in American mills and designed specifically for a remarkably consistent burn and result in perfect smoked results, every time! No fuss, no mess, just great authentic wood flavour.

How the Traeger Works

Did you know that the Traeger Grill was equipped with the industry's first brushless motor that automatically adds pellets to the fire, completely eliminating the need for guesswork when it comes to grilling and smoking? This D2 Technology uses a variable speed fan and auger to brush pellets into the fire pot where a hot rob ignites them as needed. Not only does your grill maintain its temperature, but it also circulates flavoured smoke throughout the whole grill which means no more hot spots – nothing will ever burn and the entire cooking surface of your food it surrounded by delicious smoke.

Now, the Traeger Grill takes it one step further with the addition of WIFIRE Technology. That's WIFIRE not WIFI! WIFIRE connects to the Traeger App which allows you to see exactly what is going on in your grill without being anywhere near it or lifting the lid. This way, all the heat and smoke stays inside and you can be enjoying lawn games or a dip in the pool while your dinner cooks, without worrying about overcooking or burning. This is most useful when you're slow cooking something but can be used anytime you use your grill. You can turn your grill on using the app and monitor the doneness of whatever you're cooking. This is great for pre-heating the grill and to take any concerns away about overcooking (or undercooking) your food.

The WIFIRE technology along with the D2 technology allows your grill to reach its desired temperature and maintain it, without you lifting a finger. This makes it incredibly easy to grill, smoke and even bake while imparting added flavour from the wood pellets that make the Traeger Grill so special.

Next up, we're going to walk you through all six of the available Traeger grills. You can't go wrong with any of these models, but allow us to tell you a little more about each model in depth so that you can make the best choice possible to suit your specific needs.

Types of Traeger Grills

There are six different models of Traeger to choose from – all of which have their own features and benefits. Which model you choose depends on your budget and amount of space you have in your yard. No matter which model you choose, you are making the right choice when it comes to Traeger!

Traeger Pro Series

There are two grills in the Pro Series: The Traeger Pro 575 Pellet Grill and the Traeger Pro 780 Pellet Grill. Both are budget and space friendly and come in black or bronze. The only difference between these two models is the actual size of the grill itself, but both offer the same great features including a removable grease tray and heat baffle, a double lined bottom grill, and a pellet chute to remove/change your choice of wood pellets.

Both models in the Pro Series are fuelled by an 18lb pellet hopper on the right side of the grill which you load with whatever pellets you want. If you want to change these pellets for a different flavour later, it is as easy as clicking a button on the side of your grill where there is a pellet chute for easy removal. The Pro Series models also feature a thermometer probe that runs through a port on the right side of the grill. Once the grill is lit, you can close the lid and let it come up to temp and the grill will do the rest of the work! Once you've reached your desired temp (between 165F and 450F,) the D2 technology will release the right amount of pellets to maintain the temperature and perfectly cook your food.

This cookbook will explain exactly what time and temperature you'll need for all your favourite recipes, as well as which wood pellets go best with which food.

Which is best – the Traeger Pro 575 or the 780?

The only difference in these two models is size. Both have removable top racks and feature a grease drip tray underneath the unit. The 575 Pellet Grill is great for small spaces and beginner cooks. It has everything you'll need including space for up to 24 burgers or 4 whole chickens! The 780 is slightly larger and cooks 34 burgers or 6 whole chickens… so really it's up to you what you need and have space for. Both are stunning grills with the same great features.

We recommend the Pro Series for smaller backyards/grilling areas, and for those starting out in the world of grilling and smoking. This unit is great for bachelor pads, small families and for entertaining.

If you're an experienced griller or a professional chef, then we'd recommend upgrading to the Ironwood Series for a number of added benefits which you will see outlined below.

Traeger Ironwood Series

There are two grills available in the Ironwood Series as well – again both based on the actual size of the grill. Both grills offer the same great features as the Pro Series including the same D2 technology that automatically releases your wood pellets once the grill reaches the desired temperature. Both Ironwood Series grills also offer WIFIRE technology that allows you to monitor the inside of your grill via the Traeger App, and they both offer the same removable, easy-to-clean drip tray and heat baffle.

What makes the Ironwood Series grills different is the physical size, as well as the added feature of a 20lb pellet hopper. This model also offers a Super Smoke Mode which allows you to control the temperature and flow of the actual smoke inside your grill as well. This allows you to have a *light* smoke flavour on things like fish or vegetables, or a heavier smoke on things like brisket or pork chops. The smoke ranges from 165F to 225F. When using the higher smoke settings, the Ironwood Series models feature a downdraft exhaust feature that forces air through the rear end of the grill before it exits the grill, which means whatever food you are smoking will be surrounded with smoke flavour for the entire cooking process, not just when the smoke is first burning. This is not only what makes the Traeger so different than other smoker/grills on the market, but also what makes the Ironwood models such a great investment if you're someone who loves smoked food.

Another great feature on the Ironwood Series is the 'Keep Warm' feature. This is especially great for entertaining – when you've spent all day cooking beautiful food, you can keep it just the right temperature without losing moisture or going dry, by using the 'Keep Warm' feature.

Lastly, because the Ironwood Series grills are larger than the Pro Series, there are actually two separate cooking racks which offer more versatility. The top rack is great for lighter smoked items that you want to cook slowly, and the bottom grate can be used as either a grill or can be raised to achieve a light smoke as well. If you're not using the bottom grate and are cooking something on the top rack for a long time, we recommend adding a pan of water to the bottom rack to add even more moisture to whatever you're cooking. This is something you won't find on the Pro Series.

Which is best – the Traeger Ironwood 650 or 885?

Again, the only difference in these two models is size. Both have the feature of two rack spaces allowing you to cook and grill over a variety of surfaces, or add a water pan for added moisture to your slow cooked food. Both feature that 'Keep Warm' setting, which make this the perfect model for more experienced chefs who do a lot of entertaining.

The Ironwood 650 can hold 8 chickens of 5 racks of ribs, so it is definitely a great size for party planning... but the 885 takes it one step further and can hold 10 chickens and even 9 pork roasts. Both models come in black and will look great on your patio!

If you're interested in the Ironwood Series and want to take your smoking and grilling one step further, there is one more model we'd like to share with you which you can read about below.

Traeger Timberline Series

There are two types of Timberline Series models – both are super grills with all the bells and whistles! They both feature a 24 lb hopper which means you can load your grill with enough wood pellets to smoke everything you want overnight. A full hopper (1 bag of wood pellets) can actually power your grill on low for 20 whole hours. Both models also have an added feature where there is a sensor in the belly of the grill that will warn you if your pellets are getting too low. This has basically made the art of smoking foolproof!

The Timberline Series will reach a maximum temperature of 500F and uses the same D2 technology as every other model. Once your grill reaches the desired set temp, the grill will transport the right amount of pellets onto the rod, slowly releasing smoke into your closed grill, flavouring whatever food you are cooking with subtle, delicious smoke.

What makes the Timberline Series model a super grill is the added feature of an induction fan that basically turns your grill into a convection oven! This feature rolls smoke over your food before exiting the grill's rear vent which means no matter what you're cooking or how many times you lift the lid, your grill will maintain the perfect temperature and will always end up with delicious, moist food. The lid of this model is actually an airtight gasket, along with the double wall stainless steel interior, this grill is basically better than your oven! You will find with the Timberline model, you can use your grill to make anything you can make in your oven including pastries, bread and delicate cakes.

Which is best – the Traeger Timberline 850 or 1300?

The Traeger Timberline 850 is a fantastic grill for luxury homes and anyone looking to add a grill, smoker and convection oven to their outdoor kitchen collection. The 850 model will fit 8 full racks of ribs and includes extra durable stainless steel rods which are fully removable for easy cleaning.

The Timberline 1300 is our most elite model of grill and you won't find a bigger, better model on the market! This is for serious cooks and anyone who loves to entertain. This model includes three racks which combine to provide 1300 square inches of cooking surface. The lowest rack is great for quick high temperature cooking, which we will outline in the rest of this book. The middle rack is great and can fit 12 whole chickens! The upper rack is also removable or can be used for those delicate, slow cooked items. Either way, this grill is going to yield you incredible results, especially when paired with the recipes in this book.

Which grill should I purchase?

As outlined above – any Traeger grill you buy is going to help you create exceptional smoked and grilled food for you and your family or guests. The model you choose will be based on your space and your budget. All the recipes in this book can be cooked on any of the models listed above; however the Timberline model is going to work best for any baked goods or breads, due to the True Convection capabilities. The Pro Series is great for basic grilling and smoking, and the Ironwood will uplift your grilling capabilities from novice or pro chef!

Once you have purchased your Traeger, the first step will be unboxing and assembling your grill. Decide where is the best place for your grill by deciding how far you want to walk from your kitchen area to your serving area. You will also want to make sure your grill is protected from harsh wind areas, and if you have an area that is covered but ventilated, even better! Your grill will last longer if it is protected from the elements – you can purchase our winter cover but placing it out of the elements is also a great idea. You can find lots of videos on how to assemble your grill online, and of course follow the comprehensive user manual that comes with your grill. Now is also a great time to download the Traeger app and connect to WIFIRE. Lastly, you will want to calibrate your pellet sensor and get it set up so you will know exactly when to refill your hopper.

CHAPTER 2 ONCE YOU HAVE RECEIVED THE TRAEGER

Here, we've listed a few things that will make your grilling experience more enjoyable. These are just suggestions of course – once you have your Traeger grill up and running, your entire cooking experience will improve. These suggestions are just icing on the (grilled) cake!

Accessories

The Traeger Grill Brush – While most grill brushes are made of stainless steel, the Traeger grill brush is made of a slab of polished wood, with teeth on the end to get into every nook and cranny of your grill. The reason for this is primarily for safety – although convenience and speed is also a factor. A steel brush may lose pieces of steel which may go into your food if they're not caught, which can be a hazard for your health. With wood, there is no worry.

Along with the grill brush, we also recommend the *Traeger All-Natural Grill Cleaner* which allows you to clean your grill like the pros, without the chemicals.

Extra Racks – These are a great idea if you decide to add extra vegetables or smaller items to your grill. Narrow grill racks make it easy to grill things like asparagus, shrimp and anything that is small that you don't want to skewer. We've provided heaps of recipes for this, but having the extra thin rack will make this easier.

Burger Irons – The hardest part of making great burgers is the fact that they shrink a lot when cooking. With the Traeger Burger Iron, you can flatten your burger patty part way through the cooking process making for the prefect size burger for your bun. This also makes the cooking process faster when it is thin and even, ensuring your burgers are never, ever dry.

Grilling Tongs, Shears, Flipper and Basting Brush – These tools are all optional of course, but they will make your grilling experience more fun... and will make you feel like a real pro! Since Traeger makes everything of such great quality, if you're going to purchase any of these tools, we recommend getting them from Traeger.com!

Instructions

Seasoning

Seasoning is an important first step of grill ownership. This will ensure that your grill is in the perfect state for grilling, smoking, roasting or baking. Seasoning helps lock in the non-stick coating meaning you can use less oil when cooking, and it also makes cleaning your grill easier. This is an important step that takes about 1 hour and should not be skipped.

To season your grill, follow these steps the *first time* you use your Traeger:

Step 1 – Add wood pellets of your choice to the auger at the side of your grill

Step 2 – Plug in the grill and turn the main power switch to "On"

Step 3 – Turn the dial to "Select Auger" and choose "Prime Auger." The pellets will now fall into the fire pot. Once they have all left the Auger and into the fire pot, select "Done"

Step 4 – Turn the dial to 350F and press the dial in to activate

Step 5 – Press "Ignite" and close the lid of your grill. Wait and allow the temperature to come up to 350F. Let it run at 350F for 20 minutes.

Step 6 – Next, raise the temperature dial to 450F and let it run for an additional 30 minutes.

Step 7 – Shut down your grill. This varies by model but will be clear in the user manual for your model.

Once the shutdown of your grill is complete, your grill is fully seasoned and ready to go!

Starting Up Your Grill

There are two main options for using your Traeger Grill – it is important to know the difference as it will affect the end product and your cooking experience as a whole. If you do not follow these steps, your cooking experience may result in temperature fluctuations, flames and other issues.

Both methods result in delicious, moist food that will be subtly flavoured with the smoke flavour of your choice. You can refer to the Traeger website if you are unsure of which process is best for you.

The Closed Lid Start-Up Process

This method is super simple! When you've found a recipe you want to cook, simply turn on your grill and select your desired temperature. Let the grill preheat while keeping the lid completely closed for about 15 minutes. This will allow smoke to build in the grill. During this time is a great time to get your ingredients ready – this includes patting meat dry, seasoning vegetables or draining marinade from whatever you are cooking.

The Open Lid Start-Up Process

With this method, you will turn on your grill with the lid open. Wait for about 5 minutes and let the fire start before setting the smoke setting. Next, you'll close the lid and set the temperature waiting for 15 minutes or so for it to come up to temperature. Once you add your food to the grill, you will close the grill and them allow for smoke to build up inside.

A Note About Preheating

Preheating your Traeger grill will take some time, especially with the Timberline models which are larger and therefore take longer to preheat. This is of the same importance as preheating your oven when you are baking bread, so it's a step that should not be skipped. Make sure you leave extra time when planning your meal, to allow your grill to come up to temperature (usually 15-20 minutes.) You can use this cookbook as a guide for how long the cooking process will take, but make sure you account for the preheating time!

Shut Down Your Grill

This grill will take longer to fully shutdown that your average barbeque, because they wood pellets have to burn out and because of the double lined walls of the grill, it maintains its heat for quite a long time. Each model is equipped with a special timer, so you will know exactly how long it will take for your grill to completely shut down. This is important not only for safety, but also so you know when you can add the recommended cover to your grill (when it's cooled completely.)

Cleaning

Because you are not dealing with charcoal or hardwood soot or embers, cleaning your Traeger is incredibly easy. Just like any barbeque, you can simply brush the racks of your grill with a brush or grill brick after each use. Traeger takes it one step further by making all the racks removable, so you could also opt to soak them in hot, soapy water to give them a deep clean. One of the best features of the Traeger Grill is that all the racks come out, which makes it super easy to clean the whole interior – a shop vac will do the trick in a jiffy!

The removable, sloped drip tray included on every Traeger model means that any grease will be collected, which will save on cleaning. You can simple remove this tray and empty it into the garbage or garden, and start fresh each time you cook. (You can also purchase removable drip tray liners direct from Traeger which mitigate some of the messiness of cleaning your drip tray!)

With the Timberline model of grill, the remnants in the grease tray are actually heated gently and the vapours mix with the smoke, further flavouring and moistening whatever it is that you're cooking.

Traeger also offers a wooden grill brush in their accessory shop that makes every day cleaning of your grill easy and safe.

Basically, your Traeger is an investment. Just like you love your car, you will love your grill, and you will want to keep it clean and give it some extra TLC every once in a while. We recommend deep cleaning your Traeger once a year (spring cleaning time!) and covering it when not in use to protect from the elements. This will help you keep your Traeger in tip top condition for years!

Make the Most of Traeger Grill

Know Your Wood

There are many different types of wood pellets to air with your Traeger grill. We recommend purchasing Traeger brand pellets for your grill. These pellets were designed specifically for your grill and will yield the absolute best results!

Once you have your wood pellets, it really is as easy as pouring them into the auger on the side of your grill and letting them do the rest of the work!

Flavours of wood pellets range, and this cookbook can help you decide which flavour is best for you, but as a general rule of thumb, apple, cherry and maple chips are milder in smoke flavour and add a hint of sweetness and earthy tones to your recipes. Other mild wood flavours include: alder, apricot, chestnut, mulberry, nectarine, pear and plum. For a more medium flavoured smoke we recommend almond, lemon, oak, orange or peach. Each of these pellets will add nutty or even citrus notes to your food and burn a little more heavily than the milder flavours mentioned above. Lastly, for a robust smoke, you'll want to select a hickory, mesquite or walnut wood.

Traeger also offers a variety of mixed pellets which offer a stunning harmony of flavour! *Traeger's Signature Blend* is of course our favourite – it's a mixture of cherry, hickory and maple… which is a truly amazing blend for all classic barbequed foods. Another great blend is the *Oak and Alder* – this one is particularly great for subtle flavours like seafood and desserts. There's also *A Kiss of Summer* which has a hint of lemon zest and is made from alder and maple – it's said to go great with lobster tails! If you're looking for something bolder, try *Bold To The Bone* for pork or brisket. For the wine lover in your family, there's a special *Winemaker's Blend* that imparts a sweet and spicy aromatic to vegetables or meats. And lastly, there's a *Cherry Mesquite* which is great for smoked desserts because of the sweetness it adds to the grill!

No matter what wood pellets you buy, we recommend storing them in their original, sealed bags. You want to keep these pellets in a dry place and out of direct sunlight which can dry them out and make them burn more quickly than desired. In a dark, dry place and in a sealed bag, your pellets will last indefinitely.

You can do your own experimenting with what wood flavours work best for you. We've outlined what we have found works best in these recipes, and please note if you do decided to choose a different wood, it could change the outcome of the recipe… or maybe you'll create something magical! Just be aware of what wood you're using and use the rules of thumb provided in this recipe book as your guide.

Know Your Meat

This book includes a variety of recipes to cook everything from whole poultry to chicken breasts and thighs, to all varieties of pork, different types of steaks and whole racks of ribs, to more delicate cuts like rack of lamb... the options really are endless for your Traeger grill. You can of course also grill the basic items you're used to throwing on the barbeque including burgers and sausages. You can also cook fish and seafood, your favourite vegetables and even bread or baked goods on this awesome, versatile appliance.

The outside of your recipe will start with the quality of the ingredients you choose, so starting with a butcher shop or grocer you trust is a great place to begin! Look for good marbling in your steaks, pork and chicken that is a light pink colour and firm texture. Make sure the fish or seafood you purchase is as fresh as possible or cook it from frozen. Remember that the larger the cut of meat, the longer you will need to cook it. Fast provides deeper flavour in your meat, but you can also cook very lean cuts of meat on your Traeger with great success. It is important to remember that leaner cuts of meat tend to need less time cooking, as they will dry out more easily without the fat content – this is why fattier, larger cuts of meat can be left on the grill longer and cook more slowly.

If you're unsure of what type of meat to buy, we recommend talking to your butcher as they will love to help! Using this cookbook as a guide is a great way to make the most of your cooking experience!

Your Traeger grill has many features to help cook meat as successfully as possible, but just like everything in life it takes a little TLC to be successful. While Traeger does offer the "Set It And Forget It" feature and the convenient WIFIRE app to help make sure your food is never overcooked, if you stray too far from these guidelines or the recipes in this book, you could end up with dried out or overcooked meat. By following the recipes in this book and by reading up on your Traeger before you start cooking, you will reduce the chances of overcooking or undercooking your food on your new grill!

Again – that rule of thumb is: Fat Equals Flavour – look for good marbling in your meats and if you're choosing a very lean meat or fish, it is best to cook on higher heat for less time. If you've got a large cut of meat with lots of fat, you can use the lower cooking settings and 'Set It And Forget It.'

Flavouring Your Food

Everyone knows how delicious a dry rub is on a rack of ribs, or how great a sweet and salty marinade can be on chicken thighs. Cooking with your Traeger grill is no different! The only difference is that you can cook without herbs and spices or marinades if you're looking for a straight smoke flavour, but this book does provide a number of recipes for delicious marinades and spice blends.

You really can't go wrong with dry spices – just buy them from a reputable grocer to make sure you're getting freshest option out there. If you aren't getting huge flavour from your dried spices, you can heat them up gently in a pan before adding them to your meat to help release some of the oils that create flavour.

When using herbs, fresh is also best! Look for vibrant, fresh looking herbs that have great flavour by simply rubbing the leaves together. These can be added at the beginning, middle or end of cooking – just follow the recipes outlined in this book for the best advice.

Grill Set Up

Okay, so you've got your grill set up and seasoned. You've got your recipe ready to go and your wood pellets loaded. Now it's time to get cooking!

Traeger offers a number of great accessories to make this easier including tongs, oven mitts, pans and extra racks. The most important thing to know though is the placement of your ingredients for maximum quality and ease of cooking. You may be used to shifting meat around on your grill top, finding hot spots and 'cold zones'... but with your Traeger, you no longer have to worry about that! In fact, it works a lot better if you set the meat on the grill, close the lid and walk away for the cooking process. This book will provide great tips on how to cook the best chicken, steak and pork chop, as well as how to make the most of vegetables, fish and seafood. No matter what you are cooking, with the Traeger Grill, you are working with pre-set levels of heat and smoke, taking out any guesswork with your grilling experience. Simply place your ingredients in the center of the grill and work outwards from the center – the more delicate ingredients can fan out closer to the outsides. The only decision you'll need to make is if you have the Ironwood or Timberline, and you'll need to pick which rack to cook on. Again, this book will provide solid advice and instruction on this for easy cooking and awesome results every time!

The Final Ingredient–Temperature
Your Traeger is a master at maintaining temperature, and this cookbook will help you decide exactly which temperature is best based on what you are cooking and what the desired results are.
Understanding how temperature affects food is the best way to achieve the best results. Low temperatures are used for larger cuts of meat with lots of fat – the low heat slowly breaks down the collagen and fat in the meat making it flavourful, tender and moist. This is especially great for things like brisket, pork roasts and pulled meats. For leaner cuts of meat like chicken, fish or lamb, a long, slow cooking process will effectively turn your meat into jerky! A good way to prevent drying out is to use the recipes and guidelines in this book, and to do some research before you start cooking. Also, using a water pan with the Ironwood and Timberline models is another great way to impart an added layer of moisture to the process.
Using the lower rack of the grill and high heat for a short period of time is a great way to grill lean meats like chicken, turkey, burgers or fish. They will still achieve a smoky flavour because of the circulatory nature of the Traeger so not to worry! You can also turn off the smoking feature and set your grill to a set temperature and use it as effectively as an oven when making things like pastries or breads. We've included some recipes for these items near the end of this book and invite you to try them!

Cold Smoking VS. Hot Smoking
Cold smoking differs from regular or hot smoking because the food you're cooking is imparted with smoke flavour but isn't fully cooked in the process. This is achieved by keeping the temperature in the smoking chamber at a low temperature (68F – 85F) and cooked for a long, long time. Generally, something that is cold smoked is cured first, to reduce the risk of spoilage during the cold smoking process. This is a popular way to smoke fish (cured first and then smoked, or just cold smoked) to maintain moisture and flavour of the fish. This can also be used to smoke cheese and other dairy products including yogurt, and for vegetables that you want to leave crunchy. Cold smoking is also the preferred method for smoking liquids such as alcohol for cocktails... but why stop there? Why not try cold smoking juice or coffee?! (We've provided a few smoked drink recipes to help get you started!)
Cold smoking is made possible with the Traeger using a few helpful tips! You can add a tray of ice to the bottom rack of your Ironwood or Timberline model, and keep replenishing it to maintain moisture and a cool temperate throughout the process, but you can also just set the temperature to low and place your cured ingredients in the middle of the grill.

With hot smoking, the temperature is set higher so that the food cooks while it is smoking. This is great for larger cuts of meat, especially when the smoker is set between 225-275. Most of the recipes in this book use the method of hot smoking, but we have provided some tips and recipes for cold smoking as well.

Smoke-Roasting

When you use your Traeger grill at higher temperatures, you will reach a process that is actually known as Smoke Roasting. This is similar to searing in that you get a browned exterior on the outside of your meat or vegetables, but unlike with stovetop cooking or traditional barbequing, you will also achieve a smoky flavour. This is the principal reason Joe Traeger invented the Traeger grill and we think you will find that smoke roasting offers the best of all worlds when it comes to flavouring your food!

With the Traeger grill, you can also *reverse sear* your food. This is a relatively new concept which we've outlined thoroughly in the steak chapter of this book. Reverse searing is when you slow cook your food first and allow it to fully cook and then crank up the temperature and allow it to sear. This sealed in flavours and juices and allows you to achieve perfect doneness and a delicious, crusty, caramelized sear on whatever you're cooking. Cue the drool!

In conclusion, temperature is very important to the smoking process! Follow the guidelines laid out in this book and remember the basic temperature settings:

65-85F is for cold smoking

Up to 275F is for regular smoking

275F and higher is for searing a.k.a Smoke Roasting

Smoking Tips

This book will provide loads of tips for you to add plenty of smoked food to your diet. The main thing to remember is that the smoke flavour should be *subtle.* The Traeger makes this incredibly easy, by adding just the right amount of wood pellets to the heating elements, and the fact that the air is constantly circulating makes it foolproof.

We recommend smoking fish on the top rack of your Traeger at a lower temperature. The flesh of fish is delicate and lean, but unlike leaner meats (where higher temperatures are recommended for a shorter period of time) with fish we recommend a lower heat. Salmon and trout work great as they have higher fat content, but with white fish or seafood, you will want to make sure you are using gentle heat for a medium length of time.

With very high fat items such as bacon, we recommend using a cold smoke for a longer period of time. With a hot smoke on these items, too much of the fat will melt away causing shrinkage and a dry product. Although you can use hot smoke for things like pork belly, we've provided recipes using cold smoke for these high far items.

The more you cook with your smoker, the more experienced you will become and the more comfortable you will be when it comes to knowing the temperatures and timing of your favourite foods. In the meantime, we've provided loads of recipes and tips in this book!

Grilling Tips

In this book you will find a plethora of recipes for all your favourite grilled recipes including burgers, sausages, hot dogs, steaks, pork chops, chicken breast and more. You'll also find recipes for vegetables, tofu, seafood, fish and even baked goods. Anything you can make on your stovetop or in the oven, you can make on your Traeger, so we've added all kinds of different recipes including grilled pizza and even fruit! No matter what you're grilling, you'll find it here.

When you start using your Traeger grill, you will find that grilling is actually a lot easier on this appliance than any grill you've used before. You may be tempted to move your meats around the top of the grill to find the hot spots and cold spots, but once you get rolling with the Traeger, you will begin to discover that this is not necessary.

But utilizing the pro tips we've outlined in this book and by following the recipes as well as caring for your Traeger, you will become a grill master in no time!

Baking Tips

When using the convection features of your Traeger, you will be able to use your oven less and less, and you will want to once you discover how wonderful and easy it is to bake on your Traeger.

We recommend starting with *cold* ingredients when you start baking. This will help to keep pie crusts and cookies crisp on the outside and soft on the inside – to achieve this it's best if your grill is preheated and you add your product to the inside of the "oven" while it is cold. This means if you make a pie for example, you may want to chill it before you cook it. Same goes for cookies, breads and other pastries. We have found that this yields the absolute best results, but feel free to play around with it!

A Note About Winter Grilling

One last note about your Traeger – if you live somewhere that has harsh winters, and you are worried about missing your Traeger during that time, fear no more!!

Unlike most grills that are unable to operate in the winter months, the Traeger is functional even in the harshest winter conditions. This is due to a few reasons. First, the double walled stainless steel body of your grill maintains temperature so well; it also shields the inside of your grill from freezing in the winter.

Grilling in the winter is for serious grillers – it takes a little extra work, but imagine this: You clear a path to your grill and brush the snow off the cover. You uncover the grill and preheat it to 350F. This may take a little longer but it will be well worth it! You add a pork shoulder to the grill which you've already dry rubbed and set your timer for 12 hours. The next morning, you wake up and have delicious pulled pork to serve with your cozy winter breakfast of eggs and toast... what a treat!

We've added a few other winter inspired recipes for you folks up north, and we know you'll appreciate them as much as we enjoyed writing them!

Pantry Essentials

Barbeque Sauce – A great barbeque sauce is of the keys to great barbeque food! This is totally up to your own tastes, but definitely look for one that is tangy and slightly sweet... and if you like smoke, look for one with hickory or added smoky flavour. You can use barbeque sauce to baste meat while it's cooking, or serve it afterwards with grilled chicken or pork.

You can find a variety of Traeger brand sauces and marinades online and we also provide some recipes to make your own in this book. Our favourites are the *Traeger Apricot Barbeque Sauce* (goes great with anything smoked using Peach pellets!) *Traeger Sugar Lips Glaze* goes great on chicken or fish.

Rubs - Rubs are a great substitute for a marinade because they don't burn when you are cooking something for a long time. Sometimes the sugar in a marinade will go bitter, but with a rub, you can penetrate the surface of your meat with flavour, without worrying about the burn. Traeger has some great rubs online for everything from prime rib to fish. They've got a great coffee rub and also include things like turkey brine kits. Check it out!

Lemons – Acidity is an important ingredient in most marinades because it helps break down meat proteins therefore making it more tender. Adding a squeeze of lemon to fish or seafood while it is cooking or just before it's done is a great way to add a burst of freshness and flavour.

Salt – Salting meat (especially) is a very important step. Our chefs at Traeger always, ALWAYS have salt on hand for prepping their ingredients, as well as salting during and after the cooking process. With cured foods for cold smoking, you'll want to ease up on the salt as the curing ingredients do contain a lot of salt already. But for large cuts of meat, salting them is very important!

Also adding a dash of salt to meat after its sliced/ready to serve is a great way to wow your guests and act like a real, pro chef!

Oil and Fats – With the Traeger Grill's non stick stainless steel grill racks, you will find you don't need to use much oil at all, but for foods that don't contain a lot of fat like fish or chicken, adding a brushing of good quality oil or spray is a great idea! We like to keep olive oil on hand for drizzling over lean meats and fish after cooking and a good grape seed or canola oil for brushing before we grill.

Explore Your Traeger

Now that you've read up on all things Traeger, you are finally ready to start exploring!

Remember that your Traeger is for more than just smoking and grilling – with the ease of a button (as easy as turning on your oven) you can use this appliance to bake, roast and braise. You can also use it to deep fry, slow cook and steam. Basically, if you can dream it, the Traeger can do it!

Grilling For Every Occasion

In this book, we've provided recipes for every occasion we can think of – to help you be able to spend more time doing the things that matter! From roasted root vegetables at Thanksgiving, to a whole brined turkey... from Hot Toddy's to turkey gravy. From Super bowl Sunday cheese fondue, to loaded baked buffalo chicken dip. From Irish soda bread on St. Patrick's Day to a smoked Margarita on Cinco De Mayo. From short rib chilli to maple bacon doughnuts...

And this cookbook isn't just for special occasions... it also suits every dietary restriction and diet out there! In fact, adding more grilled food to your diet is an excellent, easy way to follow a paleo or keto diet, and it's also great for low-fat diets if you are concerned about added oils to your food. Basically, this book (and this grill!) is for everyone!

The Art Of Barbeque

The art of barbequing goes as far back as cooking does – some might say that barbeque was the first method of cooking – developed by cavemen when they discovered fire! Since then, barbeque has become a staple in many cultures, and loved worldwide. With the invention of the electric smoker and the propane barbeque, it has become accessible for every home to have an affordable, easy-to-use grill in their backyards.

Barbeque is now a very important part of American culture and it is said that the founding fathers of America were huge barbeque fans, especially George Washington. Barbeque plays an especially large role in Southern American culture where it is prized for bringing bold flavours, rich sauces and age old techniques. People in the South loved it so much, they began having competitions around who made the best barbequed food which has led to a multibillion dollar industry. "Pit Masters" from all over the world join competitions every summer to show why their smoked and grilled food is the ultimate.

Barbeque food isn't just popular in the Western world though. In Japanese and Korean cultures, grilling is a communal affair with restaurants and homes sporting portable table-top grills for everyone to grill their own meat and fish as they dine. Yakitori restaurants have become so popular they've even arrived in North America! Quick grilling and barbequing is here to stay... and now you can bring it to your own home with the Traeger Grill!

One Last Thing
No matter what way you look at it, barbeque is loved around the world, and now it is going to be enjoyed and mastered in *your* home.
We think the reason barbeque culture has spread so quickly and lasted for so long, is because part of the art of barbeque is the art of *sharing* food. A large piece of smoked meat and a platter of grilled vegetables is the perfect food to serve to just about anyone. A smoked fish alongside some great appetizers, or even something as simple as hamburgers and hot dogs, or a grilled cheese sandwich... Barbeque means family! And this barbeque is going to give you more time with your family with its D2 technology, WIFIRE app and "Set It And Forget It" features. Long gone are the days of you babysitting your grill, waiting patiently for your food to cook while dancing it around the grill looking for the best spot. Long gone are the days of flavourless, bland steaks or overcooked chicken breast. Long gone are the days of missing out on time at your own pool party so that you can carefully watch the shrimp skewers. Everything is made easy with the Traeger grill, and your life is promised to improve!
We hope this book provides you with lots of great ideas! Rain or shine, sunny days or in-for-the-winter, any day is a great day to get out there and grill. Your Traeger can help you live a healthier, simpler lifestyle and help give you some of your time back. And remember, barbeque is about family.... So get out there and cook something great!

Troubleshooting
Your WIFIRE app will have some helpful tips when it comes to troubleshooting your Traeger, and you can also refer to your user manual. There are however a few things that could come up which we will cover here:
What do I do if my Traeger Grill won't start?
First, check to see if your grill is in "Demo" mode. The controller will quickly reboot and should turn on after that. If that is unsuccessful, check to see if the fan is running. DO NOT TOUCH anything inside the grill especially the Hot Rod. Just listen closely to see if the fan is running when you turn the grill on. If it's not, it could be a pellet jam.
What do I do if the pellets are not moving though?
A pellet jam is a common problem with a simple solution. Simply flush the pellets through the auger. You can check to make sure your pellets are in good condition – if they have been in the auger for a long time in the elements, they may have become dry or brittle. They should ideally have a nice sheen to them and have a "snap" if you break one. If this is not the case, we recommend starting with new, fresh wood pellets. This will help reduce the chances of them jamming in the auger.
What do I do if my grill is not maintaining smoke or temperature?
If there is too much smoke coming from your grill, this could be a similar problem with the pellets. Make sure they are fresh, shiny and have a nice break to them. If they are very dry or damp at all, they will smoke a lot and not produce an even temperature.
If there is a build-up of grease in the trap or if it is overflowing, or if you have not cleaned your grill in a long time, there could be blockages around the fan which would result in uneven smoke,

or a failure to distribute heat. This is also a simple fix by emptying the grease trap and giving your grill a good, deep clean and making sure the fan is running properly.

What do I do if my grill catches fire?

Of course, with any heating element, there is always the risk of fire and flames. The Traeger grill has many safety ratings because of its specific design, but there could always be things that come up. The most common reason a fire would start is if the grease tray had not been emptied and it came into contact with the flame. This is unlikely, but it is possible, so it's a good idea to make sure you empty and clean the grease tray regularly.

These are the most common problems you might encounter with your Traeger. Most have quick and easy solutions and will be mitigated with proper seasoning and regular cleaning of your grill. For any other problems that arise, please contact your Traeger dealership or customer service through the website immediately.

CHAPTER 3 TOP 10 RECIPES

3-2-1 Grilled BBQ Ribs

Prep time: 15 minutes | Cook time: 6 hours | Serves 6

$1/_3$ cup yellow mustard
½ cup apple juice, divided, plus more as needed
1 tablespoon Worcestershire sauce
2 rack baby back pork ribs, membrane removed
Traeger Pork &Poultry Rub, to taste
½ cup dark brown sugar
⅓ cup honey, warmed
1 cup Traeger 'Que BBQ sauce

1.   Stir together the mustard, ¼ cup of apple juice, and Worcestershire sauce in a small bowl. Spread the mustard mixture thinly on both sides of the ribs and season to taste with Traeger Pork & Poultry Rub.
2.   When ready to cook, set Traeger temperature to 180ºF (82ºC) and preheat, lid closed for 15 minutes. Smoke the ribs for 3 hours, meat-side up.
3.   Once complete, transfer the ribs to a rimmed baking sheet and increase the grill temperature to 225ºF (107ºC).
4.   Tear off four long sheets of heavy-duty aluminum foil. Top with a rack of ribs and pull up the sides to keep the liquid enclosed. Scatter the rack with half the brown sugar, then top with half the honey and half the remaining apple juice. If you want more tender ribs, you can use a bit more apple juice. Lay another piece of foil on top and tightly crimp the edges so there is no leakage. Repeat with the remaining rack of ribs.
5.   Return the foiled ribs to the grill and cook for another 2 hours.
6.   Remove the foil from the ribs and brush the ribs with Traeger 'Que Sauce on both sides. Discard the foil.
7.   Place the ribs directly on the grill and continue to grill for 30 to 60 minutes more, or until the sauce has tightened.
8.   Allow the ribs to cool for 5 to 10 minutes and serve.

Traeger Smoked Pulled Pork

Prep time: 10 minutes | Cook time: 9 hours | Serves 8

1 (6- to 9-pound / 2.7- to 4.1-kg) bone-in pork shoulder, trimmed
Traeger Big Game Rub, as needed
2 cup apple cider
Traeger 'Que BBQ sauce, to taste

1.   Season the pork butt generously with Traeger Big Game Rub on all sides and allow to sit for 20 minutes.
2.   When ready to cook, set Traeger temperature to 250ºF (121ºC) and preheat, lid closed for 15 minutes.
3.   Arrange the pork butt, fat-side up, directly on the grill and cook for about 3 to 5 hours, or until the internal temperature registers 160ºF (71ºC).
4.   Remove the pork butt from the grill.
5.   Stack 4 large pieces of aluminum foil on top of each other on a large baking sheet, ensuring they are wide enough to wrap the pork butt entirely on all sides. If not, overlap the foil pieces to create a wider base. Put the pork butt in the center on the aluminum foil, then bring up the sides of the foil a little bit before pouring the apple cider on top of the pork butt. Wrap the foil tightly around the pork butt, ensuring the cider does not escape.
6.   Return the foil-wrapped pork butt, fat-side up, to the grill and cook for about 3 to 4 hours, or until a meat thermometer inserted in the thickest part of the meat reaches 204ºF (96ºC). The cooking time depends on the size of the pork butt.
7.   Remove the pork butt from the grill. Let rest for 45 minutes in the foil packet.
8.   Remove the pork from the foil and pour off any excess liquid into a fat separator.
9.   Put the pork butt in a large dish and shred the meat, removing and discarding the bone and any excess fat. Add separated liquid back into pork and season with additional Traeger Big Game Rub to taste. Optionally, add Traeger 'Que BBQ Sauce or your favorite BBQ sauce to taste. Serve immediately.

Easy Baked Potatoes

Prep time: 15 minutes | Cook time: 1 hours | Serves 4

6 russet potatoes, scrubbed and dried
3 tablespoons canola oil
1 tablespoon kosher salt
Optional Toppings:
Butter
Sour cream
Bacon bits
Cheddar cheese
Fresh chives

1.   Place the potatoes in a large bowl and coat with the canola oil, then season with salt.
2.   When ready to cook, set Traeger temperature to 450ºF (232ºC) and preheat, lid closed for 15 minutes.
3.   Arrange the potatoes directly on the grill and bake until fork-tender, about 30 to 40 minutes. Serve the potatoes hot with the toppings, if desired.

Traeger Prime Rib Roast

Prep time: 5 minutes | Cook time: 4 hours | Serves 8
1 (5- to 7-bone) prime rib roast
Traeger Prime Rib Rub, as needed
1.   Generously season the roast with the Traeger Prime Rib Rub on all sides and wrap in plastic wrap. Place in the refrigerator for 24 hours.
2.   When ready to cook, set Traeger temperature to 500ºF (260ºC) and preheat, lid closed for 15 minutes.
3.   Put the prime rib, fat-side up, directly on the grill and cook for 30 minutes.
4.   When done, reduce the grill temperature to 300ºF (149ºC). Continue to cook for 3 to 4 hours or until cooked to the desired internal temperature, 120ºF (49ºC) for rare, 130ºF (54ºC) for medium rare, 140ºF (60ºC) for medium or 150ºF (66ºC) for well done. The cooking time depends on the size of your roast and desired finished temperature.
5.   Remove the roast from the grill and cool for 30 minutes before carving.

Beer Can Whole Chicken

Prep time: 5 minutes | Cook time: 1 hour | Serves 4
5 pounds (2.3 kg) whole chicken
Traeger Chicken Rub, as needed
1 can beer
1.   Tuck the wing tips back and truss the chicken legs together. Generously season the whole chicken, including the cavity, with Traeger Chicken Rub.
2.   Place the chicken onto the open can of beer so that the chicken is sitting upright with the can in its cavity.
3.   When ready to cook, set the Traeger to 350ºF (177ºC) and preheat, lid closed for 15 minutes.
4.   Put the chicken on a sheet tray and place directly on the grill. Cook for 60 to 75 minutes or until a meat thermometer inserted in the thickest part of the breast reaches 165ºF (74ºC).
5.   Remove the chicken from the grill and allow to cool for 5 to 10 minutes before serving.

Smoked Marinated Pork Tenderloins

Prep time: 5 minutes | Cook time: 3 hours | Serves 4
Marinade:
½ cup apple juice
¼ cup brown sugar
3 tablespoons Traeger Pork & Poultry Rub
3 tablespoons honey, warmed
2 tablespoons thyme leaves
½ tablespoon black pepper
Pork:
2 (1½-pound / 680-g) pork tenderloins, silver skin removed
1.   In a large bowl, whisk all the ingredients for the marinade to combine. Add the pork tenderloins, turning to coat well on all sides. Cover the bowl with plastic wrap. Let marinate for 2 to 3 hours in the refrigerator.
2.   When ready to cook, set Traeger temperature to 225ºF (107ºC) and preheat, lid closed for 15 minutes. For optimal flavor, use Super Smoke if available.
3.   Put the marinated pork tenderloins directly on the grill and smoke for about 2½ to 3 hours, or until the internal temperature 145ºF (63ºC) on a meat thermometer.
4.   Remove the pork from the grill and cool for 5 minutes before slicing and serving.

Traeger Brisket

Prep time: 20 minutes | Cook time: 9 hours | Serves 8
1 (12- to 14-pound / 5.4- to 6.4-kg) whole packer brisket, trimmed
Traeger Beef Rub, as needed
1.   Lightly season the brisket with Traeger Beef Rub and wrap in plastic wrap. Allow to sit for 12 to 24 hours in the refrigerator.
2.   When ready to cook, set Traeger temperature to 225ºF (107ºC) and preheat, lid closed for 15 minutes.
3.   Remove the brisket from plastic wrap and place fat-side down on the grill. Cook for 6 hours until the internal temperature reaches 160ºF (71ºC) on a meat thermometer.
4.   Remove the brisket from the grill and wrap in a double layer of foil.
5.   Return the foiled brisket to the grill and cook for another 3 to 4 hours, or until the meat registers a finished internal temperature of 204ºF (96ºC).
6.   Let the brisket sit in the foil for at least 30 minutes before slicing and serving.

Smoked Traeger Brisket

Prep time: 15 minutes | Cook time: 12 hours | Serves 6

1 tablespoon Worcestershire sauce
1 teaspoon Traeger Blackened Saskatchewan Rub
1 teaspoon Traeger Chicken Rub
1 tablespoon Traeger Beef Rub
1 (4- to 6-pound / 1.8- to 2.7-kg) flat cut brisket
1 cup beef broth

1. Whisk together the Worcestershire sauce and Traeger rubs in a bowl. Rub this mixture into the meat.
2. When ready to cook, set Traeger temperature to 180ºF (82ºC) and preheat, lid closed for 15 minutes. For optimal flavor, use Super Smoke if available.
3. Put the brisket on the grill and cook for about 5 to 7 hours, or until the internal temperature of the meat reaches 160ºF (71ºC).
4. Remove the brisket from the grill and wrap in a double layer of foil, then add the beef broth to the foil packet.
5. Return the foiled brisket to the grill. Increase the temperature to 225ºF (107ºC) and cook for an additional 4 to 5 hours, or until the internal temperature of the meat reaches 204ºF (96ºC).
6. Remove the brisket from the grill and cool for at least 30 minutes before slicing and serving.

Glazed Meatloaf

Prep time: 15 minutes | Cook time: 2 hours | Serves 6

1 cup milk
1 cup bread crumbs
2 tablespoons chopped onion
2 teaspoons salt
½ teaspoon ground sage
2 egg, beaten
2 pounds (907 g) ground beef
¼ pound (113 g) ground sausage
Glaze:
½ cup apple juice
1 cup Traeger 'Que BBQ sauce

1. Stir together the milk, bread crumbs, onion, salt, and sage in a large bowl. Pour in the beaten eggs. Fold in the ground beef and sausage and stir until well incorporated. Shape the mixture into a loaf, packing tightly.
2. When ready to cook, set Traeger temperature to 225ºF (107ºC) and preheat, lid closed for 15 minutes. For optimal flavor, use Super Smoke if available.
3. Transfer the meatloaf to a wire rack and place on the grill. Cook until it reaches an internal temperature of 160ºF (71ºC), about 2 hours.
4. Meanwhile, whisk the glaze ingredients to combine in a small bowl. Glaze the meatloaf during the last 20 minutes of cooking.
5. Allow the meatloaf to sit for 5 minutes and slice to serve.

BBQ Brisket Burnt Ends

Prep time: 10 minutes | Cook time: 9 hours | Serves 6

12 ounces (340 g) Traeger Texas Spicy BBQ Sauce
2 cup beef broth
1 (4- to 6-pound / 1.8- to 2.7-kg) point cut brisket, trimmed
Traeger Beef Rub, as needed

1. Whisk the sauce and broth together in a small bowl and set aside. Season the brisket generously with Traeger Beef Rub.
2. When ready to cook, set Traeger temperature to 250ºF (121ºC) and preheat, lid closed for 15 minutes.
3. Put the brisket on the grill and cook for about 6 to 7 hours, or until the internal temperature reaches 190ºF (88ºC).
4. Remove the brisket from the grill and cut into 1-inch cubes. Toss the brisket cubes with sauce mixture in a pan, then cover with aluminum foil.
5. Place the pan on the grill and cook for 1 hour.
6. Stir the burnt ends and cook for another 1 hour. Serve hot.

CHAPTER 4 RUB, SAUCES, AND SEASONING

Homemade Chicken Rub

Prep time: 10 minute | Cook time: 0 minute | Makes 1/4 cup

2 tablespoons packed light brown sugar
1½ teaspoons coarse kosher salt
1¼ teaspoons garlic powder
½ teaspoon onion powder
½ teaspoon freshly ground black pepper
½ teaspoon ground chipotle chile pepper
½ teaspoon smoked paprika
¼ teaspoon dried oregano leaves
¼ teaspoon mustard powder
¼ teaspoon cayenne pepper

1.　　In a small airtight container or zip-top bag, combine the brown sugar, salt, garlic powder, onion powder, black pepper, chipotle pepper, paprika, oregano, mustard, and cayenne.
2.　　Close the container and shake to mix. Unused rub will keep in an airtight container for months.

Garlicky Dill Seafood Rub

Prep time: 5 minutes | Cook time: 0 minute | Makes 5 tablespoons

2 tablespoons coarse kosher salt
2 tablespoons dried dill weed
1 tablespoon garlic powder
1½ teaspoons lemon pepper

1.　　In a small airtight container or zip-top bag, combine the salt, dill, garlic powder, and lemon pepper.
2.　　Close the container and shake to mix. Unused rub will keep in an airtight container for months.

Classic Cajun Rub

Prep time: 10 minute | Cook time: 0 minute | Makes 3 tablespoons

1 teaspoon freshly ground black pepper
1 teaspoon onion powder
1 teaspoon coarse kosher salt
1 teaspoon garlic powder
1 teaspoon sweet paprika
½ teaspoon cayenne pepper
½ teaspoon red pepper flakes
½ teaspoon dried oregano leaves
½ teaspoon dried thyme
½ teaspoon smoked paprika

1.　　In a small airtight container or zip-top bag, combine the black pepper, onion powder, salt, garlic powder, sweet paprika, cayenne, red pepper flakes, oregano, thyme, and smoked paprika.
2.　　Close the container and shake to mix. Unused rub will keep in an airtight container for months.

Simple Espresso Brisket Rub

Prep time: 10 minute | Cook time: 0 minute | Makes ½ cup

3 tablespoons coarse kosher salt
2 tablespoons ground espresso coffee
2 tablespoons freshly ground black pepper
1 tablespoon garlic powder
1 tablespoon light brown sugar
1½ teaspoons dried minced onion
1 teaspoon ground cumin

1.　　In a small airtight container or zip-top bag, combine the salt, espresso, black pepper, garlic powder, brown sugar, minced onion, and cumin.
2.　　Close the container and shake to mix. Unused rub will keep in an airtight container for months.

Brown Sugar Rub

Prep time: 10 minute | Cook time: 0 minute | Makes ¼ cup

2 tablespoons light brown sugar
1 teaspoon coarse kosher salt
1 teaspoon garlic powder
1 teaspoon onion powder
1 teaspoon sweet paprika
½ teaspoon freshly ground black pepper
½ teaspoon cayenne pepper
½ teaspoon dried oregano leaves
¼ teaspoon smoked paprika

1.　　In a small airtight container or zip-top bag, combine the brown sugar, salt, garlic powder, onion powder, sweet paprika, black pepper, cayenne, oregano, and smoked paprika.
2.　　Close the container and shake to mix. Unused rub will keep in an airtight container for months.

Easy All-Purpose Dry Rub

Prep time: 10 minute | Cook time: 0 minute | Makes 2 and ½ cups

½ cup paprika, or ⅓ cup smoked paprika
¼ cup kosher salt
¼ cup freshly ground black pepper
¼ cup brown sugar
¼ cup chile powder
3 tablespoons ground cumin

2 tablespoons ground coriander
1 tablespoon cayenne pepper, or to taste
1.   Combine all ingredients in a bowl and mix well with a fork to break up the sugar and combine the spices. Mixture will keep in an airtight container, out of the light, for a few months.

California Beef Rub

Prep time: 10 minute | Cook time: 0 minute | Makes ⅓ cups

2 tablespoons finely ground coffee
1½ tablespoons kosher salt
1½ tablespoons granulated garlic
1 heaping teaspoon black pepper
1 tablespoon brown sugar
¼ teaspoon cayenne pepper
¼ teaspoon ground cloves
¼ teaspoon cinnamon
1.   Combine all ingredients in a bowl and mix well with a fork to break up the sugar and combine the spices. Mixture will keep in an airtight container, out of the light, for a few months.

Sweet-Spicy Cinnamon Rub

Prep time: 10 minute | Cook time: 0 minute | Makes ¼ cups

2 tablespoons light brown sugar
1 teaspoon coarse kosher salt
1 teaspoon garlic powder
1 teaspoon onion powder
1 teaspoon sweet paprika
½ teaspoon freshly ground black pepper
½ teaspoon cayenne pepper
½ teaspoon dried oregano leaves
½ teaspoon ground ginger
½ teaspoon ground cumin
¼ teaspoon smoked paprika
¼ teaspoon ground cinnamon
¼ teaspoon ground coriander
¼ teaspoon chili powder
1.   In a small airtight container or zip-top bag, combine the brown sugar, salt, garlic powder, onion powder, sweet paprika, black pepper, cayenne, oregano, ginger, cumin, smoked paprika, cinnamon, coriander, and chili powder.
2.   Close the container and shake to mix. Unused rub will keep in an airtight container for months.

Spicy Coffee Rub

Prep time: 5 minutes | Cook time: 0 minute | Makes 1 cups

¼ cup finely ground dark-roast coffee
¼ cup ancho chile powder

¼ cup dark brown sugar, tightly packed
2 tablespoons smoked paprika
2 tablespoons kosher salt
1 tablespoon ground cumin
1.   In a small bowl, mix all the ingredients thoroughly, massaging the mixture with your fingers to break down the dark brown sugar into fine crystals.
2.   Liberally sprinkle a thin layer of the rub onto the steak, then pat it in with your fingers so it adheres.

Fast Cumin Salt

Prep time: 5 minutes | Cook time: 0 minute | Makes ¼ cups

1 teaspoon cumin seeds
¼ cup medium-coarse or flaky sea salt
Pinch red pepper flakes (optional)
Pinch cayenne or hot paprika (optional)
1.   Toast cumin seeds in a dry skillet over medium-high heat until fragrant and lightly colored, about 1 minute.
2.   Grind very coarsely in a mortar or spice mill.
3.   Combine in a bowl with salt and stir together.
4.   Add red pepper flakes or cayenne, if using.

Burger Seasoning

Prep time: 10 minute | Cook time: 0 minute | Makes 2 tablespoons

1 teaspoon coarse kosher salt
1 teaspoon garlic powder
1 teaspoon dried minced onion
1 teaspoon onion powder
½ teaspoon sweet paprika
¼ teaspoon mustard powder
¼ teaspoon celery seed
1 teaspoon freshly ground black pepper
1.   In a small airtight container or zip-top bag, combine the salt, garlic powder, minced onion, onion powder, black pepper, sweet paprika, mustard powder, and celery seed.
2.   Close the container and shake to mix. Unused burger shake will keep in an airtight container for months.

Simple Jerk Seasoning

Prep time: 10 minute | Cook time: 0 minute | Makes ¼ cup

1 tablespoon allspice berries
¼ teaspoon nutmeg pieces (crack a whole nutmeg with a hammer)
1 teaspoon black peppercorns
2 teaspoons dried thyme

1 teaspoon cayenne, or to taste
1 tablespoon paprika
1 tablespoon sugar
1 tablespoon salt
2 teaspoons minced garlic
2 teaspoons minced ginger (or 2 teaspoons ground ginger)
1.   Put allspice, nutmeg, peppercorns and thyme in a spice or coffee grinder and grind to a fine powder.
2.   Mix in remaining ingredients and use immediately. To use later, omit garlic and ginger and store in a tightly covered container; add garlic and ginger immediately before using.

Rosemary Lamb Seasoning

Prep time: 5 minutes | Cook time: 0 minute | Makes 2 tablespoons
2 teaspoons dried rosemary leaves
2 teaspoons coarse kosher salt
1 teaspoon garlic powder
1 teaspoon freshly ground black pepper
½ teaspoon onion powder
½ teaspoon dried minced onion
1.   In a small airtight container or zip-top bag, combine the rosemary, salt, garlic powder, black pepper, onion powder, and minced onion.
2.   Close the container and shake to mix. Unused seasoning will keep in an airtight container for months.

Classic Tea Injectable

Prep time: 10 minute | Cook time: 0 minute | Makes 2 cups
¼ cup favorite spice rub or shake
2 cups water
1.   Place the rub in a standard paper coffee filter and tie it up with kitchen string to seal.
2.   In a small pot over high heat, bring the water to a boil.
3.   Drop the filter into the boiling water and remove the pot from the heat. Let it steep for 30 minute.
4.   Remove and discard the filter. Discard any unused tea after injecting the meat.

Buttered Garlicky Injectable

Prep time: 5 minutes | Cook time: 0 minute | Makes 2 cups
16 tablespoons (2 sticks) salted butter
2 tablespoons salt
1½ tablespoons garlic powder

1.   Use this injectable quickly and clean up with hot water. Because butter solidifies so quickly, it can easily clog your injector.

Herbed Compound Butter

Prep time: 10 minute | Cook time: 0 minute | Makes ½ cup
8 tablespoons unsalted butter
1 tablespoon herb leaves, minced
1 small shallot, peeled and minced
2 teaspoons freshly squeezed lemon or lime juice
Splash Champagne or white-wine vinegar
1.   Put the butter on a cutting board and, using a fork, cut the other ingredients into it until the butter is creamy and smooth. Scrape the butter together with a chef's knife, and form it into a rough log. If making ahead of time, roll it tightly in a sheet of plastic wrap and refrigerate or freeze until ready to use.

Homemade Lobster Butter

Prep time: 5 minutes | Cook time: 40 minute | Makes ½ cup
Shells of cooked lobsters, crushed into small pieces
8 tablespoons (1 stick) unsalted butter per lobster
1.   Heat grill to 300ºF (149ºC). Put lobster shells on the largest sheet pan you can fit in the oven, and allow them to dry and roast, about 15 to 20 minute. Remove and set aside.
2.   Meanwhile, melt 1 stick butter per lobster in a large bowl or double boiler set over simmering water, making sure bowl does not touch the surface of water. Add lobster shells to the melted butter and simmer gently, without boiling, for about 20 minute.
3.   Strain the melted butter through a cheesecloth-lined sieve into another bowl, then set that bowl into ice to chill. Cover bowl and refrigerate to set, then skim off the top and discard any liquids. Use within a few days, or freeze for up to a few weeks.

Teriyaki Marinade

Prep time: 5 minutes | Cook time: 0 minute | Makes 1 cup
¼ cup water
¼ cup soy sauce
¼ cup packed light brown sugar
¼cup Worcestershire sauce
2 garlic cloves, sliced
1.   In a small bowl, whisk the water, soy sauce, brown sugar, Worcestershire sauce, and garlic until combined. Refrigerate any unused marinade in an airtight container for 2 or 3 days.

Classic Italian Marinade

Prep time: 15 minutes | Cook time: 0 minute | Makes 1 cup

1 cup extra-virgin olive oil
¾ cup red wine vinegar
Zest of 1 lemon
¼ cup freshly squeezed lemon juice (about 2 lemons)
4 cloves garlic, peeled, smashed and roughly chopped
1 bay leaf
1 tablespoon thyme leaves
1 tablespoon oregano leaves
1 tablespoon basil leaves, rolled and chopped into chiffonade
1 teaspoon granulated sugar
1 teaspoon kosher salt
1 teaspoon freshly cracked black pepper
1 teaspoon red pepper flakes, or to taste

1.   Whisk together all the ingredients in a large bowl. Refrigerate any unused marinade in an airtight container for 2 or 3 days.

Asian Chili Tofu Marinade

Prep time: 10 minute | Cook time: 0 minute | Makes ½ cup

¼ cup soy sauce
1 tablespoon rice vinegar
1 teaspoon brown sugar
2 tablespoons mirin (sweet Japanese rice wine)
1 to 2 garlic cloves, to taste, minced or puréed
1 tablespoon minced or grated fresh ginger
1 teaspoon Asian chili paste or cayenne to taste
2 tablespoons dark sesame oil

1.   Whisk together all of the ingredients in a bowl. Use as a marinade and/or dipping sauce for pan-seared, grilled or plain tofu.

Turkey Brine

Prep time: 5 minutes | Cook time: 0 minute | Makes 1 brine

2 gallons water
2 cups coarse kosher salt
2 cups packed light brown sugar

1.   In a clean 5-gallon bucket, stir together the water, salt, and brown sugar until the salt and sugar dissolve completely.

Lemony Butter Mop for Seafood

Prep time: 5 minutes | Cook time: 2 minutes | Makes 1½ cups

8 tablespoons (1 stick) butter
Juice of 1 small lemon
1 tablespoon fine salt
1½ teaspoons garlic powder
1½ teaspoons dried dill weed

1.   In a small skillet over medium heat, melt the butter.
2.   Stir in the lemon juice, salt, garlic powder, and dill, stirring until well mixed. Use immediately.

Worcestershire Spritz

Prep time: 5 minutes | Cook time: 0 minute | Makes 1 cup

½ cup water
½ cup Worcestershire sauce
2 garlic cloves, sliced

1.   In a small bowl, stir together the water, Worcestershire sauce, and garlic until mixed.
2.   Transfer to a spray bottle for spritzing. Refrigerate any unused spritz for up to 3 days and use for all kinds of meats.

Barbecue Sauce

Prep time: 10 minute | Cook time: 30 minute | Makes 3 cups

1 small onion, finely chopped
2 garlic cloves, finely minced
2 cups ketchup
1 cup water
½ cup molasses
½ cup apple cider vinegar
5 tablespoons granulated sugar
5 tablespoons light brown sugar
1 tablespoon Worcestershire sauce
1 tablespoon freshly squeezed lemon juice
2 teaspoons liquid smoke
1½ teaspoons freshly ground black pepper
1 tablespoon yellow mustard

1.   On the stovetop, in a saucepan over medium heat, combine the onion, garlic, ketchup, water, molasses, apple cider vinegar, granulated sugar, brown sugar, Worcestershire sauce, lemon juice, liquid smoke, black pepper, and mustard. Bring to a boil, then reduce the heat to low and simmer for 30 minute, straining out any bigger chunks, if desired.
2.   Let the sauce cool completely, then transfer to an airtight container and refrigerate for up to 2 weeks, or use a canning process to store for longer.

Carolina Barbecue Sauce

Prep time: 5 minutes | Cook time: 0 minute | Makes 1 cup

½ cup white vinegar
½ cup cider vinegar
½ tablespoon sugar
½ tablespoon crushed red pepper flakes
½ tablespoon Tabasco sauce
Salt and freshly cracked black pepper, to taste

1. Whisk ingredients together in a bowl. Drizzle on barbecued meat. Covered, sauce will keep about 2 months.

White Barbecue Sauce

Prep time: 5 minutes | Cook time: 0 minute | Makes 3 cups

1½ cups mayonnaise
⅓ cup plus 2 tablespoons apple-cider vinegar
2 tablespoons lemon juice
2 tablespoons prepared horseradish
1 teaspoon mustard powder
Kosher salt and freshly ground black pepper, to taste
Cayenne pepper, to taste

1. Combine the mayonnaise, vinegar, lemon juice, horseradish and mustard powder in a medium nonreactive bowl, and whisk until smooth.
2. Add salt, pepper and cayenne to taste. Brush on grilled or roasted chicken during the end of the cooking process, and pass remaining sauce at the table.

Hot Sauce

Prep time: 10 minute | Cook time: 0 minute | Serves 4

½ teaspoons coriander
½ teaspoons cumin seeds
¼ teaspoons black pepper
2 green cardamom pods
2 garlic cloves
1 teaspoons salt
1 ounces. parsley
2 tablespoons olive oil

1. In a blender place all ingredients and blend until smooth
2. Pour sauce in a bowl and serve.

Parmesan Basil Pesto Sauce

Prep time: 5 minutes | Cook time: 0 minute | Serves 4

•
2 cloves garlic
2 ounces. basil leaves
1 tablespoon pine nuts
1 ounces (28 g) Parmesan cheese
½ cup olive oil

1. In a blender place all ingredients and blend until smooth
2. Pour sauce in a bowl and serve.

Vegetarian Pesto

Prep time: 10 minute | Cook time: 0 minute | Serves 4

•

1 cup cilantro leaves
1 cup basil leaves
1 cup parsley leaves
½ cup mint leaves
½ cup walnuts
1 teaspoons miso
1 teaspoons lemon juice
¼ cup olive oil

1. In a blender place all ingredients and blend until smooth
2. Pour sauce in a bowl and serve.

Almonds and Fennel Sauce

Prep time: 5 minutes | Cook time: 0 minute | Serves 4

1 cup fennel bulb
1 cup olive oil
1 cup almonds
1 cup fennel fronds

1. In a blender place all ingredients and blend until smooth
2. Pour sauce in a bowl and serve.

Honey kimchi Dipping

Prep time: 5 minutes | Cook time: 0 minute | Serves 4

5 tablespoons unsalted butter
8 tablespoons kimchi paste
2 tablespoons honey
1 teaspoon sesame seeds

1. In a blender place all ingredients and blend until smooth
2. Pour sauce in a bowl and serve.

Japan Dipping Sauce

Prep time: 5 minutes | Cook time: 0 minute | Serves 4

•
6 tablespoons ponzu sauce
2 tablespoons scallions
2 teaspoon ginger
2 teaspoon mirin
1 teaspoon sesame oil
¼ teaspoon salt

1. In a blender place all ingredients and blend until smooth
2. Pour sauce in a bowl and serve.

Thai Tangy Dipping Sauce

Prep time: 5 minutes | Cook time: 0 minute | Serves 4

6 teaspoon garlic sauce
2 tablespoons fish sauce
2 tablespoons lime juice

1 tablespoon brown sugar
1 teaspoon chili flakes
1.   In a blender place all ingredients and blend until smooth
2.   Pour sauce in a bowl and serve.

Tangy Coconut Dipping Sauce

Prep time: 5 minutes | Cook time: 0 minute | Serves
4 tablespoons coconut milk
1 tablespoon curry paste
2 tablespoons lime juice
2 teaspoon soy sauce
1 ounce (28 g) parsley
2 tablespoons olive oil
1.   In a blender place all ingredients and blend until smooth
2.   Pour sauce in a bowl and serve.

Maple Black Bean Dipping Sauce

Prep time: 5 minutes | Cook time: 0 minute | Serves 4
2 tablespoons black bean paste
2 tablespoons peanut butter
1 tablespoon maple syrup
2 tablespoons olive oil
1.   In a blender place all ingredients and blend until smooth
2.   Pour sauce in a bowl and serve.

Maple Dipping Sauce

Prep time: 5 minutes | Cook time: 0 minute | Serves 4
2 tablespoons peanut butter
2 tablespoons maple syrup
2 teaspoon olive oil
2 tablespoon Korean black bean paste
1.   In a blender place all ingredients and blend until smooth
2.   Pour sauce in a bowl and serve.

Soy-Sugar Dipping Sauce

Prep time: 5 minutes | Cook time: 0 minute | Serves 4
¼ cup soy sauce
¼ cup sugar
¼ cup rice vinegar
½ cup scallions
½ cup cilantro
1.   In a blender place all ingredients and blend until smooth
2.   Pour sauce in a bowl and serve.

Avocado and Parsley Salsa

Prep time: 10 minutes | Cook time: 0 minute | Serves 4
2 avocados
1 onion
1 jalapeno
2 garlic cloves
¼ cup red wine vinegar
1 tablespoon lime juice
¼ cup parsley leaves
1.   In a blender place all ingredients and blend until smooth
2.   Pour sauce in a bowl and serve.

Smoked Salt

Prep time: 2 minutes | Cook time: 4 hours | Makes 1 pound
1 pound (454 g) coarse sea salt
1.   Supply your smoker with wood pellets and follow the manufacturer's specific start-up procedure. Preheat the grill, with the lid closed, to 120ºF (49ºC).
2.   Pour the salt onto a rimmed baking sheet and smoke for 4 hours, stirring every hour.
3.   Remove the salt from the smoker, let it cool, and store in an airtight container.

CHAPTER 5 MEATS

Classic Texas Smoked Brisket

Prep time: 15 minutes | Cook time: 16 to 20 hours | Serves 12 to 15

1 (12-pound / 340-g) full packer brisket
2 tablespoons yellow mustard
1 batch espresso brisket rub
Worcestershire mop and spritz, for spritzing

1.	Supply your Traeger with wood pellets and follow the start-up procedure. Preheat the grill, with the lid closed, to 225ºF (107ºC).
2.	Using a boning knife, carefully remove all but about ½ inch of the large layer of fat covering one side of your brisket.
3.	Coat the brisket all over with mustard and season it with the rub. Using your hands, work the rub into the meat. Pour the mop into a spray bottle.
4.	Place the brisket directly on the grill grate and smoke until its internal temperature reaches 195°F (91ºC), spritzing it every hour with the mop.
5.	Pull the brisket from the grill and wrap it completely in aluminum foil or butcher paper. Place the wrapped brisket in a cooler, cover the cooler, and let it rest for 1 or 2 hours.
6.	Remove the brisket from the cooler and unwrap it.
7.	Separate the brisket point from the flat by cutting along the fat layer and slice the flat. The point can be saved for burnt ends (see Sweet Heat Burnt Ends), or sliced and served as well.

Homemade Mesquite Smoked Brisket

Prep time: 15 minutes | Cook time: 12 to 16 hours | Serves 8 to 12

1 (12-pound / 340-g) full packer brisket
2 tablespoons yellow mustard (you can also use soy sauce)
Salt, to taste
Freshly ground black pepper, to taste

1.	Supply your Traeger with wood pellets and follow the start-up procedure. Preheat the grill, with the lid closed, to 225ºF (107ºC).
2.	Using a boning knife, carefully remove all but about ½ inch of the large layer of fat covering one side of your brisket.
3.	Coat the brisket all over with mustard and season it with salt and pepper.
4.	Place the brisket directly on the grill grate and smoke until its internal temperature reaches 160ºF (71ºC) and the brisket has formed a dark bark.
5.	Pull the brisket from the grill and wrap it completely in aluminum foil or butcher paper.

6.	Increase the grill's temperature to 350ºF (177ºC) and return the wrapped brisket to it. Continue to cook until its internal temperature reaches 190ºF (88ºC).
7.	Transfer the wrapped brisket to a cooler, cover the cooler, and let the brisket rest for 1 or 2 hours.
8.	Remove the brisket from the cooler and unwrap it.
9.	Separate the brisket point from the flat by cutting along the fat layer, and slice the flat. The point can be saved for burnt ends (see Sweet Heat Burnt Ends), or sliced and served as well.

Smoked Burnt Ends

Prep time: 30 minute | Cook time: 6 hours | Serves 8 to 10

1 (6-pound / 170-g) brisket point
2 tablespoons yellow mustard
1 batch sweet brown sugar rub
2 tablespoons honey
1 cup barbecue sauce
2 tablespoons light brown sugar

1.	Supply your Traeger with wood pellets and follow the start-up procedure. Preheat the grill, with the lid closed, to 225ºF (107ºC).
2.	Using a boning knife, carefully remove all but about ½ inch of the large layer of fat covering one side of your brisket point.
3.	Coat the point all over with mustard and season it with the rub. Using your hands, work the rub into the meat.
4.	Place the point directly on the grill grate and smoke until its internal temperature reaches 165ºF (74ºC).
5.	Pull the brisket from the grill and wrap it completely in aluminum foil or butcher paper.
6.	Increase the grill's temperature to 350ºF (177ºC) and return the wrapped brisket to it. Continue to cook until its internal temperature reaches 185ºF (85ºC).
7.	Remove the point from the grill, unwrap it, and cut the meat into 1-inch cubes. Place the cubes in an aluminum pan and stir in the honey, barbecue sauce, and brown sugar.
8.	Place the pan in the grill and smoke the beef cubes for 1 hour more, uncovered. Remove the burnt ends from the grill and serve immediately.

Reverse-Seared Tri-Tip Roast

Prep time: 10 minute | Cook time: 2 to 3 hours | Serves 4

1½ pounds (680 g) Tri-Tip roast
1 batch Espresso Brisket Rub
1.   Supply your Traeger with wood pellets and follow the start-up procedure. Preheat the grill, with the lid closed, to 180ºF (82ºC).
2.   Season the Tri-Tip roast with the rub. Using your hands, work the rub into the meat.
3.   Place the roast directly on the grill grate and smoke until its internal temperature reaches 140°F (60ºC).
4.   Increase the grill's temperature to 450°F and continue to cook until the roast's internal temperature reaches 145°F (63ºC). This same technique can be done over an open flame or in a cast-iron skillet with some butter.
5.   Remove the Tri-Tip roast from the grill and let it rest 10 to 15 minutes, before slicing and serving.

Smoked Tri-Tip Roast

Prep time: 25 minutes | Cook time: 5 hours | Serves 4
1½ pounds (680 g) Tri-Tip roast
Salt, to taste
Freshly ground black pepper, to taste
2 teaspoons garlic powder
2 teaspoons lemon pepper
½ cup apple juice
1.   Supply your Traeger with wood pellets and follow the start-up procedure. Preheat the grill, with the lid closed, to 180ºF (82ºC).
2.   Season the Tri-Tip roast with salt, pepper, garlic powder, and lemon pepper. Using your hands, work the seasoning into the meat.
3.   Place the roast directly on the grill grate and smoke for 4 hours.
4.   Pull the Tri-Tip from the grill and place it on enough aluminum foil to wrap it completely.
5.   Increase the grill's temperature to 375°F (191ºC).
6.   Fold in three sides of the foil around the roast and add the apple juice. Fold in the last side, completely enclosing the Tri-Tip and liquid. Return the wrapped Tri-Tip to the grill and cook for 45 minutes more.
7.   Remove the Tri-Tip roast from the grill and let it rest for 10 to 15 minutes, before unwrapping, slicing, and serving.

Santa Maria Tri-Tip Bottom Sirloin

Prep time: 15 minutes | Cook time: 45 minutes to 1 hour | Serves 4
2 teaspoons sea salt
2 teaspoons freshly ground black pepper
2 teaspoons onion powder

2 teaspoons garlic powder
2 teaspoons dried oregano
1 teaspoon cayenne pepper
1 teaspoon ground sage
1 teaspoon finely chopped fresh rosemary
1 (1½- to 2-pound / 680- to 907-g) tri-tip bottom sirloin
1.   Supply your Traeger with wood pellets and follow the start-up procedure. Preheat the grill, with the lid closed, to 425ºF (218ºC).
2.   In a small bowl, combine the salt, pepper, onion powder, garlic powder, oregano, cayenne pepper, sage, and rosemary to create a rub.
3.   Season the meat all over with the rub and lay it directly on the grill.
4.   Close the lid and smoke for 45 minutes to 1 hour, or until a meat thermometer inserted in the thickest part of the meat reads 120ºF (49ºC) for rare, 130ºF (54ºC) for medium-rare, or 140ºF (60ºC) for medium, keeping in mind that the meat will come up in temperature by about another 5ºF (-15ºC) during the rest period.
5.   Remove the tri-tip from the heat, tent with aluminum foil, and let rest for 15 minutes before slicing against the grain.

Mustard Pulled Beef

Prep time: 25 minutes | Cook time: 12 to 14 hours | Serves 5 to 8
1 (4-pound / 1.8-kg) top round roast
2 tablespoons yellow mustard
1 batch Espresso Brisket Rub
½ cup beef broth
1.   Supply your Traeger with wood pellets and follow the start-up procedure. Preheat the grill, with the lid closed, to 225ºF (107ºC).
2.   Coat the top round roast all over with mustard and season it with the rub. Using your hands, work the rub into the meat.
3.   Place the roast directly on the grill grate and smoke until its internal temperature reaches 160ºF (71ºC) and a dark bark has formed.
4.   Pull the roast from the grill and place it on enough aluminum foil to wrap it completely.
5.   Increase the grill's temperature to 350ºF (177ºC).
6.   Fold in three sides of the foil around the roast and add the beef broth. Fold in the last side, completely enclosing the roast and liquid. Return the wrapped roast to the grill and cook until its internal temperature reaches 195ºF (91ºC).
7.   Pull the roast from the grill and place it in a cooler. Cover the cooler and let the roast rest for 1 or 2 hours.

8.	Remove the roast from the cooler and unwrap it. Pull apart the beef using just your fingers. Serve immediately.

Smoked Top Round Roast Beef

Prep time: 10 minute | Cook time: 12 to 14 hours | Serves 5 to 8

1 (4-pound / 1.8-kg) top round roast
1 batch Espresso Brisket Rub
1 tablespoon butter

1.	Supply your Traeger with wood pellets and follow the start-up procedure. Preheat the grill, with the lid closed, to 180ºF (82ºC).
2.	Season the top round roast with the rub. Using your hands, work the rub into the meat.
3.	Place the roast directly on the grill grate and smoke until its internal temperature reaches 140ºF (60ºC). Remove the roast from the grill.
4.	Place a cast-iron skillet on the grill grate and increase the grill's temperature to 450ºF (232ºC). Place the roast in the skillet, add the butter, and cook until its internal temperature reaches 145°F (63ºC), flipping once after about 3 minutes.
5.	Remove the roast from the grill and let it rest for 10 to 15 minutes, before slicing and serving.

Smoked Mustard Beef Ribs

Prep time: 25 minutes | Cook time: 4 to 6 hours | Serves 4 to 8

2 (2- or 3-pound / 907- or 1360-g) racks beef ribs
2 tablespoons yellow mustard
1 batch sweet and spicy cinnamon rub

1.	Supply your Traeger with wood pellets and follow the start-up procedure. Preheat the grill, with the lid closed, to 225ºF (107ºC).
2.	Remove the membrane from the backside of the ribs. This can be done by cutting just through the membrane in an X pattern and working a paper towel between the membrane and the ribs to pull it off.
3.	Coat the ribs all over with mustard and season them with the rub. Using your hands, work the rub into the meat.
4.	Place the ribs directly on the grill grate and smoke until their internal temperature reaches between 190°F (88ºC) and 200°F (93ºC).
5.	Remove the racks from the grill and cut them into individual ribs. Serve immediately.

Braised Beef Short Ribs

Prep time: 25 minutes | Cook time: 4 hours | Serves 2 to 4

4 beef short ribs
Salt, to taste
Freshly ground black pepper, to taste
½ cup beef broth

1.	Supply your Traeger with wood pellets and follow the start-up procedure. Preheat the grill, with the lid closed, to 180ºF (82ºC).
2.	Season the ribs on both sides with salt and pepper.
3.	Place the ribs directly on the grill grate and smoke for 3 hours.
4.	Pull the ribs from the grill and place them on enough aluminum foil to wrap them completely.
5.	Increase the grill's temperature to 375°F (191ºC).
6.	Fold in three sides of the foil around the ribs and add the beef broth. Fold in the last side, completely enclosing the ribs and liquid. Return the wrapped ribs to the grill and cook for 45 minutes more. Remove the short ribs from the grill, unwrap them, and serve immediately.

Roasted Prime Rib

Prep time: 15 minutes | Cook time: 4 or 5 hours | Serves 8 to 12

1 (3-bone) rib roast
Salt, to taste
Freshly ground black pepper, to taste
1 garlic clove, minced

1.	Supply your Traeger with wood pellets and follow the start-up procedure. Preheat the grill, with the lid closed, to 360ºF (182ºC).
2.	Season the roast all over with salt and pepper and, using your hands, rub it all over with the minced garlic.
3.	Place the roast directly on the grill grate and smoke for 4 or 5 hours, until its internal temperature reaches 145°F (63ºC) for medium-rare.
4.	Remove the roast from the grill and let it rest for 15 minutes, before slicing and serving.

Smoked Pastrami

Prep time: 15 minutes | Cook time: 12 to 16 hours | Serves 6 to 8

1 (8-pound / 3.6-kg) corned beef brisket
2 tablespoons yellow mustard
1 batch Espresso Brisket Rub
Worcestershire Mop and Spritz, for spritzing

1.	Supply your Traeger with wood pellets and follow the start-up procedure. Preheat the grill, with the lid closed, to 225ºF (107ºC).
2.	Coat the brisket all over with mustard and season it with the rub. Using your hands, work the rub into the meat. Pour the mop into a spray bottle.

3.	Place the brisket directly on the grill grate and smoke until its internal temperature reaches 195°F (91ºC), spritzing it every hour with the mop.
4.	Pull the corned beef brisket from the grill and wrap it completely in aluminum foil or butcher paper. Place the wrapped brisket in a cooler, cover the cooler, and let it rest for 1 or 2 hours.
5.	Remove the corned beef from the cooler and unwrap it. Slice the corned beef and serve.

New York Steaks

Prep time: 15 minutes | Cook time: 1 to 2 hours | Serves 4

4 (1-inch-thick) New York steaks
2 tablespoons olive oil
Salt, to taste
Freshly ground black pepper, to taste
1.	Supply your Traeger with wood pellets and follow the start-up procedure. Preheat the grill, with the lid closed, to 180ºF (82ºC).
2.	Rub the steaks all over with olive oil and season both sides with salt and pepper.
3.	Place the steaks directly on the grill grate and smoke for 1 hour.
4.	Increase the grill's temperature to 375°F (191ºC) and continue to cook until the steaks' internal temperature reaches 145°F (63ºC) for medium-rare.
5.	Remove the steaks and let them rest 5 minutes, before slicing and serving.

T-Bones Steak

Prep time: 10 minute | Cook time: 30 minute | Serves 4

4 (1½- to 2-inch-thick) T-bone steaks
2 tablespoons olive oil
1 batch Espresso Brisket Rub or Chili-Coffee Rub
1.	Supply your Traeger with wood pellets and follow the start-up procedure. Preheat the grill, with the lid closed, to 500ºF (260ºC).
2.	Coat the steaks all over with olive oil and season both sides with the rub. Using your hands, work the rub into the meat.
3.	Place the steaks directly on a grill grate and smoke until their internal temperature reaches 135ºF (57ºC) for rare, 145ºF (63ºC) for medium-rare, and 155ºF (68ºC) for well-done. Remove the steaks from the grill and serve hot.

Reverse-Seared Sirlion Steaks

Prep time: 15 minutes | Cook time: 1 or 2 hours | Serves 4

4 (4-ounce / 113-g) sirloin steaks
2 tablespoons olive oil

Salt, to taste
Freshly ground black pepper, to taste
4 tablespoons butter
1.	Supply your Traeger with wood pellets and follow the start-up procedure. Preheat the grill, with the lid closed, to 180ºF (82ºC).
2.	Rub the steaks all over with olive oil and season both sides with salt and pepper.
3.	Place the steaks directly on the grill grate and smoke until their internal temperature reaches 135ºF (57ºC). Remove the steaks from the grill.
4.	Place a cast-iron skillet on the grill grate and increase the grill's temperature to 450ºF (232ºC).
5.	Place the steaks in the skillet and top each with 1 tablespoon of butter. Cook the steaks until their internal temperature reaches 145°F (63ºC), flipping once after 2 or 3 minutes. (I recommend reverse-searing over an open flame rather than in the cast-iron skillet, if your grill has that option.) Remove the steaks and serve immediately.

Asian Sirloin Steak Skewers

Prep time: 10 minute | Cook time: 1⅓ hours | Serves 6

1½ pounds (680 g) top sirloin steak
6 garlic cloves, minced
1 red onion
⅓ cup sugar
¾ cup soy sauce
1 tablespoon ground ginger
¼ cup sesame oil
3 tablespoon sesame seeds
¼ cup vegetable oil
Bamboo skewers
1.	Cut sirloin steak into cubes, about 1 inch.
2.	Cut red onion into chunks similar in size to the sirloin steak cubes.
3.	In a bowl, combine and whisk soy sauce, sesame oil, vegetable oil, minced garlic, sugar, ginger, and sesame seeds.
4.	Add steak to sauce bowl and toss to coat until steak is covered in the sauce.
5.	Marinate for at least 1 hour in a refrigerator (if you are in a rush it's ok to skip this part, but you'll sacrifice a little bit of flavor).
6.	Preheat pellet grill to 350ºF (177ºC).
7.	Thread marinated beef and red onion pieces onto bamboo skewers.
8.	Grill the skewers, turning after about 4 minutes. Cook for 8 minutes total or until meat reaches your desired doneness.

Tomahawk Ribeye Steak

Prep time: 45 minutes | Cook time: 1 or 2 hours | Serves 4 to 6

1 (2½- to 3½-lbs / 1.1- to 1.6-kg) tomahawk ribeye steak
5 garlic cloves, minced
2 tablespoon kosher salt
1 bundle fresh thyme
2 tablespoon ground black pepper
8 ounces butter stick
1 tablespoon garlic powder
⅛ cup olive oil

1.	Mix rub ingredients (salt, black pepper, and garlic powder) in a small bowl. Use this mixture to season all sides of the ribeye steak generously. You can also substitute your favorite steak seasoning. After applying seasoning, let the steak rest at room temperature for at least 30 minute.
2.	While the steak rests, preheat your pellet grill to 450ºF (232ºC) to 500ºF (260ºC) for searing.
3.	Sear the steak for 5 minutes on each side. Halfway through each side (so after 2½ minutes), rotate the steak 90º to form grill marks on the tomahawk.
4.	After the tomahawk steak has seared for 5 minutes on each side (10 minute total), move the steak to a raised rack.
5.	Adjust your pellet grill's temperature to 250ºF (121ºC) and turn up smoke setting if applicable. Leave the lid open for a moment to help allow some heat to escape.
6.	Stick your probe meat thermometer into the very center of the cut to measure internal temperature.
7.	Place butter stick, garlic cloves, olive oil, and thyme in the aluminum pan. Then place the aluminum pan under the steak to catch drippings. After a few minutes, the steak drippings and ingredients will mix together
8.	Baste the steak with the aluminum pan mixture every 10 minute until the tomahawk steak reaches your desired doneness
9.	Once the steak reaches its desired doneness, remove from the grill and place on a cutting board or serving dish. The steak should rest for 10-15 minutes before cutting/serving.

Spicy Beef Tenderloin

Prep time: 25 minutes | Cook time: 1¼ hours | Serves 6

2½ pounds (1.1 kg) center cut beef tenderloin, trimmed and tied if uneven
2 tablespoon unsalted butter, room temperature
6 tablespoon peppercorns, mixed colors
1 tablespoon kosher salt

1 cup parsley, chopped
Horseradish sauce, on the side
4 tablespoon Dijon mustard

1.	Coarsely grind peppercorn mixture into a bowl. Add parsley, mustard, butter, and salt. Mix until thoroughly combined.
2.	Rub spiced butter mixture generously and thoroughly on all sides of the tenderloin. Coat completely and roll tenderloin in bowl if necessary to soak up as much seasoning as possible.
3.	Preheat pellet grill to 450ºF (232ºC).
4.	Place tenderloin on an elevated rack (important) and roast. Use a probe meat thermometer to measure internal temperature. Cook until the center of the tenderloin reaches a temperature of 130ºF (54ºC). This typically takes 30-45 minutes but could be more or less depending on the size of your tenderloin.
5.	Once tenderloin reaches desired doneness, remove from grill and allow to rest for at least 15 minutes.
6.	Move tenderloin to a cutting board and slice. Try to catch as many juices as possible. Garnish with additional parsley.

Korean Short Ribs

Prep time: 15 minutes | Cook time: 8 hours | Serves 5

3 lbs (1.4kg) beef short ribs
2 tablespoon sugar
¾ cup water
1 tablespoon ground black pepper
3 tablespoon white vinegar
2 tablespoon sesame oil
3 tablespoon soy sauce
6 cloves garlic, minced
⅓ cup light brown sugar
½ yellow onion, finely chopped

1.	Combine soy sauce, water, and vinegar in a bowl. Mix and whisk in brown sugar, white sugar, pepper, sesame oil, garlic, and onion. Whisk until the sugars have completely dissolved.
2.	Pour marinade into large bowl or baking pan with high sides. Dunk the short ribs in the marinade, coating completely. Cover marinaded short ribs with plastic wrap and refrigerate for 6 to 12 hours.
3.	Preheat pellet grill to 225ºF (107ºC).
4.	Remove plastic wrap from ribs and pull ribs out of marinade. Shake off any excess marinade and dispose of the contents left in the bowl.
5.	Place ribs on grill and cook for about 6-8 hours, until ribs reach an internal temperature of

203ºF (95ºC). Measure using a probe meat thermometer.

6.	Once ribs reach temperature, remove from grill and allow to rest for about 20 minute. Slice, serve, and enjoy!

Swiss Cheese Beef Meatloaf

Prep time: 15 minutes | Cook time: 2 hours | Serves 4

1 tablespoon canola oil
2 garlic cloves, finely chopped
1 medium onion, finely chopped
1 poblano chile, stemmed, seeded, and finely chopped
2 pounds extra-lean ground beef
2 tablespoons Montreal steak seasoning
1 tablespoon A.1. steak sauce
½ pound bacon, cooked and crumbled
2 cups shredded Swiss cheese
1 egg, beaten
2 cups breadcrumbs
½ cup Tiger Sauce

1.	On your stove top, heat the canola oil in a medium sauté pan over medium-high heat. Add the garlic, onion, and poblano, and sauté for 3 to 5 minutes, or until the onion is just barely translucent.
2.	Supply your smoker with wood pellets and follow the manufacturer's specific start-up procedure. Preheat, with the lid closed, to 225ºF (107ºC).
3.	In a large bowl, combine the sautéed vegetables, ground beef, steak seasoning, steak sauce, bacon, Swiss cheese, egg, and breadcrumbs. Mix with your hands until well incorporated, then shape into a loaf.
4.	Put the meatloaf in a cast iron skillet and place it on the grill. Close the lid and smoke for 2 hours, or until a meat thermometer inserted in the loaf reads 165ºF (74ºC).
5.	Top with the meatloaf with the Tiger Sauce, remove from the grill, and let rest for about 10 minute before serving.

Homemade London Broil

Prep time: 15 minutes | Cook time: 12 to 16 minutes | Serves 4

1 (1½- to 2-pound / 680- to 907-g) London broil or top round steak
¼ cup soy sauce
2 tablespoons white wine
2 tablespoons extra-virgin olive oil
¼ cup chopped scallions
2 tablespoons packed brown sugar
2 garlic cloves, minced
2 teaspoons red pepper flakes
1 teaspoon freshly ground black pepper

1.	Using a meat mallet, pound the steak lightly all over on both sides to break down its fibers and tenderize. You are not trying to pound down the thickness.
2.	In a medium bowl, make the marinade by combining the soy sauce, white wine, olive oil, scallions, brown sugar, garlic, red pepper flakes, and black pepper.
3.	Put the steak in a shallow plastic container with a lid and pour the marinade over the meat. Cover and refrigerate for at least 4 hours.
4.	Remove the steak from the marinade, shaking off any excess, and discard the marinade.
5.	Supply your smoker with wood pellets and follow the manufacturer's specific start-up procedure. Preheat, with the lid closed, to 350ºF (177ºC).
6.	Place the steak directly on the grill, close the lid, and smoke for 6 minutes. Flip, then smoke with the lid closed for 6 to 10 minute more, or until a meat thermometer inserted in the meat reads 130ºF (54ºC) for medium-rare.
7.	Let the steak rest for about 10 minute before slicing and serving. The meat's temperature will rise by about 5 degrees while it rests

Texas Beef Shoulder Clod

Prep time: 15 minutes | Cook time: 12 to 16 hours | Serves 16 to 20

½ cup sea salt
½ cup freshly ground black pepper
1 tablespoon red pepper flakes
1 tablespoon minced garlic
1 tablespoon cayenne pepper
1 tablespoon smoked paprika
1 (13- to 15-pound / 5.9- to 6.8-kg) beef shoulder clod

1.	In a small bowl, combine the salt, pepper, red pepper flakes, minced garlic, cayenne pepper, and smoked paprika to create a rub. Generously apply it to the beef shoulder.
2.	Supply your smoker with wood pellets and follow the manufacturer's specific start-up procedure. Preheat, with the lid closed, to 250ºF (121ºC).
3.	Put the meat on the grill grate, close the lid, and smoke for 12 to 16 hours, or until a meat thermometer inserted deeply into the beef reads 195ºF (91ºC). You may need to cover the clod with aluminum foil toward the end of smoking to prevent overbrowning.
4.	Let the meat rest for about 15 minutes before slicing against the grain and serving.

Somked Cheeseburger Hand Pies

Prep time: 35 minutes | Cook time: 10 minute | Serves 4

½ pound lean ground beef
1 tablespoon minced onion
1 tablespoon steak seasoning
1 cup shredded Monterey Jack and Colby cheese blend
8 slices white American cheese, divided
2 (14-ounce / 397-g) refrigerated prepared pizza dough sheets, divided
2 eggs, beaten with 2 tablespoons water (egg wash), divided
24 hamburger dill pickle chips
2 tablespoons sesame seeds
6 slices tomato, for garnish
Ketchup and mustard, for serving

1. Supply your smoker with wood pellets and follow the manufacturer's specific start-up procedure. Preheat, with the lid closed, to 325ºF (163ºC).
2. On your stove top, in a medium sauté pan over medium-high heat, brown the ground beef for 4 to 5 minutes, or until cooked through. Add the minced onion and steak seasoning.
3. Toss in the shredded cheese blend and 2 slices of American cheese, and stir until melted and fully incorporated.
4. Remove the cheeseburger mixture from the heat and set aside.
5. Make sure the dough is well chilled for easier handling. Working quickly, roll out one prepared pizza crust on parchment paper and brush with half of the egg wash.
6. Arrange the remaining 6 slices of American cheese on the dough to outline 6 hand pies.
7. Top each cheese slice with ¼ cup of the cheeseburger mixture, spreading slightly inside the imaginary lines of the hand pies.
8. Place 4 pickle slices on top of the filling for each pie.
9. Top the whole thing with the other prepared pizza crust and cut between the cheese slices to create 6 hand pies.
10. Using kitchen scissors, cut the parchment to further separate the pies, but leave them on the paper.
11. Using a fork dipped in egg wash, seal the edges of the pies on all sides. Baste the tops of the pies with the remaining egg wash and sprinkle with the sesame seeds.
12. Remove the pies from the parchment paper and gently place on the grill grate. Close the lid and smoke for 5 minutes, then carefully flip and smoke with the lid closed for 5 more minutes, or until browned.

13. Top with the sliced tomato and serve with ketchup and mustard.

Spiced Brisket

Prep time: 15 minutes | Cook time: 9 hours | Serves 8

Rub:
2 tablespoons onion powder
2 tablespoons garlic powder
2 teaspoons chile powder
2 tablespoons paprika
⅓ cup coarse ground black pepper
⅓ cup jacobsen salt or kosher salt

Brisket:
1 (12- to 14-pound / 5.4- to 6.4-kg) whole packer brisket, trimmed
1½ cup beef broth

1. In a small bowl, thoroughly combine all the rub ingredients. Season the brisket with the rub on all sides.
2. When ready to cook, set Traeger temperature to 225ºF (107ºC) and preheat, lid closed for 15 minutes. For optimal flavor, use Super Smoke if available.
3. Place the brisket, fat-side down, on the grill and cook for about 5 to 6 hour, or until it reaches an internal temperature of 160ºF (71ºC).
4. Remove the brisket from the grill and wrap in a double layer of foil, then add the beef broth to the foil packet.
5. Return the foiled brisket to the grill and cook for about another 3 hours, or until it reaches an internal temperature of 204ºF (96ºC).
6. Remove the brisket from grill and unwrap from foil. Allow to rest for 15 minutes. Slice the brisket against the grain and serve warm.

Dijon Corned Beef Brisket

Prep time: 15 minutes | Cook time: 5 hours | Serves 4

1 (3-pound / 1.4-kg) flat cut corned beef brisket, fat cap at least ¼ inch thick
¼ cup Dijon mustard
1 bottle Traeger Apricot BBQ Sauce

1. Remove the brisket from its packaging and discard the spice packet, if any. Soak the brisket in water for at least 8 hours, changing the water every 2 hours.
2. When ready to cook, set Traeger temperature to 275ºF (135ºC) and preheat, lid closed for 15 minutes.
3. Place the brisket, fat-side up, directly on the grill and cook for 2 hours.

4.	Meanwhile, whisk the remaining ingredients together in a medium bowl. Pour half of the sauce mixture into the bottom of a disposable aluminum foil pan.

5.	Using tongs, transfer the brisket, fat-side up, to the pan. Pour the remaining sauce mixture over the top of the brisket, spreading the sauce evenly with a spatula. Cover the pan tightly with aluminum foil.

6.	Return the brisket to the grill and cook for an additional 2 to 3 hours, or until the brisket is tender and reaches an internal temperature of 203ºF (95ºC).

7.	Let the brisket cool for 15 to 20 minutes. Slice the brisket across the grain and serve warm.

Smoked Wagyu Tri-Tip

Prep time: 5 minutes | Cook time: 1 hour | Serves 4

1 Wagyu beef tri-tip, trimmed
½ cup Traeger Prime Rib Rub

1.	Generously season the tri-tip with Traeger Prime Rib Rub.

2.	When ready to cook, set temperature to 225ºF (107ºC) and preheat, lid closed for 15 minutes. For optimal flavor, use Super Smoke if available.

3.	Put the tri-tip on the grill and cook for 1 to 1½ hours, or until it reaches an internal temperature of 130ºF (54ºC).

4.	Remove the tri-tip from the grill and set aside.

5.	Increase the grill temperature to 475ºF (246ºC). After 15 minutes, return the tri-tip to the grill and cook each side for 3 minutes.

6.	Remove the tri-tip from the grill and slice to serve.

Brined Brisket

Prep time: 20 minutes | Cook time: 7 hours | Serves 4

1 cup brown sugar
½ cup kosher salt
1 (5- to 7-pound / 2.3- to 3.2-kg) flat cut brisket
¼ cup Traeger Beef Rub

1.	Dissolve the sugar and salt in 6 quarts boiling water. Add 6 cups ice then let it cool. Put the brisket into the brine and cover. Place the brine in the refrigerator overnight.

2.	Remove the brisket from the brine and pat dry with paper towels. Evenly sprinkle Traeger Beef Rub on the brisket.

3.	When ready to cook, set Traeger temperature to 250ºF (121ºC) and preheat, lid closed for 15 minutes.

4.	Put the brisket, fat-cap down, on the grill and smoke for 3 hours.

5.	Remove the brisket from the grill and wrap in a double layer of foil. Increase the grill temperature to 275ºF (135ºC) and cook for an additional 3 to 4 hours, or until the internal temperature reaches 204ºF (96ºC) on a meat thermometer.

6.	Unwrap the brisket and place it on the grill and cook for 30 minutes more.

7.	Remove the brisket from the grill and cool for 15 minutes before slicing against the grain and serving.

Garlic-Parmesan Crusted Filet Mignon

Prep time: 15 minutes | Cook time: 10 minutes | Serves 4

8 filet Mignon steaks
2 teaspoons garlic salt
2 teaspoons black pepper
2 teaspoons salt
2 cup grated Parmesan cheese
8 garlic, minced
2 tablespoons Dijon mustard

1.	Season the filets with garlic salt, pepper, and salt. Combine the cheese and minced garlic in a shallow bowl.

2.	When ready to cook, set Traeger temperature to High and preheat, lid closed for 15 minutes.

3.	Put the filets on the grill and cook each side for 4 minutes. When done, spread the Dijon mustard onto the filets, then dredge in the cheese-garlic mixture. Return the filets to the grill and cook for an additional 1 to 2 minutes, or until the cheese melts.

4.	Cool for 5 minutes before serving.

Coffee Rub Brisket

Prep time: 15 minutes | Cook time: 9 hours | Serves 8

15 pounds (6.8 kg) whole packer brisket
1½ cups water, divided
2 tablespoons Traeger Coffee Rub, divided
2 tablespoons salt, divided

1.	Trim the excess fat off the brisket, leaving a ¼-inch cap on the bottom.

2.	In a small bowl, mix together 1 cup of water, 1 tablespoon of rub, and 1 tablespoon of salt. Keep stirring until most of the salt is dissolved.

3.	Inject the brisket every square inch or so with the rub mixture. Season the exterior of the brisket with the remaining 1 tablespoon of rub and salt.

4.	When ready to cook, set the Traeger to 250ºF (121ºC) and preheat, lid closed for 15 minutes.
5.	Put the brisket directly on the grill and cook until it reaches an internal temperature of 160ºF (71ºC), about 6 hours.
6.	Wrap the brisket in two layers of foil and pour the remaining ½ cup of water into the foil packet. Secure tin foil tightly to contain the liquid. Increase the grill temperature to 275ºF (135ºC) and place the brisket back on the grill. Cook for another 3 hours, or until the internal temperature reaches 204ºF (96ºC).
7.	Remove the brisket from the grill and slice to serve.

Porterhouse Steaks with Creamed Greens

Prep time: 10 minutes | Cook time: 1 hour 20 minutes | Serves 4

2 Porterhouse steaks
Kosher salt and cracked black pepper, to taste
6 tablespoons butter, divided
1 shallot, thinly sliced
2 clove garlic, minced
1 cup heavy cream
1 pinch ground nutmeg
3 pounds (1.4 kg) mixed salad greens
1.	Generously season the steaks with salt and pepper on both sides.
2.	When ready to cook, set the Traeger to 225ºF (107ºC) and preheat, lid closed for 15 minutes.
3.	Put the seasoned steaks directly on the grill and cook until the internal temperature registers 120ºF (49ºC), for 45 minutes.
4.	Remove the steaks from the grill and increase the temperature to 450ºF (232ºC). Let the grill preheat with the lid closed for 15 minutes.
5.	Return the steaks to the hot grill and cook for an additional 5 to 6 minutes per side, or until the internal temperature reaches 130ºF (54ºC) for medium rare. Remove the steaks from the grill and set aside to cool.
6.	For the creamed greens: Heat 2 tablespoons of the butter in a saucepan over high heat until it foams. Add the shallot and garlic and cook over medium-low heat for about 5 minutes, stirring often, or until softened.
7.	Stir in the heavy cream and bring to a simmer. Cook for about 10 minutes until slightly thickened. Sprinkle with the nutmeg and season with salt to taste. Purée the ingredients with a hand blender until smooth. Set aside.
8.	Heat the remaining 4 tablespoons of butter in a large pot over high heat until it foams. Add the greens and cook for about 5 minutes, stirring

constantly, or until they are tender but still bright green.
9.	Season as needed with salt and add the cream mixture. Reduce the heat, cover, and allow to simmer for 5 minutes more until cooked through.
10.	To serve, slice the steaks and serve on top of the creamed greens.

Bacon-Onion Jam Strip Steaks

Prep time: 10 minutes | Cook time: 1 hour | Serves 2

2 whole New York strip steaks, room temperature
Traeger Prime Rib Rub, to taste
½ pound (227 g) bacon, cut into small pieces
1 small sweet onion
¼ cup brown sugar
¼ cup apple juice
3 tablespoons strong brewed coffee
½ tablespoon balsamic vinegar
Extra-virgin olive oil, as needed
1.	Season the steaks with Traeger Prime Rib Rub on both sides. Set aside.
2.	When ready to cook, start the Traeger to 350ºF (177ºC) and preheat, lid closed for 15 minutes.
3.	Put the bacon pieces in a cast iron pan and place on the hot grill. Cook for 10 to 15 minutes until the fat is rendered.
4.	Remove the bacon from the pan and drain out all but 1 tablespoon of the bacon grease from the pan.
5.	Add the onion to the cast iron pan and cook for about 10 minutes on the grill, or until the onion is tender. Add the brown sugar and cook for about another 15 to 20 minutes, or until the onion begins to caramelize.
6.	Stir in the apple juice, coffee, and cooked bacon and continue to cook for about 20 minutes, stirring occasionally.
7.	Pour in the balsamic vinegar and spoon into a bowl and set aside.
8.	Turn the heat on the Traeger to High and allow to preheat for 15 minutes with the lid closed.
9.	Lightly drizzle the olive oil over the steaks and place them on the grill. Cook each side for about 4 to 5 minutes, for medium-rare, or until cooked to your desired doneness.
10.	Remove the steaks from the grill and cool for about 10 minutes before slicing. Serve the steaks topped with the bacon-onion jam.

Texas Smoked Brisket

Prep time: 15 minutes | Cook time: 10 hours | Serves 8

1 (14- to 18-pound / 6.4- to 8.2-kg) whole packer brisket, trimmed
Meat Church Holy Cow BBQ Rub
Meat Church Holy Gospel BBQ Rub

1. Season the brisket with Meat Church Holy Cow Rub on all sides. Optionally add a light layer of Meat Church Holy Gospel Rub. Allow the brisket to sit for 20 to 30 minutes.
2. When ready to cook, set the Traeger temperature to 275ºF (135ºC) and preheat, lid closed for 15 minutes.
3. Put the brisket, fat side up, on the grill and cook for about 5 to 6 hours, or until it reaches an internal temperature of 165ºF (74ºC).
4. Remove the brisket from the grill and wrap tightly in Traeger Butcher Paper.
5. Return the wrapped brisket to the grill and continue to cook for about 3 to 4 hours, or until it reaches an internal temperature of 204ºF (96ºC).
6. Remove the brisket from the grill and rest for 30 minutes. Unwrap the brisket and slice against the grain before serving.

Bacon-Wrapped Tenderloin Roast

Prep time: 10 minutes | Cook time: 1 hour | Serves 4
4 pounds (1.8 kg) beef tenderloin
4 ounces (113 g) Traeger Beef Rub
4 ounces (113 g) Traeger Coffee Rub
8 strips bacon

1. When ready to cook, set the Traeger to 275ºF (135ºC) and preheat, lid closed for 15 minutes.
2. Lightly season the beef tenderloin with the beef rub and wrap with the bacon. Season again with another layer of coffee rub.
3. Put the tenderloin directly on the grill and cook for 30 minutes, or until it reaches an internal temperature of 120ºF (49ºC). If not, continue to cook, checking every 5 minutes until cooked to the desired temperature.
4. Remove the tenderloin from the grill and increase the temperature to 450ºF (232ºC).
5. After 10 minutes, place the tenderloin back on the grill and sear for 5 minutes, or until it reaches a finished internal temperature of 135ºF (57ºC). If not, flip the tenderloin and cook for another 5 minutes.
6. Remove the tenderloin from the grill and cool for 10 minutes before slicing and serving.

Buttered Smoked Porterhouse Steak

Prep time: 15 minutes | Cook time: 45 minutes | Serves 2
4 tablespoons butter, melted

2 teaspoons Dijon mustard
2 tablespoons Worcestershire sauce
40 ounces (1.1 kg) Porterhouse steaks
1 teaspoon Traeger Coffee Rub

1. When ready to cook, set the Traeger to 180ºF (82ºC) and preheat, lid closed for 15 minutes. For optimal flavor, use Super Smoke if available.
2. Whisk the melted butter, mustard, and Worcestershire sauce together in a small bowl until smooth. Brush the mixture on both sides of the steaks. Season both sides of the steaks with Traeger Coffee Rub.
3. Place the steaks directly on the grill and smoke for 30 minutes. With tongs, transfer the steaks to a plate.
4. Increase the grill temperature to High and preheat. For optimal results, set to 500ºF (260ºC) if available. Brush the steaks again with the butter mixture.
5. Place the steaks back on the grill and continue to cook until the desired internal temperature is reached, 130ºF (54ºC) for medium rare, 135ºF (57ºC) for medium-well.
6. Cool for 5 minutes before serving.

Marinated London Broil with Butter Cheese

Prep time: 10 minutes | Cook time: 1 hour 20 minutes | Serves 4
Marinade:
¼ cup water
¼ cup soy sauce
1 clove garlic, minced
1 small onion, coarsely chopped
2 tablespoons vegetable oil or extra-virgin olive oil
2 tablespoons red wine vinegar
1 tablespoon ketchup
1 teaspoon sugar
1 teaspoon Worcestershire sauce
1 teaspoon freshly ground black pepper
Steak:
1 (2-pound / 907-g) top round London broil steak
Traeger Beef Rub, as needed
Butter Cheese:
8 tablespoons butter, softened
¼ cup crumbled blue cheese
1 teaspoon Worcestershire sauce
1 scallion, minced
Freshly ground black pepper, to taste

1. Whisk all the marinade ingredients to combine in a small bowl.
2. Put the steak into a large resealable plastic bag and pour in the marinade. Let sit in the refrigerator for 6 hours to overnight.

3. Remove the steak from the refrigerator and rest to room temperature.

4. In a separate bowl, combine all the ingredients for the butter cheese and stir to mix well. Cover and refrigerate, if not using immediately.

5. When steak is at room temperature, discard the marinade and pat dry with paper towels, then season with Traeger Beef Rub on all sides.

6. When ready to cook, set the Traeger temperature to 180ºF (82ºC) and preheat, lid closed for 15 minutes.

7. Arrange the steak directly on the grill and smoke for 60 minutes. With tongs, transfer the steak to a platter.

8. Increase the temperature to 500ºF (260ºC) and preheat with the lid closed for 10 to 15 minutes.

9. Place the steak back on the grill and cook for about 15 to 20 minutes, or until the desired internal temperature is reached, 130ºF (54ºC) for medium-rare.

10. Let the steak rest for 5 minutes before thinly slicing on a diagonal. Serve the steak alongside the prepared butter cheese.

Grilled Bloody Mary Flank Steak

Prep time: 8 hours | Cook time: 15 minutes | Serves 4

1½ pounds (680 g) flank steak
Marinade:
2 cup Traeger Smoked Bloody Mary Mix
½ cup vodka
½ cup vegetable oil
3 clove garlic, minced
1 whole lemon or lime, juiced
1 tablespoon Worcestershire sauce
1 teaspoon celery salt
1 teaspoon coarse ground black pepper
Hot sauce, to taste

1. Whisk together all the ingredients except the steak in a small bowl until combined.

2. Place the steak in a resealable plastic bag and pour half the marinade over it. Allow to marinate for at least 6 hours or overnight. Refrigerate the remaining half of the marinade in an airtight container.

3. When ready to cook, set the Traeger temperature to High and preheat.

4. Pour the remaining marinade into a small saucepan and let simmer over medium heat until it has reduced by half. Keep warm and set aside.

5. Drain the steak and discard the marinade. Pat it dry with paper towels.

6. Arrange the steak directly on the grill and cook each side for 7 to 10 minutes.

7. Transfer the steak to a cutting board and cool for 3 minutes before thinly slicing on a sharp diagonal. Serve the steak with the warmed marinade on the side.

Smoked Tomahawk Steak

Prep time: 5 minutes | Cook time: 1 hour | Serves 4

1 (32-ounce / 907-g) bone-in Tomahawk rib-eye steak, 2 inch thick
Kosher salt, to taste
Meat Church Holy Cow BBQ Rub
3 tablespoons butter

1. Lightly season the steak on all sides with salt. Let sit at room temperature for 1 hour.

2. When ready to cook, set Traeger temperature to 225ºF (107ºC) and preheat, lid closed for 15 minutes. For optimal flavor, use Super Smoke if available.

3. Rinse the steak and pat it dry with paper towels. Liberally season both sides of the steak with Meat Church Holy Cow BBQ Rub.

4. Arrange the steak directly on the grill and cook for about 45 minutes, or until it reaches an internal temperature of 120ºF (49ºC). The cooking time depends on the thickness.

5. Remove the steak from the grill and rest for 10 minutes lightly tented with aluminum foil.

6. Meanwhile, put a cast iron skillet on the grill. Increase the grill temperature to 500ºF (260ºC).

7. Put the steak on the dry cast iron griddle and sear for 1 minute. Flip the steak and sear for 1 minute more. Doing this should bring your steak to an internal temperature of no more than 130ºF (54ºC).

8. Remove the steak and top with a generous amount of butter. Continue to cook for about 5 minutes, or until the internal temperature registers 130ºF (54ºC), for medium-rare.

9. Let the steak rest for 10 minutes before slicing and serving.

Cocoa-Rubbed Steak for Two

Prep time: 50 minutes | Cook time: 50 minutes | Serves 4

2 whole rib-eye roast, trimmed
1 cup Traeger Coffee Rub
¼ cup cocoa powder

1. Cut the roast into 2½-inch-thick steaks. Reserve 2 steaks and freeze the remaining steaks for later use.

2. Mix the Traeger Coffee rub and cocoa powder in a bowl. Season the steaks lightly with the rub mixture. Reserve the remaining rub mixture for

later use. Allow the steaks to sit at room temperature for 45 minutes.

3.   When ready to cook, set the Traeger to 225ºF (107ºC) and preheat, lid closed for 15 minutes.

4.   Lay the steaks on the hot grill and cook for 40 minutes, flipping the steaks halfway through, or until the desired internal temperature is reached, between 105 to 110ºF (41 to 43ºC).

5.   Remove the steaks from the grill and allow to rest on the counter.

6.   Increase the temperature to High and preheat, lid closed for 15 minutes. For optimal results, set to 500ºF (260ºC) if available.

7.   Return the steaks to the grill and cook for 8 minutes, flipping the steaks halfway through the cooking time, or until it reaches a finished temperature of 130ºF (54ºC), for medium rare.

8.   Cool for 5 minutes before serving.

Smoked Rib-Eye Caps

Prep time: 5 minutes | Cook time: 45 minutes | Serves 4

1½ pounds (680 g) rib-eye cap, trimmed
2 tablespoons Traeger Beef Rub
2 tablespoons Traeger Coffee Rub

1.   Cut the cap into 4 even portions and roll into steaks. Tie with butcher's twine to secure.

2.   Mix both rubs in a small bowl, then lightly season the steaks with the rub mixture.

3.   When ready to cook, set Traeger to 225ºF (107ºC) and preheat, lid closed for 15 minutes. For optimal flavor, use Super Smoke if available.

4.   Lay the steaks directly on the grill and smoke for 30 to 45 minutes, or until the internal temperature reaches 120ºF (49ºC).

5.   Remove the steaks from the grill and set aside to rest.

6.   Increase the grill temperature to 450ºF (232ºC). Return the steaks to the grill and cook each side for 3 to 4 minutes, or until the internal temperature reaches 130ºF (54ºC).

7.   Remove the steaks from the grill. Rest for 5 minutes and serve.

Spiced Tomahawk Steaks

Prep time: 5 minutes | Cook time: 1 hour | Serves 4

2 tablespoons ground black pepper
2 tablespoons kosher salt
1 tablespoon paprika
½ tablespoon brown sugar
½ tablespoon onion powder
½ tablespoon garlic powder
1 teaspoon ground mustard

¼ teaspoon cayenne pepper
2 large Tomahawk steaks

1.   Stir together all the ingredients except the steaks in a small bowl. Liberally season the steaks with the rub mixture.

2.   When ready to cook, set Traeger temperature to 225ºF (107ºC) and preheat, lid closed for 15 minutes. For optimal flavor, use Super Smoke if available.

3.   Arrange the steaks directly on the grill and smoke until the internal temperature reaches 120ºF (49ºC), 45 minutes to 1 hour.

4.   Remove the steaks from the grill and set aside to rest.

5.   Increase the grill temperature to 450ºF (232ºC). Return the steaks to the grill and cook each side for 7 to 10 minutes, or until the internal temperature registers 130ºF (54ºC).

6.   Remove the steaks from the grill cool for 5 minutes before serving.

Beef Tenderloin with Cherry Tomato Vinaigrette

Prep time: 10 minutes | Cook time: 40 minutes | Serves 6

1 whole beef tenderloin
Extra-virgin olive oil, as needed
1 bottle Traeger Prime Rib Rub
Salt and pepper, to taste
Vinaigrette:
6 whole plum tomatoes
2 tablespoons balsamic vinegar
1 teaspoon thyme, minced

1.   When ready to cook, set the temperature to 450ºF (232ºC) and preheat, lid closed for 15 minutes.

2.   Tuck the thin end of the tenderloin underneath the roast and secure it with butcher's string. Rub the tenderloin with olive oil and season both sides with Prime Rib Rub or salt and pepper. Put the tenderloin on a rack in a shallow roasting pan.

3.   Place the pan with the tenderloin on the preheated grill and roast for 20 minutes.

4.   Adjust the temperature to 350ºF (177ºC) and roast for an additional 20 minutes until cooked to the desired doneness, 130ºF (54ºC) for medium rare, 140ºF (60ºC) for medium or 150ºF (66ºC) for well done.

5.   Meanwhile, make the vinaigrette by combining the tomatoes, balsamic vinegar, olive oil, and thyme in a food processor. Pulse until smoothly puréed. Season with Prime Rib Rub or salt and pepper to taste.

6.   Remove the tenderloin from the grill and serve with the vinaigrette.

Grilled Beef Short Ribs

Prep time: 15 minutes | Cook time: 8 to 10 hours | Serves 8

4 (4-bone) beef short rib racks, membrane removed
½ cup Traeger Beef Rub
1 cup apple juice

1.   Season the ribs with Traeger Beef Rub on both sides.
2.   When ready to cook, set Traeger temperature to 225ºF (107ºC) and preheat, lid closed for 15 minutes.
3.   Place the ribs, bone-side down, on the grill and cook for 8 to 10 hours, spritzing or mopping with apple juice every 60 minutes, or until the internal temperature reaches 205ºF (96ºC).
4.   Remove the ribs from the grill and let rest for 5 minutes before slicing and serving.

Smoked Beef Brisket with Mop Sauce

Prep time: 15 minutes | Cook time: 12 hours | Serves 4

1 (6-pound / 2.7-kg) flat cut brisket, trimmed
Traeger Beef Rub, as needed
Traeger Texas Spicy BBQ Sauce, for serving
Mop Sauce:
2 cup beef broth
2 tablespoons Worcestershire sauce
¼ cup apple cider vinegar, apple cider or apple juice

1.   When ready to cook, set Traeger temperature to 180ºF (82ºC) and preheat, lid closed for 15 minutes.
2.   Season the brisket with Traeger Beef Rub on both sides. Whisk all the mop sauce ingredients together in a spray bottle.
3.   Place the brisket, fat-side down, on the grill and smoke for 3 to 4 hours, spraying the brisket with the mop sauce every hour.
4.   Remove the brisket from the grill and increase the temperature to 225ºF (107ºC).
5.   Place the brisket back on the grill and continue to cook for about 6 to 8 hours, spraying occasionally with the mop sauce, or until an instant-read thermometer inserted in the thickest part of the meat registers 204ºF (96ºC).
6.   Wrap the brisket with foil and allow to rest for 30 minutes. Slice the brisket across the grain and serve alongside the BBQ Sauce.

Steak Skewers with Cherry BBQ Sauce

Prep time: 20 minutes | Cook time: 25 minutes | Serves 4

2 tablespoons butter
1 medium onion, chopped
2 clove garlic, minced
2 cup fresh or frozen dark sweet cherries, pitted and coarsely chopped
1 cup ketchup
¼ cup cider vinegar
⅔ cup brown sugar
1 tablespoon Worcestershire sauce
½ teaspoon pepper
2 teaspoons ground mustard
1½ pounds (680 g) flank steak, cut into about 16 slices
Olive oil, as needed
Traeger Prime Rib Rub, to taste
Chopped scallions, for serving

1.   Melt the butter in a large saucepan over medium heat. Add the onion and sauté for 2 minutes until softened. Add the garlic and cook for 1 minute more.
2.   Add the cherries, ketchup, vinegar, brown sugar, Worcestershire sauce, pepper, and mustard and stir well. Cook, uncovered, over medium-low heat for 20 minutes, stirring occasionally, or until the cherries are softened and the sauce has thickened.
3.   Carefully stab each slice of steak through the center, lengthwise, with a Traeger skewer. Using a meat pounder, smash each steak skewer until about ½ inch thick.
4.   Drizzle the beef skewers with olive oil and season with Prime Rib Rub on both sides.
5.   When ready to cook, set the temperature to High and preheat, lid closed for 10 to 15 minutes.
6.   Arrange the steak skewers on the grill and cook each side for about 1 to 2 minutes.
7.   Remove the steak skewers from the grill and let rest for 5 to 10 minutes. Use a spoon to mash the cherries in the sauce. Brush the steak with the cherry barbecue sauce and serve sprinkled with the chopped scallions.

Seared Strip Steak with Butter

Prep time: 15 minutes | Cook time: 1 hour 10 minutes | Serves 4

4 (1½ inch thick) New York strip steaks
Traeger Beef Rub, as needed
4 tablespoons butter, melted

1.   When ready to cook, set Traeger temperature to 225ºF (107ºC) and preheat, lid closed for 15 minutes. For optimal flavor, use Super Smoke if available.
2.   Season the steaks with Traeger Beef Rub.
3.   Arrange the steaks directly on the grill and smoke for 60 minutes, or until they reach an internal temperature of 105 to 110ºF (41 to 43ºC).
4.   Remove the steaks from the grill and set aside to rest.

5. Increase the grill temperature to 500ºF (260ºC) and preheat, lid closed for 15 minutes.

6. Place the steaks back on the grill and sear for 4 minutes. Flip the steaks and spread 1 tablespoon of melted butter onto each steak. Continue to sear for 4 minutes more, or until cooked to the desired temperature, 130ºF (54ºC) to 135ºF (57ºC) for medium-rare.

7. Remove the steaks from the grill and cool for 5 minutes before serving.

Seared Rib-Eye Steaks

Prep time: 5 minutes | Cook time: 50 minutes | Serves 2

2 (1½ inch thick) rib-eye steaks
Meat Church Gourmet Garlic and Herb Seasoning
Meat Church Holy Cow BBQ Rub
2 tablespoons butter

1. When ready to cook, set Traeger temperature to 225ºF (107ºC) and preheat, lid closed for 15 minutes. For optimal flavor, use Super Smoke if available.

2. Season the steaks on both sides with the seasoning and rub.

3. Arrange the steaks on the grill and cook for 30 to 45 minutes, or until an instant-read thermometer inserted in the thickest part of the meat registers 120ºF (49ºC).

4. Remove the steaks from the grill and set aside to cool.

5. Increase the grill temperature to 500ºF (260ºC) and return the steaks to the grill and sear for 3 minutes.

6. Remove the steaks from the grill and top with the butter. Lightly tent the steaks with foil to melt the butter. Cool for 5 minutes before slicing and slicing.

Garlic-Mustard Roasted Prime Rib

Prep time: 15 minutes | Cook time: 4 hours | Serves 6

1 (8- to 10-pounds / 3.6- to 4.5-kg) 4-bone prime rib roast, trimmed
4 clove garlic, mashed to a paste
3 tablespoons Dijon mustard
2 tablespoons Worcestershire sauce
2 teaspoons dried rosemary
2 teaspoons dried thyme
Coarse salt and freshly ground black pepper, to taste
Prepared horseradish, for serving (optional)

1. Tie the prime rib roast between the bones with butcher's twine.

2. Stir together the garlic, mustard, Worcestershire sauce, rosemary, and thyme in a small bowl until well incorporated.

3. Slather the outside of the prime rib roast with the garlic mixture and generously season both sides with salt and black pepper. Place the prime rib roast in the refrigerator, uncovered, for up to 8 hours.

4. When ready to cook, set Traeger temperature to 250ºF (121ºC) and preheat, lid closed for 15 minutes.

5. Arrange the prime rib, fat-side up, on the grill and roast for 3½ to 4 hours, or until the internal temperature of the meat (the tip of the temperature probe should be in the center of the meat) registers 120ºF (49ºC) for rare, 130ºF (54ºC) for medium rare.

6. Transfer the prime rib to a cutting board and loosely tent with foil. Let rest for 30 minutes.

7. When ready, remove the twine. Using a sharp knife, remove the rack of bone following the curvature of the meat. Carve the meat across the grain into ½-inch-thick slices. Serve the meat alongside the horseradish, if desired.

Barbecue Baby Back Ribs

Prep time: 15 minutes | Cook time: 5 to 6 hours | Serves 12 to 15

2 full slabs baby back ribs, back membranes removed
1 cup prepared table mustard
1 cup Pork Rub
1 cup apple juice, divided
1 cup packed light brown sugar, divided
1 cup of The Ultimate BBQ Sauce, divided

1. Supply your Traeger with wood pellets and follow the manufacturer's specific start-up procedure. Preheat, with the lid closed, to 150°F (66ºC) to 180ºF (82ºC), or to the "Smoke" setting.

2. Coat the ribs with the mustard to help the rub stick and lock in moisture.

3. Generously apply the rub.

4. Place the ribs directly on the grill, close the lid, and smoke for 3 hours5. Increase the temperature to 225ºF (107ºC).

5. Remove the ribs from the grill and wrap each rack individually with aluminum foil, but before sealing tightly, add ½ cup apple juice and ½ cup brown sugar to each package.

6. Return the foil-wrapped ribs to the grill, close the lid, and smoke for 2 more hours.

7. Carefully unwrap the ribs and remove the foil completely. Coat each slab with ½ cup of barbecue sauce and continue smoking with the lid closed for 30 minute to 1 hour, or until the meat tightens and has a reddish bark. For the perfect rack, the internal temperature should be 190°F (88ºC).

Maple Baby Back Ribs

Prep time: 25 minutes | Cook time: 4 hours | Serves 4 to 6

2 (2- or 3-pound / 907- or 1360-g) racks baby back ribs
2 tablespoons yellow mustard
1 batch Sweet Brown Sugar Rub
½ cup plus 2 tablespoons maple syrup, divided
2 tablespoons light brown sugar
1 cup Pepsi or other non-diet cola
¼ cup The Ultimate BBQ Sauce

1. Supply your smoker with wood pellets and follow the manufacturer's specific start-up procedure. Preheat the grill, with the lid closed, to 180ºF (82ºC).
2. Remove the membrane from the backside of the ribs. This can be done by cutting just through the membrane in an X pattern and working a paper towel between the membrane and the ribs to pull it off.
3. Coat the ribs on both sides with mustard and season them with the rub. Using your hands, work the rub into the meat.
4. Place the ribs directly on the grill grate and smoke for 3 hours.
5. Remove the ribs from the grill and place them, bone-side up, on enough aluminum foil to wrap the ribs completely. Drizzle 2 tablespoons of maple syrup over the ribs and sprinkle them with 1 tablespoon of brown sugar. Flip the ribs and repeat the maple syrup and brown sugar application on the meat side.
6. Increase the grill's temperature to 300ºF (149ºC).
7. Fold in three sides of the foil around the ribs and add the cola. Fold in the last side, completely enclosing the ribs and liquid. Return the ribs to the grill and cook for 30 to 45 minutes.
8. Remove the ribs from the grill and unwrap them from the foil.
9. In a small bowl, stir together the barbecue sauce and remaining 6 tablespoons of maple syrup. Use this to baste the ribs. Return the ribs to the grill, without the foil, and cook for 15 minutes to caramelize the sauce.
10. Cut into individual ribs and serve immediately.

Smoked Mustard Baby Back Rids

Prep time: 25 minutes | Cook time: 4 to 6 hours | Serves 4 to 8

2 (2- or 3-pound / 907- or 1360-g) racks baby back ribs
2 tablespoons yellow mustard
1 batch Pork Rub

1. Supply your smoker with wood pellets and follow the manufacturer's specific start-up procedure. Preheat the grill, with the lid closed, to 225ºF (107ºC).
2. Remove the membrane from the backside of the ribs. This can be done by cutting just through the membrane in an X pattern and working a paper towel between the membrane and the ribs to pull it off.
3. Coat the ribs on both sides with mustard and season them with the rub. Using your hands, work the rub into the meat.
4. Place the ribs directly on the grill grate and smoke until their internal temperature reaches between 190°F (88ºC) and 200°F (93ºC).
5. Remove the racks from the grill and cut into individual ribs. Serve immediately.

Smoked Mustard Spare Ribs

Prep time: 25 minutes | Cook time: 4 to 6 hours | Serves 4 to 8

2 (2- or 3-pound / 907- or 1360-g) racks spare ribs
2 tablespoons yellow mustard
1 batch Sweet Brown Sugar Rub
¼ cup The Ultimate BBQ Sauce

1. Supply your smoker with wood pellets and follow the manufacturer's specific start-up procedure. Preheat the grill, with the lid closed, to 225ºF (107ºC).
2. Remove the membrane from the backside of the ribs. This can be done by cutting just through the membrane in an X pattern and working a paper towel between the membrane and the ribs to pull it off.
3. Coat the ribs on both sides with mustard and season with the rub. Using your hands, work the rub into the meat.
4. Place the ribs directly on the grill grate and smoke until their internal temperature reaches between 190°F (88ºC) and 200°F (93ºC).
5. Baste both sides of the ribs with barbecue sauce.
6. Increase the grill's temperature to 300ºF (149ºC) and continue to cook the ribs for 15 minutes more.
7. Remove the racks from the grill, cut them into individual ribs, and serve immediately.

Brown Sugar Country Ribs

Prep time: 25 minutes | Cook time: 4 hours | Serves 12 to 15

2 pounds (907 g) country-style ribs
1 batch Sweet Brown Sugar Rub
2 tablespoons light brown sugar

1 cup Pepsi or other cola
¼ cup The Ultimate BBQ Sauce
1.   Supply your smoker with wood pellets and follow the manufacturer's specific start-up procedure. Preheat the grill, with the lid closed, to 180ºF (82ºC).
2.   Sprinkle the ribs with the rub and use your hands to work the rub into the meat.
3.   Place the ribs directly on the grill grate and smoke for 3 hours.
4.   Remove the ribs from the grill and place them on enough aluminum foil to wrap them completely. Dust the brown sugar over the ribs.
5.   Increase the grill's temperature to 300ºF (149ºC).
6.   Fold in three sides of the foil around the ribs and add the cola. Fold in the last side, completely enclosing the ribs and liquid. Return the ribs to the grill and cook for 45 minutes.
7.   Remove the ribs from the foil and place them on the grill grate. Baste all sides of the ribs with barbecue sauce. Cook for 15 minutes more to caramelize the sauce.
8.   Remove the ribs from the grill and serve immediately.

Classic Pulled Pork Shoulder

Prep time: 15 minutes | Cook time: 16 to 20 hours | Serves 8 to 12
1 (6- to 8-pound / 2.7- to 3.6-kg) bone-in pork shoulder
2 tablespoons yellow mustard
1 batch Pork Rub
Supply your smoker with wood pellets and follow the manufacturer's specific start-up procedure. Preheat the grill, with the lid closed, to 225ºF (107ºC).
Coat the pork shoulder all over with mustard and season it with the rub. Using your hands, work the rub into the meat.
Place the shoulder on the grill grate and smoke until its internal temperature reaches 195°F (91ºC).
Pull the shoulder from the grill and wrap it completely in aluminum foil or butcher paper. Place it in a cooler, cover the cooler, and let it rest for 1 or 2 hours.
Remove the pork shoulder from the cooler and unwrap it. Remove the shoulder bone and pull the pork apart using just your fingers. Serve immediately as desired. Leftovers are encouraged.

Prok-Rub Injected Pork Shoulder

Prep time: 15 minutes | Cook time: 16 to 20 hours | Serves 8 to 12
1 (6- to 8-pound / 2.7- to 3.6-kg) bone-in pork shoulder

2 cups Tea Injectable made with Pork Rub
2 tablespoons yellow mustard
1 batch Pork Rub
1.   Supply your smoker with wood pellets and follow the manufacturer's specific start-up procedure. Preheat the grill, with the lid closed, to 225ºF (107ºC).
2.   Inject the pork shoulder throughout with the tea injectable.
3.   Coat the pork shoulder all over with mustard and season it with the rub. Using your hands, work the rub into the meat.
4.   Place the shoulder directly on the grill grate and smoke until its internal temperature reaches 160ºF (71ºC) and a dark bark has formed on the exterior.
5.   Pull the shoulder from the grill and wrap it completely in aluminum foil or butcher paper.
6.   Increase the grill's temperature to 350ºF (177ºC).
7.   Return the pork shoulder to the grill and cook until its internal temperature reaches 195°F (91ºC).
8.   Pull the shoulder from the grill and place it in a cooler. Cover the cooler and let the pork rest for 1 or 2 hours.
9.   Remove the pork shoulder from the cooler and unwrap it. Remove the shoulder bone and pull the pork apart using just your fingers. Serve immediately.

Smoked Pork Chops

Prep time: 10 minute | Cook time: 55 minutes | Serves 4
1 (12-pound / 5.4-g) full packer brisket
2 tablespoons yellow mustard
1 batch Espresso Brisket Rub
Worcestershire Mop and Spritz, for spritzing
1.   Supply your smoker with wood pellets and follow the manufacturer's specific start-up procedure. Preheat the grill, with the lid closed, to 180ºF (82ºC).
2.   Season the pork chops on both sides with salt and pepper.
3.   Place the chops directly on the grill grate and smoke for 30 minute.
4.   Increase the grill's temperature to 350ºF (177ºC). Continue to cook the chops until their internal temperature reaches 145°F (63ºC).
5.   Remove the pork chops from the grill and let them rest for 5 minutes before serving.

Smoked Pork Tenderloin

Prep time: 15 minutes | Cook time: 4 to 5 hours | Serves 4 to 6

2 (1-pound / 454-g) pork tenderloins
1 batch Pork Rub
1.   Supply your smoker with wood pellets and follow the manufacturer's specific start-up procedure. Preheat the grill, with the lid closed, to 180ºF (82ºC).
2.   Generously season the tenderloins with the rub. Using your hands, work the rub into the meat.
3.   Place the tenderloins directly on the grill grate and smoke for 4 or 5 hours, until their internal temperature reaches 145°F (63ºC).
4.   Remove the tenderloins from the grill and let them rest for 5 to 10 minute before thinly slicing and serving.

Homemade Teriyaki Pork Tenderloin

Prep time: 30 minute | Cook time: 1½ to 2 hours | Serves 12 to 15

2 (1-pound / 454-g) pork tenderloins
1 batch Quick and Easy Teriyaki Marinade
Smoked salt, to taste
1.   In a large zip-top bag, combine the tenderloins and marinade. Seal the bag, turn to coat, and refrigerate the pork for at least 30 minute—I recommend up to overnight.
2.   Supply your smoker with wood pellets and follow the manufacturer's specific start-up procedure. Preheat the grill, with the lid closed, to 180ºF (82ºC).
3.   Remove the tenderloins from the marinade and season them with smoked salt.
4.   Place the tenderloins directly on the grill grate and smoke for 1 hour.
5.   Increase the grill's temperature to 300ºF (149ºC) and continue to cook until the pork's internal temperature reaches 145°F (63ºC).
6.   Remove the tenderloins from the grill and let them rest for 5 to 10 minute, before thinly slicing and serving.

Barbecued Pork Tenderloin

Prep time: 5 minutes | Cook time: 30 minute | Serves 4 to 6

2 (1-pound / 454-g) pork tenderloins
1 batch sweet and spicy cinnamon rub
1.   Supply your smoker with wood pellets and follow the manufacturer's specific start-up procedure. Preheat the grill, with the lid closed, to 350ºF (177ºC).
2.   Generously season the tenderloins with the rub. Using your hands, work the rub into the meat.
3.   Place the tenderloins directly on the grill grate and smoke until their internal temperature reaches 145°F (63ºC).

4.   Remove the tenderloins from the grill and let them rest for 5 to 10 minute, before thinly slicing and serving.

Barbecued Pork Belly Burnt Ends

Prep time: 30 minute | Cook time: 6 hours | Serves 8 to 10

1 (3-pound / 1.4-kg) skinless pork belly (if not already skinned, use a sharp boning knife to remove the skin from the belly), cut into 1½- to 2-inch cubes
1 batch Sweet Brown Sugar Rub
½ cup honey
1 cup The Ultimate BBQ Sauce
2 tablespoons light brown sugar
Supply your smoker with wood pellets and follow the manufacturer's specific start-up procedure. Preheat the grill, with the lid closed, to 250ºF (121ºC).
2. Generously season the pork belly cubes with the rub. Using your hands, work the rub into the meat.
3. Place the pork cubes directly on the grill grate and smoke until their internal temperature reaches 195°F (91ºC).
4. Transfer the cubes from the grill to an aluminum pan. Add the honey, barbecue sauce, and brown sugar. Stir to combine and coat the pork.
5. Place the pan in the grill and smoke the pork for 1 hour, uncovered. Remove the pork from the grill and serve immediately.

Cajun-Honey Smoked Ham

Prep time: 20 minute | Cook time: 4 or 5 hours | Serves 12 to 15

•
1 (5- or 6-pound / 2.3- or 2.7-kg) bone-in smoked ham
1 batch Cajun Rub
3 tablespoons honey
1.   Supply your smoker with wood pellets and follow the manufacturer's specific start-up procedure. Preheat the grill, with the lid closed, to 225ºF (107ºC).
2.   Generously season the ham with the rub and place it either in a pan or directly on the grill grate. Smoke it for 1 hour.
3.   Drizzle the honey over the ham and continue to smoke it until the ham's internal temperature reaches 145°F (63ºC).
4.   Remove the ham from the grill and let it rest for 5 to 10 minute, before thinly slicing and serving.

Rosemary-Garlic Smoked Ham

Prep time: 15 minutes | Cook time: 5 or 6 hours | Serves 12 to 15

1 (10-pound / 4.5-kg) fresh ham, skin removed
2 tablespoons olive oil
1 batch Rosemary-Garlic Lamb Seasoning
1.   Supply your smoker with wood pellets and follow the manufacturer's specific start-up procedure. Preheat the grill, with the lid closed, to 180ºF (82ºC).
2.   Rub the ham all over with olive oil and sprinkle it with the seasoning.
3.   Place the ham directly on the grill grate and smoke for 3 hours.
4.   Increase the grill's temperature to 375ºF (191ºC) and continue to smoke the ham until its internal temperature reaches 170ºF (77ºC).
5.   Remove the ham from the grill and let it rest for 10 minute, before carving and serving.

Spiced Breakfast Grits

Prep time: 20 minute | Cook time: 30 to 40 minute | Serves 12 to 15
2 cups chicken stock
1 cup water
1 cup quick-cooking grits
3 tablespoons unsalted butter
2 tablespoons minced garlic
1 medium onion, chopped
1 jalapeño pepper, stemmed, seeded, and chopped
1 teaspoon cayenne pepper
2 teaspoons red pepper flakes
1 tablespoon hot sauce
1 cup shredded Monterey Jack cheese
1 cup sour cream
Salt, to taste
Freshly ground black pepper, to taste
2 eggs, beaten
⅓ cup half-and-half
3 cups leftover pulled pork (preferably smoked)
1.   Supply your smoker with wood pellets and follow the manufacturer's specific start-up procedure. Preheat, with the lid closed, to 350ºF (177ºC).
2.   On your kitchen stove top, in a large saucepan over high heat, bring the chicken stock and water to a boil.
3.   Add the grits and reduce the heat to low, then stir in the butter, garlic, onion, jalapeño, cayenne, red pepper flakes, hot sauce, cheese, and sour cream. Season with salt and pepper, then cook for about 5 minutes.
4.   Temper the beaten eggs (see Tip below) and incorporate into the grits. Remove the saucepan from the heat and stir in the half-and-half and pulled pork.
5.   Pour the grits into a greased grill-safe 9-by-13-inch casserole dish or aluminum pan.

6.   Transfer to the grill, close the lid, and bake for 30 to 40 minute, covering with aluminum foil toward the end of cooking if the grits start to get too brown on top.

Roasted Lip-Smackin' Pork Loin

Prep time: 10 minute | Cook time: 3 hours | Serves 8
¼ cup finely ground coffee
¼ cup paprika
¼ cup garlic powder
2 tablespoons chili powder
1 tablespoon packed light brown sugar
1 tablespoon ground allspice
1 tablespoon ground coriander
1 tablespoon freshly ground black pepper
2 teaspoons ground mustard
1½ teaspoons celery seeds
1 (1½- to 2-pound) pork loin roast
1.   Supply your smoker with wood pellets and follow the manufacturer's specific start-up procedure. Preheat, with the lid closed, to 250ºF (121ºC).
2.   In a small bowl, combine the ground coffee, paprika, garlic powder, chili powder, brown sugar, allspice, coriander, pepper, mustard, and celery seeds to create a rub, and generously apply it to the pork loin roast.
3.   Place the pork loin on the grill, fat-side up, close the lid, and roast for 3 hours, or until a meat thermometer inserted in the thickest part of the meat reads 160ºF (71ºC).
4.   Let the pork rest for 5 minutes before slicing and serving.

Pork, Pineapple, and Sweet Pepper Kebabs

Prep time: 20 minute | Cook time: 1 to 4 hours | Serves 12 to 15
1 (20-ounce / 567-g) bottle hoisin sauce
½ cup Sriracha
¼ cup honey
¼ cup apple cider vinegar
2 tablespoons canola oil
2 teaspoons minced garlic
2 teaspoons onion powder
1 teaspoon ground ginger
1 teaspoon salt
1 teaspoon freshly ground black pepper
2 pounds thick-cut pork chops or pork loin, cut into 2-inch cubes
10 ounces fresh pineapple, cut into chunks
1 red onion, cut into wedges
1 bag mini sweet peppers, tops removed and seeded

12 metal or wooden skewers (soaked in water for 30 minute if wooden)

1. In a small bowl, stir together the hoisin, Sriracha, honey, vinegar, oil, minced garlic, onion powder, ginger, salt, and black pepper to create the marinade. Reserve ¼ cup for basting.

2. Toss the pork cubes, pineapple chunks, onion wedges, and mini peppers in the remaining marinade. Cover and refrigerate for at least 1 hour or up to 4 hours.

3. Supply your smoker with wood pellets and follow the manufacturer's specific start-up procedure. Preheat, with the lid closed, to 450ºF (232ºC).

4. Remove the pork, pineapple, and veggies from the marinade; do not rinse. Discard the c.

5. Use the double-skewer technique to assemble the kebabs (see Tip below). Thread each of 6 skewers with a piece of pork, a piece of pineapple, a piece of onion, and a sweet mini pepper, making sure that the skewer goes through the left side of the ingredients. Repeat the threading on each skewer two more times. Double-skewer the kebabs by sticking another 6 skewers through the right side of the ingredients.

6. Place the kebabs directly on the grill, close the lid, and smoke for 10 to 12 minutes, turning once. They are done when a meat thermometer inserted in the pork reads 160ºF (71ºC).

Jalapeño Bacon-Wrapped Tenderloin

Prep time: 25 minutes | Cook time: 2½ hours | Serves 4 to 6

¼ cup yellow mustard
2 (1-pound / 454-g) pork tenderloins
¼ cup Pork Rub
8 ounces (227 g) cream cheese, softened
1 cup grated Cheddar cheese
1 tablespoon unsalted butter, melted
1 tablespoon minced garlic
2 jalapeño peppers, seeded and diced
1½ pounds bacon

1. Slather the mustard all over the pork tenderloins, then sprinkle generously with the dry rub to coat the meat.

2. Supply your smoker with wood pellets and follow the manufacturer's specific start-up procedure. Preheat, with the lid closed, to 225ºF (107ºC).

3. Place the tenderloins directly on the grill, close the lid, and smoke for 2 hours.

4. Remove the pork from the grill and increase the temperature to 375°F (191ºC).

5. In a small bowl, combine the cream cheese, Cheddar cheese, melted butter, garlic, and jalapeños.

6. Starting from the top, slice deeply along the center of each tenderloin end to end, creating a cavity.

7. Spread half of the cream cheese mixture in the cavity of one tenderloin. Repeat with the remaining mixture and the other piece of meat.

8. Securely wrap one tenderloin with half of the bacon. Repeat with the remaining bacon and the other piece of meat.

9. Transfer the bacon-wrapped tenderloins to the grill, close the lid, and smoke for about 30 minute, or until a meat thermometer inserted in the thickest part of the meat reads 160ºF (71ºC) and the bacon is browned and cooked through.

10. Let the tenderloins rest for 5 to 10 minute before slicing and serving.

Brown Sugar-Glazed Ham

Prep time: 30 minute | Cook time: 5 hours | Serves 12 to 15

1 (12- to 15-pound / 5.4- to 6.8-kg) whole bone-in ham, fully cooked
¼ cup yellow mustard
1 cup pineapple juice
½ cup packed light brown sugar
1 teaspoon ground cinnamon
½ teaspoon ground cloves

1. Supply your smoker with wood pellets and follow the manufacturer's specific start-up procedure. Preheat, with the lid closed, to 275ºF (135ºC).

2. Trim off the excess fat and skin from the ham, leaving a ¼-inch layer of fat. Put the ham in an aluminum foil–lined roasting pan.

3. On your kitchen stove top, in a medium saucepan over low heat, combine the mustard, pineapple juice, brown sugar, cinnamon, and cloves and simmer for 15 minutes, or until thick and reduced by about half.

4. Baste the ham with half of the pineapple–brown sugar syrup, reserving the rest for basting later in the cook.

5. Place the roasting pan on the grill, close the lid, and smoke for 4 hours.

6. Baste the ham with the remaining pineapple–brown sugar syrup and continue smoking with the lid closed for another hour, or until a meat thermometer inserted in the thickest part of the ham reads 140ºF (60ºC).

7. Remove the ham from the grill, tent with foil, and let rest for 20 minute before carving.

Stuffed Pork Ribs

Prep time: 1 hour | Cook time: 3 hours | Serves 2 to 4

10 pound (4.5 kg) crown roast of pork, 12-14 ribs

1 cup apple juice or cider
2 tablespoon apple cider vinegar
2 tablespoon Dijon mustard
1 tablespoon brown sugar
2 clove garlic, minced
2 tablespoon thyme or rosemary, fresh
1 teaspoon salt
1 teaspoon coarse ground black pepper, divided
½ cup olive oil
8 cup your favorite stuffing, prepared according to the package directions, or homemade

1.	Set the pork on a flat rack in a shallow roasting pan. Cover the end of each bone with a small piece of foil.
2.	Make the marinade: Bring the apple cider to a boil over high heat and reduce by half. Remove from the heat, and whisk in the vinegar, mustard, brown sugar, garlic, thyme, and salt and pepper. Slowly whisk in the oil.
3.	Using a pastry brush, apply the marinade to the roast, coating all surfaces. Cover it with plastic wrap and allow it to sit until the meat comes to room temperature, about 1 hour.
4.	When ready to cook, set grill temperature to High and preheat, lid closed for 15 minutes.
5.	Arrange the roasting pan with the pork on the grill grate. Roast for 30 minute.
6.	Reduce the heat to 325ºF (163ºC). Loosely fill the crown with the stuffing, mounding it at the top. Cover the stuffing with foil. (Alternatively, you can bake the stuffing in a separate pan alongside the roast.)
7.	Roast the pork for another 1-½ hours. Remove the foil from the stuffing and continue to roast until the internal temperature of the meat is 150°F (66ºC), about 30 minute to an hour. Make sure the temperature probe doesn't touch bone or you will get a false reading.
8.	Remove roast from grill and allow to rest for 15 minutes. Remove the foil covering the bones, but leave the butcher's string on the roast until ready to carve. Transfer to a warm platter.
9.	To serve, carve between the bones. Enjoy.

Stuffed Pork Loin wwith Bacon

Prep time: 20 minute | Cook time: 1 hour | Serves 4 to 6

•
3 pound (1.4 kg) pork loin, butterflied
As needed pork rub
¼ cup Walnuts, chopped
⅓ cup Craisins
1 tablespoon oregano, fresh
1 tablespoon fresh thyme
6 pieces Asparagus, fresh
6 slices Bacon, sliced
1/3 cup Parmesan cheese, grated
As needed bacon grease

1.	Lay down 2 large pieces of butcher's twine on your work surface. Place butterflied pork loin perpendicular to twine.
2.	Season the inside of the pork loin with the pork rub.
3.	On one end of the loin, layer in a line all of the ingredients, beginning with the chopped walnuts, craisins, oregano, thyme, and asparagus.
4.	Add bacon and top with the parmesan cheese.
5.	Starting at the end with all of the fillings, carefully roll up the pork loin and secure on both ends with butcher's twine.
6.	Roll the pork loin in the reserved bacon grease and season the outside with more Pork Rub.
7.	When ready to cook, set temperature to 180ºF (82ºC) and preheat, lid closed for 15 minutes. Place stuffed pork loin directly on the grill grate and smoke for 1 hour.
8.	Remove the pork loin; increase the temperature to 350ºF (177ºC) and allow to preheat.
9.	Place the loin back on the Traeger and grill for approximately 30 to 45 minutes or until the temperature reads 135ºF (57ºC) on an instant-read thermometer.
10.	Move the pork loin to a plate and tent it with aluminum foil. Let it rest for 15 minutes before slicing and serving. Enjoy!

Porchetta with Italian Salsa Verde

Prep time: 30 minute | Cook time: 3 hours | Serves 8 to 12

3 tablespoon dried fennel seed
2 tablespoon red pepper flakes
2 tablespoon sage, minced
1 tablespoon rosemary, minced
3 clove garlic, minced
As needed lemon zest
As needed orange zest
Salt and pepper, to taste
6 pound (2.7 kg) pork belly, skin on
1 whole shallot, thinly sliced
6 tablespoon parsley, minced
2 tablespoon freshly minced chives
1 tablespoon oregano, fresh
3 tablespoon white wine vinegar
½ teaspoon kosher salt
¾ cup olive oil
½ teaspoon Dijon mustard
As needed fresh lemon juice

1. Prepare herb mixture: In a medium bowl, mix together fennel seeds, red pepper flakes, sage, rosemary, garlic, citrus zest, salt and pepper.
2. Place pork belly skin side up on a clean work surface and score in a crosshatch pattern. Flip the pork belly over and season flesh side with salt, pepper and half of the herb mixture.
3. Place trimmed pork loin in the center of the belly and rub with remaining herb mixture. Season with salt and pepper.
4. Roll the pork belly around the loin to form a cylindrical shape and tie tightly with kitchen twine at 1" intervals.
5. Season the outside with salt and pepper and transfer to refrigerator, uncovered and let air dry overnight.
6. When ready to cook, start the Traeger grill and set to smoke.
7. Fit a rimmed baking sheet with a rack and place the pork on the rack seam side down.
8. Place the pan directly on the grill grate and smoke for 1 hour.
9. Increase the grill temperature to 325ºF (163ºC) and roast until the internal temperature of the meat reaches 135ºF (57ºC), about 2½ hours. If the exterior begins to burn before the desired internal temperature is reached, tent with foil.
10. Remove from grill and let stand 30 minute before slicing.
11. To make the Italian salsa verde: Combine shallot, parsley, chives, vinegar, oregano and salt in a medium bowl. Whisk in olive oil then stir in mustard and lemon juice.
12. Drizzle slices with Italian salsa verde and enjoy!

BBQ St. Louis-Style Ribs

Prep time: 5 minutes | Cook time: 6 hours 10 minutes | Serves 4

2 racks of St. Louis-style ribs
¼ cup Traeger Pork & Poultry Rub
1 cup apple juice
1 bottle Traeger Sweet & Heat BBQ Sauce

1. Trim the ribs and peel off the membrane from the back of the ribs. Brush the Traeger Pork & Poultry Rub all over the ribs. Let marinate for 20 minutes and up to 4 hours if refrigerated.
2. When ready to cook, set Traeger temperature to 225ºF (107ºC) and preheat, lid closed for 15 minutes.
3. Place the ribs, bone-side down, on the grill grate. Pour the apple juice in a spray bottle and spritz the ribs evenly. Smoke for 3 hours.

4. Remove the ribs from the grill and wrap in aluminum foil. Leave an opening at one end, pour in the remaining apple juice into the foil and wrap tightly.
5. Place the ribs back on the grill, meat-side down. Smoke for an additional 3 hours.
6. After 1 hour, start checking the internal temperature of the ribs. The ribs are done when the internal temperature reaches 203ºF (95ºC).
7. When done, remove from the foil and brush the Traeger Sweet & Heat BBQ Sauce all over the ribs.
8. Return to the grill and cook for an additional 10 minutes to set the sauce.
9. After sauce has set, take the ribs off the grill and let rest for 10 minutes.
10. Slice the ribs in between the bones and serve warm.

Balsamic Smoked Pork Chops

Prep time: 10 minutes | Cook time: 65 to 70 minutes | Serves 4

4 (8-ounce / 227-g) bone-in pork rib chops
Traeger Pork & Poultry Rub, as needed
Olive oil, as needed
Glaze:
½ cup balsamic vinegar
¼ cup brown sugar
2 sprigs rosemary, finely chopped
Ginger ale beer, as needed

1. When ready to cook, set Traeger temperature to 180ºF (82ºC) and preheat, lid closed for 15 minutes.
2. Brush the pork chops all over with the Traeger Pork & Poultry Rub, gently pressing the seasoning into the meat.
3. Place the pork chops on the grill grate and smoke for 30 minutes.
4. Meanwhile, make the glaze: Place all the ingredients in a saucepan over medium-low heat. Cook for about 15 to 20 minutes, or until it thickens to the point that it can coat the back of a spoon but still be pourable. Keep the glaze warm while the pork chops finish smoking.
5. Remove the pork chops and set the Traeger to High and preheat, lid closed for 10 to 15 minutes.
6. Lightly drizzle the chops with olive oil and return to the grill grate.
7. Cook the chops for 20 minutes, or until an instant-read thermometer inserted in the thickest part of the meat registers at least 145ºF (63ºC).
8. Let the pork chops cool for 10 minutes and baste with the glaze.
9. Remove from the grill and let rest for 10 minutes before cutting. Serve warm.

Juicy BBQ Ribs

Prep time: 10 minutes | Cook time: 2 hours 20 minutes | Serves 6

4 rack baby back ribs
½ cup white grape juice
½ cup apple juice
Honey, as needed
Traeger BBQ Sauce, as needed

Rub:

⅔ cup brown sugar
½ cup paprika
⅓ cup garlic powder
2 tablespoons chili powder
2 tablespoons onion powder
1 tablespoon freshly ground white pepper
1 tablespoon cayenne pepper
1 tablespoon ground black pepper
1½ teaspoons ground cumin
1½ teaspoons dried oregano

1. In a bowl, stir together all the ingredients for the rub. Season the ribs with the rub on both sides.
2. When ready to cook, set Traeger temperature to 275ºF (135ºC) and preheat, lid closed for 15 minutes.
3. Place the seasoned ribs on the grill and cook for 45 minutes.
4. Meanwhile, combine the grape and apple juices in a small bowl and set aside.
5. Remove the ribs from the grill and place them, bone-side down, on a large disposable foil pan. Pour the juice mixture over the ribs.
6. Drizzle with the honey. Wrap up the ribs completely with the foil and seal the edges. Return the ribs to the grill and cook for 1 hour.
7. Remove the ribs from the foil and place directly on the grill grate. Set the temperature to 350ºF (177ºC) and cook for 30 additional minutes.
8. Rub the ribs with the Traeger BBQ Sauce and cook for an additional 5 minutes to set the sauce.
9. Transfer the ribs to a cutting board. Slice into single serving-size pieces and serve.

Traeger Smoked Queso

Prep time: 10 minutes | Cook time: 1 hour | Serves 8

1 pound (454 g) hot pork sausage
1 pound (454 g) smoked Gouda cheese
1 (2-pound / 907-g) block Velveeta cheese
1 (10-ounce / 284-g) can RO*TEL Fire Roasted Diced Tomatoes & Green Chilies
1 (10-ounce / 284-g) can RO*TEL Original Diced Tomatoes & Green Chilies
1 (10-ounce / 284-g) can cream of mushroom soup
4 tablespoons Traeger Coffee Rub
½ cup chopped cilantro

1. In a skillet over medium heat, cook the pork sausage for 15 minutes, breaking into small chunks. Remove the sausage from the skillet. Drain the sausage and discard the grease.
2. When ready to cook, set Traeger temperature to 350ºF (177ºC) and preheat, lid closed for 15 minutes.
3. Cut the smoked Gouda into 1-inch cubes and cut the block of Velveeta into 5 to 6 large pieces.
4. Place the cheeses in an oven safe dish. Add the canned tomatoes and chilies with the liquid. Pour in the cream of mushroom soup. Add the cooked sausage and Traeger Coffee Rub.
5. Place the dish on the grill and smoke the queso for 45 minutes, stirring 3 to 4 times.
6. After 40 minutes, add most of the cilantro to the dish and continue smoking for 5 minutes.
7. Top with the remaining cilantro and serve hot.

BBQ Honey Pork Belly

Prep time: 5 minutes | Cook time: 4 hours | Serves 8

1 (about 5- to 7-pound / 2.3- to 3.2-kg) skinless pork belly, cut into 1-inch cubes
Meat Church Honey Hog, as needed
1 cup apple juice, for spritzing
1½ cups Traeger Apricot BBQ Sauce
½ cup clover honey

1. When ready to cook, set Traeger temperature to 275ºF (135ºC) and preheat, lid closed for 15 minutes.
2. In a large bowl, toss together the pork belly cubes and Meat Church Honey Hog until well coated. Let sit for at least 15 minutes.
3. Place the pork belly cubes, fat-side down, on the grill. Cook for 3 hours, spritzing with apple juice every 45 minutes or whenever it starts to look dry.
4. Remove the pork when the internal temperature of the meat reaches 195ºF (91ºC) on a meat thermometer.
5. Transfer the cubes to a half-size aluminum pan. Season with more Meat Church Honey Hog.
6. Cover the cubes with the Traeger Apricot BBQ Sauce. Drizzle clover honey over the top. Toss the cubes thoroughly until completely coated.
7. Place the pan back to the grill and cook uncovered for 1 more hour, or until all liquid has reduced and caramelized.
8. Let cool for 15 minutes before serving. Serve warm.

Spicy Smoked St. Louis Ribs

Prep time: 10 minutes | Cook time: 4 hours | Serves 4

2 rack St. Louis-style ribs
2 cups apple juice

Rub:

¼ cup brown sugar
1 tablespoon onion powder
1 tablespoon cumin
1 tablespoon smoked paprika
1 tablespoon garlic salt
½ tablespoon red pepper flakes
1 teaspoon ground coriander

1. When ready to cook, set Traeger temperature to 250ºF (121ºC) and preheat, lid closed for 15 minutes.
2. In a small bowl, whisk together all the ingredients for the rub. Season the ribs generously on all sides with the rub.
3. Place the seasoned ribs on the grill and smoke for 2 hours.
4. Remove from the grill and wrap the ribs in a double layer of foil. Pour the apple juice over the ribs into the foil pack. Place the ribs back to the grill and cook for 2 more hours.
5. Remove the ribs from grill and let rest for 10 minutes. Serve warm.

Chile Verde Braised Pork Shoulder

Prep time: 20 minutes | Cook time: 2 hours | Serves 6

1 pork shoulder, bone removed and cut into 1½-inch cubes (about 2 to 3 pounds / 0.9 to 1.4 kg)
1 tablespoon all-purpose flour
Salt, to taste
Black pepper, to taste
1 pound (454 g) tomatillos, husked and washed
1 medium yellow onion, peeled and cut into 1-inch chunks
2 jalapeños
4 cloves garlic
4 tablespoons olive oil, divided
2 cans green chiles
2 cups chicken stock
1 tablespoon cumin
1 tablespoon dried oregano
¼ cup chopped cilantro
½ lime, juiced

1. In a medium bowl, toss the pork shoulder with the flour, salt and pepper until well coated.
2. When ready to cook, set Traeger temperature to 500ºF (260ºC) and preheat, lid closed for 15 minutes.
3. Place a large cast iron skillet directly on the bottom rack of the grill and let preheat for 20 minutes.
4. Place the tomatillos, onion, jalapeños and garlic on a parchment-lined sheet tray. Drizzle with 2 tablespoons of the olive oil and season with salt and pepper. Stir to coat.
5. Pour the remaining 2 tablespoons of the olive oil in the cast iron skillet and add the pork shoulder. Spread the meat out evenly.
6. Place the sheet tray on the top rack. Close the lid and cook for 20 minutes, undisturbed. The pork should be evenly browned on the bottom and the veggies should be tender and lightly browned.
7. Remove the vegetables from the grill and transfer to a blender. Pulse until smooth. Pour the puréed vegetables into the skillet with the pork along with the green chiles, chicken stock, cumin and oregano.
8. Close the lid and reduce the temperature to 325ºF (163ºC). Cook for 60 to 90 minutes, or until the liquid has reduced and the pork is fork tender.
9. Remove from the grill. Top with the chopped cilantro and drizzle with the lime juice. Serve immediately.

Traeger Grilled Pork Chops

Prep time: 5 minutes | Cook time: 30 minutes | Serves 2

2 (1½-inch thick) pork chops
¼ cup red wine
¼ cup olive oil
3 tablespoons chopped fresh rosemary
Traeger Blackened Saskatchewan Rub, as needed
Salt, to taste

1. In a large bowl, stir together all the ingredients, except for the pork chops. Add the pork chops to the bowl and let marinate in the refrigerator for 2 hours.
2. When ready to cook, set Traeger temperature to 500ºF (260ºC) and preheat, lid closed for 15 minutes.
3. Place the marinated chops directly on the grill grate and cook for 30 minutes, or until an instant-read thermometer inserted in the thickest part of the meat registers 140ºF (60ºC).
4. Remove from the grill and let cool for 5 minutes before serving.

Butter-Sugar Glazed BBQ Pork Ribs

Prep time: 5 minutes | Cook time: 4 hours 50 minutes| Serves 6

2 rack St. Louis-style ribs, membrane removed
1 cup Traeger Pork & Poultry Rub

4 tablespoons agave, divided
4 tablespoons butter, divided
2 tablespoons brown sugar, divided
1 bottle Traeger Sweet & Heat BBQ Sauce

1.   When ready to cook, set Traeger temperature to 225ºF (107ºC) and preheat, lid closed for 15 minutes.
2.   Brush the ribs all over with the Traeger Pork & Poultry Rub. Let marinate for 15 to 20 minutes.
3.   Place the ribs, bone-side down, on the grill and cook for 3 hours.
4.   Meanwhile, prepare the brown sugar wrap. Spread 2 tablespoons of the agave, 2 tablespoons of the butter and 1 tablespoon of the brown sugar on top of a double layer of aluminum foil. Repeat for the second foil.
5.   After 3 hours, place one rack of ribs, meat-side down, in the prepared foil and wrap. Repeat with the second rack.
6.   Increase the temperature of the grill to 250ºF (121ºC) and place the wrapped ribs, meat-side down, on the grill. Cook for another 1½ hours, or until an instant-read thermometer inserted in the meat registers 205ºF (96ºC).
7.   Remove the ribs from the grill and discard the foil. Return the unwrapped ribs to the grill and cook for 10 more minutes.
8.   Remove from the grill and rub with the Traeger Sweet & Heat BBQ Sauce. Return the ribs to the grill and cook for another 10 minutes.
9.   Let cool for 10 minutes before slicing. Serve warm.

Traeger Braised BBQ Ribs

Prep time: 5 minutes | Cook time: 5 hours 10 minutes | Serves 4
2 rack St. Louis-style ribs, patted dry and membrane removed
¼ cup Traeger Big Game Rub
1 cup apple juice
Traeger BBQ Sauce, as needed

1.   Brush the ribs all over with the Traeger Big Game Rub. Let marinate for 20 minutes and up to 4 hours if refrigerated.
2.   When ready to cook, set Traeger temperature to 225ºF (107ºC) and preheat, lid closed for 15 minutes.
3.   Arrange the ribs, bone-side down, on the grill and cook for 5 hours.
4.   After 1 hour, put the apple juice in a spray bottle and spritz the ribs. Spritz every 45 minutes thereafter.

5.   After 4½ hours, check the internal temperature of ribs. The ribs are done when the internal temperature reaches 200ºF (93ºC). If not, check back in another 30 minutes.
6.   When done, brush the ribs all over with the Traeger BBQ Sauce. Cook for 10 more minutes to set the sauce.
7.   Remove the ribs from the grill and let rest for 10 minutes. Slice the ribs in between the bones and serve warm.

Apricot BBQ Smoked Pork Tenderloin

Prep time: 5 minutes | Cook time: 48 minutes | Serves 4
2 pounds (907 g) pork tenderloin, trimmed
3 ounces (85 g) Traeger Big Game Rub
1 cup Traeger Apricot BBQ Sauce

1.   Brush the pork tenderloin all over with the Traeger Big Game Rub and let marinate for 30 minutes.
2.   When ready to cook, set Traeger temperature to 180ºF (82ºC) and preheat, lid closed for 15 minutes.
3.   Arrange the pork tenderloin on the grill grate and smoke for 45 minutes.
4.   Remove the pork from the grill. Set Traeger temperature to High and preheat, lid closed for 15 minutes.
5.   Place the pork back to the grill grate and grill each side of the pork tenderloin for 90 seconds, or until an instant-read thermometer inserted in the thickest part of the meat registers 145ºF (63ºC).
6.   Brush the pork with the Traeger Apricot BBQ Sauce. Transfer to a plate and let cool for 20 minutes before serving.

Brown Sugar Baked Pork Belly

Prep time: 5 minutes | Cook time: 2o to 30 minutes | Serves 2
½ cup brown sugar
1 tablespoon ground fennel
2 teaspoons kosher salt
1 teaspoon ground black pepper
1 pound (454 g) pork belly, diced

1.   Fold a piece of aluminum foil in half and crimp the edges so there is a rim. Using a fork, poke holes in the bottom of the foil.
2.   When ready to cook, set Traeger temperature to 350ºF (177ºC) and preheat, lid closed for 15 minutes.
3.   In a large bowl, stir together all the ingredients, except for the pork belly.

4.	Add the diced pork belly to the bowl and toss until well coated. Transfer the pork pieces to the foil.
5.	Place the foil on the grill and bake for 20 to 30 minutes, or until the pork belly is crispy, glazed and bubbly.
6.	Let rest for 5 minutes before serving.

Sriracha Lamb Chops

Prep time: 15 minutes | Cook time: 10 to 20 minute | Serves 4 to 6
½ cup rice wine vinegar
1 teaspoon liquid smoke
2 tablespoons extra-virgin olive oil
2 tablespoons dried minced onion
1 tablespoon chopped fresh mint
8 (4-ounce / 113-g) lamb chops
½ cup hot pepper jelly
1 tablespoon Sriracha
1 teaspoon salt
1 teaspoon freshly ground black pepper
1.	In a small bowl, whisk together the rice wine vinegar, liquid smoke, olive oil, minced onion, and mint. Place the lamb chops in an aluminum roasting pan. Pour the marinade over the meat, turning to coat thoroughly. Cover with plastic wrap and marinate in the refrigerator for 2 hours.
2.	Supply your smoker with wood pellets and follow the manufacturer's specific start-up procedure. Preheat, with the lid closed, to 165ºF (74ºC), or the "Smoke" setting.
3.	On the stove top, in a small saucepan over low heat, combine the hot pepper jelly and Sriracha and keep warm.
4.	When ready to cook the chops, remove them from the marinade and pat dry. Discard the marinade.
5.	Season the chops with the salt and pepper, then place them directly on the grill grate, close the lid, and smoke for 5 minutes to "breathe" some smoke into them.
6.	Remove the chops from the grill. Increase the pellet cooker temperature to 450ºF (232ºC), or the "High" setting. Once the grill is up to temperature, place the chops on the grill and sear, cooking for 2 minutes per side to achieve medium-rare chops. A meat thermometer inserted in the thickest part of the meat should read 145°F (63ºC). Continue grilling, if necessary, to your desired doneness.
7.	Serve the chops with the warm Sriracha pepper jelly on the side.

Christmas Garlicky Lamb

Prep time: 1 hour | Cook time: 1 to 2 hours | Serves 4
•
2 racks of lamb, trimmed, frenched, and tied into a crown
1¼ cups extra-virgin olive oil, divided
2 tablespoons chopped fresh basil
2 tablespoons chopped fresh rosemary
2 tablespoons ground sage
2 tablespoons ground thyme
8 garlic cloves, minced
2 teaspoons salt
2 teaspoons freshly ground black pepper
1.	Set the lamb out on the counter to take the chill off, about an hour.
2.	In a small bowl, combine 1 cup of olive oil, the basil, rosemary, sage, thyme, garlic, salt, and pepper.
3.	Baste the entire crown with the herbed olive oil and wrap the exposed frenched bones in aluminum foil.
4.	Supply your smoker with wood pellets and follow the manufacturer's specific start-up procedure. Preheat, with the lid closed, to 275ºF (135ºC).
5.	Put the lamb directly on the grill, close the lid, and smoke for 1 hour 30 minute to 2 hours, or until a meat thermometer inserted in the thickest part reads 140ºF (60ºC).
6.	Remove the lamb from the heat, tent with foil, and let rest for about 15 minutes before serving. The temperature will rise about 5ºF (-15ºC) during the rest period, for a finished temperature of 145°F (63ºC).

Lamb with Pitas

Prep time: 20 minute | Cook time: 40 minute | Serves 4
1 pound (454 g) ground lamb
2 teaspoons salt
1 teaspoon freshly ground black pepper
2 tablespoons chopped fresh oregano
1 tablespoon minced garlic
1 tablespoon onion powder
4 to 6 pocketless pitas
Tzatziki sauce, for serving
1 tomato, chopped, for serving
1 small onion, thinly sliced, for serving
1.	In a medium bowl, combine the lamb, salt, pepper, oregano, garlic, and onion powder; mix well. Cover with plastic wrap and refrigerate overnight.
2.	Supply your smoker with wood pellets and follow the manufacturer's specific start-up procedure. Preheat, with the lid closed, to 300ºF (149ºC).

3.   Remove the meat mixture from the refrigerator and, on a Frogmat or a piece of heavy-duty aluminum foil, roll and shape it into a rectangular loaf about 8 inches long by 5 inches wide.

4.   Place the loaf directly on the grill, close the lid, and smoke for 35 minutes, or until a meat thermometer inserted in the center reads 155°F (68°C).

5.   Remove the loaf from the heat and increase the temperature to 450°F (232°C).

6.   Cut the loaf into ⅛-inch slices and place on a Frogmat or a piece of heavy-duty foil.

7.   Return the meat (still on the Frogmat or foil) to the smoker, close the lid, and continue cooking for 2 to 4 minutes, or until the edges are crispy.

8.   Warm the pitas in the smoker for a few minutes and serve with the lamb, tzatziki sauce, chopped tomato, and sliced onion.

Smoked Venison Steaks

Prep time: 20 minute | Cook time: 1 hour 20 minute | Serves 4

4 (8-ounce / 227-g) venison steaks
2 tablespoons extra-virgin olive oil
4 garlic cloves, minced
1 tablespoon ground sage
2 teaspoons sea salt
2 teaspoons freshly ground black pepper

1.   Supply your smoker with wood pellets and follow the manufacturer's specific start-up procedure. Preheat, with the lid closed, to 225°F (107°C).

2.   Rub the venison steaks well with the olive oil and season with the garlic, sage, salt, and pepper.

3.   Arrange the venison steaks directly on the grill grate, close the lid, and smoke for 1 hour and 20 minute, or until a meat thermometer inserted in the center reads 130°F (54°C) to 140°F (60°C), depending on desired doneness. If you want a better sear, remove the steaks from the grill at an internal temperature of 125°F (52°C), crank up the heat to 450°F (232°C), or the "High" setting, and cook the steaks on each side for an additional 2 to 3 minutes.

Garlicky Rosemary Lamb Leg

Prep time: 15 minutes | Cook time: 20 to 25 minutes per pound | Serves 12 to 16

2 tablespoons finely chopped fresh rosemary
1 tablespoon ground thyme
5 garlic cloves, minced
2 tablespoons sea salt
1 tablespoon freshly ground black pepper
Butcher's string
1 whole boneless (6- to 8-pound / 2.7- to 3.6-kg) leg of lamb

¼ cup extra-virgin olive oil
1 cup red wine vinegar
½ cup canola oil

1.   In a small bowl, combine the rosemary, thyme, garlic, salt, and pepper; set aside.

2.   Using butcher's string, tie the leg of lamb into the shape of a roast. Your butcher should also be happy to truss the leg for you.

3.   Rub the lamb generously with the olive oil and season with the spice mixture. Transfer to a plate, cover with plastic wrap, and refrigerate for 4 hours.

4.   Remove the lamb from the refrigerator but do not rinse.

5.   Supply your smoker with wood pellets and follow the manufacturer's specific start-up procedure. Preheat, with the lid closed, to 325°F (163°C).

6.   In a small bowl, combine the red wine vinegar and canola oil for basting.

7.   Place the lamb directly on the grill, close the lid, and smoke for 20 to 25 minutes per pound (depending on desired doneness), basting with the oil and vinegar mixture every 30 minute. Lamb is generally served medium-rare to medium, so it will be done when a meat thermometer inserted in the thickest part reads 140°F (60°C) to 145°F (63°C).

8.   Let the lamb rest for about 15 minutes before slicing to serve.

Rosemary Lamb Chops

Prep time: 15 minutes | Cook time: 2 hours | Serves 4

4½ pounds (2 kg) bone-in lamb chops
2 tablespoons olive oil
Salt, to taste
Freshly ground black pepper, to taste
1 bunch fresh rosemary

1.   Supply your smoker with wood pellets and follow the manufacturer's specific start-up procedure. Preheat the grill, with the lid closed, to 180°F (82°C).

2.   Rub the lamb chops all over with olive oil and season on both sides with salt and pepper.

3.   Spread the rosemary directly on the grill grate, creating a surface area large enough for all the chops to rest on. Place the chops on the rosemary and smoke until they reach an internal temperature of 135°F (57°C).

4.   Increase the grill's temperature to 450°F (232°C), remove the rosemary, and continue to cook the chops until their internal temperature reaches 145°F (63°C).

5.   Remove the chops from the grill and let them rest for 5 minutes before serving.

Rosemary-Garlic Rack of Lamb

Prep time: 25 minutes | Cook time: 4 to 6 hours | Serves 6

1 (2-pound / 907-g) rack of lamb
1 batch Rosemary-Garlic Lamb Seasoning

1. Supply your smoker with wood pellets and follow the manufacturer's specific start-up procedure. Preheat the grill, with the lid closed, to 225ºF (107ºC).
2. Using a boning knife, score the bottom fat portion of the rib meat.
3. Using your hands, rub the rack of lamb all over with the seasoning, making sure it penetrates into the scored fat.
4. Place the rack directly on the grill grate, fat-side up, and smoke until its internal temperature reaches 145°F (63ºC).
5. Remove the rack from the grill and let it rest for 20 to 30 minute, before slicing it into individual ribs to serve.

Grilled Lamb and Apricot Kabobs

Prep time: 15 minutes | Cook time: 8 to 10 minutes | Serves 4

½ cup olive oil
½ cup lemon juice
2 tablespoons minced fresh mint
1 tablespoon lemon zest
½ tablespoon finely chopped cilantro
½ tablespoon salt
2 teaspoons black pepper
1 teaspoon cumin
3 pounds (1.4 kg) boneless leg of lamb, cut into 2-inch cubes
15 whole dried apricots
2 whole red onions, cut into ⅛-inch thick

1. In a medium bowl, stir together the olive oil, lemon juice, mint, lemon zest, cilantro, salt, pepper and cumin. Add the lamb shoulder to the bowl and toss to coat. Set in the refrigerator and marinate overnight.
2. Remove the lamb from the marinade and thread lamb, apricots, and red onion alternatively until the skewer is full.
3. When ready to cook, set Traeger temperature to 400ºF (204ºC) and preheat, lid closed for 15 minutes.
4. Lay the skewers on the grill grate and cook for 8 to 10 minutes, or until the onions are lightly browned and the lamb is cooked to the desired temperature.
5. Remove the skewers from the grill and serve immediately.

Spicy Braised Lamb Shoulder

Prep time: 10 minutes | Cook time: 5 hours 2 minutes | Serves 4

2 ounces (57 g) guajillo peppers, deseeded
2 tablespoons plus ½ cup water, divided
3 cloves garlic
2 tablespoons olive oil
1 tablespoon lime juice
1 tablespoon smoked paprika
1 tablespoon fresh oregano
1 tablespoon salt
¼ tablespoon ground coriander seeds
¼ tablespoon ground cumin seeds
¼ tablespoon ground pumpkin seeds
3 pounds (1.4 kg) lamb shoulders

1. In a microwave-safe bowl, cover the guajillo chilies with water and microwave on high for 2 minutes. Let cool slightly, then transfer the soft chilies and 2 tablespoons of the water to a blender.
2. Add the remaining ingredients, except for the lamb shoulders, to the blender. Pulse until smooth.
3. Arrange the lamb in a roast pan and rub ½ cup of the sauce all over the meat. Let marinate at room temperature for at least 2 hours and up to 12 hours.
4. When ready to cook, set Traeger temperature to 325ºF (163ºC) and preheat, lid closed for 15 minutes.
5. Add ½ cup of the water to the roast pan and cover the pan loosely with foil. Cook the lamb for 2½ hours, adding water to the pan a few times.
6. Remove the foil and cook for another 2½ hours, or until the lamb is browned and tender, occasionally spooning the juices on top.
7. Remove from the grill and let cool for 20 minutes before shredding. Spoon the remaining liquid in the bottom of the pan over the lamb.
8. Serve immediately.

Grilled Lamb Leg

Prep time: 10 minutes | Cook time: 30 to 40 minutes | Serves 8

5 pounds (2.3 kg) leg of lamb, butterflied and boneless
1 whole onion, sliced into rings
Marinade:
1 whole lemon, juiced and rinds reserved
4 cloves garlic, minced
1 cup olive oil
¼ cup red wine vinegar
2½ teaspoons minced rosemary
1 teaspoon thyme
1 teaspoon salt
1 teaspoon ground black pepper

1. In a mixing bowl, whisk together all the ingredients for the marinade.
2. Remove any netting from the lamb and place into a large resealable plastic bag. Pour the marinade into the bag and add the onion. Massage the bag to distribute the marinade and herbs. Refrigerate for several hours or overnight.
3. Remove the lamb from the marinade and pat dry with paper towels. Discard the marinade.
4. When ready to cook, set the Traeger to High and preheat, lid closed for 15 minutes.
5. Arrange the lamb on the grill grate, fat-side down. Grill for 30 to 40 minutes per side, or until the internal temperature reaches 135ºF (57ºC) for medium-rare.
6. Let the lamb leg cool for 5 minutes before slicing. Serve warm.

Roasted Breaded Rack of Lamb

Prep time: 10 minutes | Cook time: 20 minutes | Serves 4

1 rack of lamb, frenched (about 1½ pounds / 680 g)
½ cup yellow mustard
1 tablespoon salt
1 teaspoon ground black pepper
1 cup panko bread crumbs
1 tablespoon minced Italian parsley
1 teaspoon minced rosemary
1 teaspoon minced sage

1. Rub the rack of lamb with the mustard and season with salt and pepper.
2. In a shallow baking dish, combine the remaining ingredients. Dredge the lamb in the bread crumb mixture.
3. When ready to cook, set Traeger temperature to 500ºF (260ºC) and preheat, lid closed for 15 minutes.
4. Place the rack of lamb on the grill grate, bone-side down, and cook for 20 minutes, or until the internal temperature reaches 120ºF (49ºC).
5. Remove from the grill and let rest for 5 to 10 minutes before slicing. Serve warm.

Garlicky Grilled Rack of Lamb

Prep time: 5 minutes | Cook time: 30 minutes | Serves 4

8 cloves garlic
1 bunch fresh thyme
1 tablespoon kosher salt
2 teaspoons extra-virgin olive oil
1 teaspoon sherry vinegar
2 pounds (907 g) rack of lamb

1. In a blender, combine all the ingredients, except for the rack of lamb. Pulse until smooth. Rub the paste all over the rack of lamb.
2. When ready to cook, set Traeger temperature to 450ºF (232ºC) and preheat, lid closed for 15 minutes.
3. Lay the rack of lamb, fat-side down, on the grill and cook for 20 minutes. Turn over so the fat side is up and cook for an additional 10 minutes. A thermometer inserted in the center of the lamb should register 160ºF (71ºC).
4. Let cool for 10 minutes before slicing into chops. Serve warm.

Smoked Brats with Buds

Prep time: 10 minute | Cook time: 1 to 2 hours | Serves 12 to 15

4 (12-ounce / 340-g) cans of beer
2 onions, sliced into rings
2 green bell peppers, sliced into rings
2 tablespoons unsalted butter, plus more for the rolls
2 tablespoons red pepper flakes
10 brats, uncooked
10 hoagie rolls, split
Mustard, for serving

1. On your kitchen stove top, in a large saucepan over high heat, bring the beer, onions, peppers, butter, and red pepper flakes to a boil.
2. Supply your smoker with wood pellets and follow the manufacturer's specific start-up procedure. Preheat, with the lid closed, to 225ºF (107ºC).
3. Place a disposable pan on one side of grill, and pour the warmed beer mixture into it, creating a "brat tub" (see Tip below).
4. Place the brats on the other side of the grill, directly on the grate, and close the lid and smoke for 1 hour, turning 2 or 3 times.
5. Add the brats to the pan with the onions and peppers, cover tightly with aluminum foil, and continue smoking with the lid closed for 30 minute to 1 hour, or until a meat thermometer inserted in the brats reads 160ºF (71ºC).
6. Butter the cut sides of the hoagie rolls and toast cut-side down on the grill.
7. Using a slotted spoon, remove the brats, onions, and peppers from the cooking liquid and discard the liquid.
8. Serve the brats on the toasted buns, topped with the onions and peppers and mustard (ketchup optional)

Traeger Smoked Pork Sausage

Prep time: 30 minute | Cook time: 3 hours | Serves 4 to 6

3 pounds (1.4 kg) ground pork
½ tablespoon ground mustard
1 tablespoon onion powder
1 tablespoon garlic powder
1 teaspoon pink curing salt
1 tablespoon salt
4 teaspoon black pepper
½ cup ice water
Hog casings, soaked and rinsed in cold water

1.   In a medium bowl, combine the meat and seasonings, mix well.
2.   Add ice water to meat and mix with hands working quickly until everything is incorporated.
3.   Place mixture in a sausage stuffer and follow manufacturer's instructions for operating. Use caution not to overstuff or the casing might burst.
4.   Once all the meat is stuffed, determine your desired link length and pinch and twist a couple of times or tie it off. Repeat for each link.
5.   When ready to cook, set Traeger temperature to 225°F (107°C) and preheat, lid closed for 15 minutes. For optimal flavor, use Super Smoke if available.
6.   Place links directly on the grill grate and cook for 1 to 2 hours or until the internal temperature registers 155°F (68°C). Let sausage rest a few minutes before slicing. Enjoy!

Hot Sausage and Potato

Prep time: 15 minutes | Cook time: 50 minute | Serves 4 to 6
●
2 pounds (907 g) hot sausage links
2 pounds (907 g) potatoes, fingerling
1 tablespoon fresh thyme
4 tablespoon butter

1.   When ready to cook, set the Traeger to 375°F (191°C) and preheat, lid closed for 15 minutes.
2.   Put your sausage links on the grill to get some color. This should take about 3 minutes on each side.
3.   While sausage is cooking, cut the potatoes into bite size pieces all about the same size so they cook evenly. Chop the thyme and butter, then combine all the ingredients into a Traeger cast iron skillet.
4.   Pull your sausage off the grill, slice into bite size pieces and add to your cast iron.
5.   Turn grill down to 275°F (135°C) and put the cast iron in the grill for 45 minutes to an hour or until the potatoes are fully cooked.
6.   After 45 minutes, use a butter knife to test your potatoes by cutting into one to see if its done.

To speed up cook time you can cover cast iron will a lid or foil. Serve. Enjoy!

Bacon-Wrapped Hot Dog

Prep time: 20 minute | Cook time: 25 minutes | Serves 4 to 6
16 Hot Dogs
16 Slices Bacon, sliced
2 Onion, sliced
16 hot dog buns
As Needed The Ultimate BBQ Sauce
As Needed Cheese

1.   When ready to cook, set the Traeger to 375°F (191°C) and preheat, lid closed for 15 minutes.
2.   Wrap bacon strips around the hot dogs, and grill directly on the grill grate for 10 minute each side. Grill onions at the same time as the hot dogs, and cook for 10 to15 minutes.
3.   Open hot dog buns and spread BBQ sauce, the grilled hot dogs, cheese sauce and grilled onions. Top with vegetables. Serve, enjoy!

Andouille Sausage and Pepper Skewers

Prep time: 15 minutes | Cook time: 10 minute | Serves 6 to 8
12 ounces (340 g) andouille sausage, cut into 2 inch slices
½ whole red onion, sliced
1 whole green bell pepper, sliced
1 whole yellow bell pepper, sliced
Olive oil, to taste
Cajun shake, to taste
½ cup minced tomatoes
½ tablespoon minced chipotle in adobo sauce
¼ teaspoon cracked black pepper
1 teaspoon honey
¼ teaspoon ancho chile powder
¼ teaspoon garlic powder
¼ teaspoon onion powder
¼ teaspoon kosher sea salt

1.   If using wooden skewers, soak skewers in water for about 30 minute prior to cooking.
2.   Start the Traeger on High heat, lid closed, for 10 to 15 minutes.
3.   Cut pepper, onion and sausage into chunks. Thread skewer alternating between meat and vegetables.
4.   Drizzle each of the skewers with olive oil and season on all sides with the Traeger Cajun Rub.
5.   Put skewers directly on grill grate and cook for about 5 minutes. Flip skewers over and cook for an additional 5 minutes.
6.   Spicy Ketchup Dipping: Mix together sauce ingredients and transfer to a small serving bowl.

7. Pull skewers off grill and serve with spicy dipping sauce. Enjoy!

Polish Kielbasa with Smoked Cabbage

Prep time: 1 hour | Cook time: 1 to 2 hours | Serves 8

4 pounds (1.8 kg) ground pork
½ cup water
2 garlic cloves, minced
4 teaspoons salt
1 teaspoon freshly ground black pepper
1 teaspoon dried marjoram
½ teaspoon ground allspice
14 feet natural hog casings, medium size

1. In a large bowl, combine the pork, water, garlic, salt, pepper, marjoram, and allspice.
2. Stuff the casings according to the instructions on your sausage stuffing device, or use a funnel (see Tip).
3. Twist the casings according to your desired length and prick each with a pin in several places so the kielbasa won't burst.
4. Transfer the kielbasa to a plate, cover with plastic wrap, and refrigerate for at least 8 hours or overnight.
5. Remove from the refrigerator and allow the links to come to room temperature.
6. Supply your smoker with wood pellets and follow the manufacturer's specific start-up procedure. Preheat, with the lid closed, to 225ºF (107ºC).
7. Place the kielbasa directly on the grill grate, close the lid, and smoke for 1 hour 30 minute to 2 hours, or until a meat thermometer inserted in each link reads 155°F (68ºC). (The internal temperature will rise about 5ºF (-15ºC) when resting, for a finished temp of 160ºF (71ºC).)

Serve with buns and condiments of your choosing, or cut up the kielbasa and serve with smoked cabbage

CHAPTER 6 POULTRY

Beer Can Chicken

Prep time: 30 minute | Cook time: 3 to 4 hours | Serves 3 to 4

8 tablespoons (1 stick) unsalted butter, melted
½ cup apple cider vinegar
½ cup Cajun seasoning, divided
1 teaspoon garlic powder
1 teaspoon onion powder
1 (4-pound / 1.8-kg) whole chicken, giblets removed
Extra-virgin olive oil, for rubbing
1 (12-ounce / 340-g) can beer
1 cup apple juice
½ cup extra-virgin olive oil

1.	In a small bowl, whisk together the butter, vinegar, ¼ cup of Cajun seasoning, garlic powder, and onion powder.
2.	Use a meat-injecting syringe to inject the liquid into various spots in the chicken. Inject about half of the mixture into the breasts and the other half throughout the rest of the chicken.
3.	Rub the chicken all over with olive oil and apply the remaining ¼ cup of Cajun seasoning, being sure to rub under the skin as well.
4.	Drink or discard half the beer and place the opened beer can on a stable surface.
5.	Place the bird's cavity on top of the can and position the chicken so it will sit up by itself. Prop the legs forward to make the bird more stable, or buy an inexpensive, specially made stand to hold the beer can and chicken in place.
6.	Supply your smoker with wood pellets and follow the manufacturer's specific start-up procedure. Preheat, with the lid closed, to 250ºF (121ºC).
7.	In a clean 12-ounce spray bottle, combine the apple juice and olive oil. Cover and shake the mop sauce well before each use.
8.	Carefully put the chicken on the grill. Close the lid and smoke the chicken for 3 to 4 hours, spraying with the mop sauce every hour, until golden brown and a meat thermometer inserted in the thickest part of the thigh reads 165ºF (74ºC). Keep a piece of aluminum foil handy to loosely cover the chicken if the skin begins to brown too quickly.
9.	Let the meat rest for 5 minutes before carving.

Buffalo Chicken Tortilla

Prep time: 30 minute | Cook time: 20 minute | Serves 4

2 teaspoons poultry seasoning
1 teaspoon freshly ground black pepper
1 teaspoon garlic powder
1 to 1½ pounds chicken tenders
4 tablespoons (½ stick) unsalted butter, melted
½ cup hot sauce (such as Frank's RedHot)
4 (10-inch) flour tortillas
1 cup shredded lettuce
½ cup diced tomato
½ cup diced celery
½ cup diced red onion
½ cup shredded Cheddar cheese
¼ cup blue cheese crumbles
¼ cup prepared ranch dressing
2 tablespoons sliced pickled jalapeño peppers (optional)

1.	Supply your smoker with wood pellets and follow the manufacturer's specific start-up procedure. Preheat, with the lid closed, to 350ºF (177ºC).
2.	In a small bowl, stir together the poultry seasoning, pepper, and garlic powder to create an all-purpose rub, and season the chicken tenders with it.
3.	Arrange the tenders directly on the grill, close the lid, and smoke for 20 minute, or until a meat thermometer inserted in the thickest part of the meat reads 170ºF (77ºC).
4.	In another bowl, stir together the melted butter and hot sauce and coat the smoked chicken with it.
5.	To serve, heat the tortillas on the grill for less than a minute on each side and place on a plate.
6.	Top each tortilla with some of the lettuce, tomato, celery, red onion, Cheddar cheese, blue cheese crumbles, ranch dressing, and jalapeños (if using).
7.	Divide the chicken among the tortillas, close up securely, and serve.

Smoked Whole Chicken

Prep time: 15 minutes | Cook time: 1 to 2 hours | Serves 6 to 8

1 whole chicken
2 tablespoons olive oil
1 batch chicken rub

1.	Supply your smoker with wood pellets and follow the manufacturer's specific start-up procedure. Preheat the grill, with the lid closed, to 375°F (191ºC).
2.	Coat the chicken all over with olive oil and season it with the rub. Using your hands, work the rub into the meat.
3.	Place the chicken directly on the grill grate and smoke until its internal temperature reaches 170ºF (77ºC).

4.   Remove the chicken from the grill and let it rest for 10 minute, before carving and serving.

Tea Injectable Chicken

Prep time: 25 minutes | Cook time: 4 hours | Serves 6 to 8

1 whole chicken
2 cups tea injectable (using not-just-for-pork rub)
2 tablespoons olive oil
1 batch chicken rub
2 tablespoons butter, melted

1.   Supply your smoker with wood pellets and follow the manufacturer's specific start-up procedure. Preheat the grill, with the lid closed, to 180ºF (82ºC).
2.   Inject the chicken throughout with the tea injectable.
3.   Coat the chicken all over with olive oil and season it with the rub. Using your hands, work the rub into the meat.
4.   Place the chicken directly on the grill grate and smoke for 3 hours.
5.   Baste the chicken with the butter and increase the grill's temperature to 375ºF (191ºC). Continue to cook the chicken until its internal temperature reaches 170ºF (77ºC).
6.   Remove the chicken from the grill and let it rest for 10 minute, before carving and serving.

Smoked Skinless Chicken Breast

Prep time: 15 minutes | Cook time: 1½ hours | Serves 4 to 6

2½ pounds (1.1 kg) boneless, skinless chicken breasts
Salt, to taste
Freshly ground black pepper, to taste

1.   Supply your smoker with wood pellets and follow the manufacturer's specific start-up procedure. Preheat the grill, with the lid closed, to 180ºF (82ºC).
2.   Season the chicken breasts all over with salt and pepper.
3.   Place the breasts directly on the grill grate and smoke for 1 hour.
4.   Increase the grill's temperature to 325ºF (163ºC) and continue to cook until the chicken's internal temperature reaches 170ºF (77ºC). Remove the breasts from the grill and serve immediately.

Smoked Chicken Breast

Prep time: 10 minute | Cook time: 45 minutes | Serves 2 to 4

2 (1-pound / 454-g) bone-in, skin-on chicken breasts
1 batch Chicken Rub

1.   Supply your smoker with wood pellets and follow the manufacturer's specific start-up procedure. Preheat the grill, with the lid closed, to 350ºF (177ºC).
2.   Season the chicken breasts all over with the rub. Using your hands, work the rub into the meat.
3.   Place the breasts directly on the grill grate and smoke until their internal temperature reaches 170ºF (77ºC). Remove the breasts from the grill and serve immediately.

Chicken Breast Tenders

Prep time: 15 minutes | Cook time: 1⅓ hours | Serves 2 to 4

1 pound (454 g) boneless, skinless chicken breast tenders
1 batch Chicken Rub

1.   Supply your smoker with wood pellets and follow the manufacturer's specific start-up procedure. Preheat the grill, with the lid closed, to 180ºF (82ºC).
2.   Season the chicken tenders with the rub. Using your hands, work the rub into the meat.
3.   Place the tenders directly on the grill grate and smoke for 1 hour.
4.   Increase the grill's temperature to 300ºF (149ºC) and continue to cook until the tenders' internal temperature reaches 170ºF (77ºC). Remove the tenders from the grill and serve immediately.

Buffalo Chicken Wings

Prep time: 15 minutes | Cook time: 35 minutes | Serves 2 to 3

1 pound (454 g) chicken wings
1 batch Chicken Rub
1 cup Frank's Red-Hot Sauce, Buffalo wing sauce, or similar

1.   Supply your smoker with wood pellets and follow the manufacturer's specific start-up procedure. Preheat the grill, with the lid closed, to 300ºF (149ºC).
2.   Season the chicken wings with the rub. Using your hands, work the rub into the meat.
3.   Place the wings directly on the grill grate and smoke until their internal temperature reaches 160ºF (71ºC).
4.   Baste the wings with the sauce and continue to smoke until the wings' internal temperature reaches 170ºF (77ºC).

Cinnamon Rub Chicken Wings

Prep time: 20 minute | Cook time: 1½ hours | Serves 2 to 4

1 pound (454 g) chicken wings
1 batch sweet and spicy cinnamon rub
1 cup barbecue sauce

1. Supply your smoker with wood pellets and follow the manufacturer's specific start-up procedure. Preheat the grill, with the lid closed, to 325ºF (163ºC).
2. Season the chicken wings with the rub. Using your hands, work the rub into the meat.
3. Place the wings directly on the grill grate and cook until they reach an internal temperature of 165ºF (74ºC).
4. Transfer the wings into an aluminum pan. Add the barbecue sauce and stir to coat the wings.
5. Reduce the grill's temperature to 250ºF (121ºC) and put the pan on the grill. Smoke the wings for 1 hour more, uncovered. Remove the wings from the grill and serve immediately.

Smoked Chicken Drumsticks

Prep time: minutes | Cook time: | Serves
1 pound (454 g) chicken drumsticks
2 tablespoons olive oil
1 batch sweet and spicy cinnamon rub
1. Supply your smoker with wood pellets and follow the manufacturer's specific start-up procedure. Preheat the grill, with the lid closed, to 350ºF (177ºC).
2. Coat the drumsticks all over with olive oil and season with the rub. Using your hands, work the rub into the meat.
3. Place the drumsticks directly on the grill grate and smoke until their internal temperature reaches 170ºF (77ºC). Remove the drumsticks from the grill and serve immediately.

Smoked Chicken Quarters

Prep time: 15 minutes | Cook time: 2 hours | Serves 2 to 4
4 chicken quarters
2 tablespoons olive oil
1 batch Chicken Rub
2 tablespoons butter
1. Supply your smoker with wood pellets and follow the manufacturer's specific start-up procedure. Preheat the grill, with the lid closed, to 180ºF (82ºC).
2. Coat the chicken quarters all over with olive oil and season them with the rub. Using your hands, work the rub into the meat.
3. Place the quarters directly on the grill grate and smoke for 1½ hours.
4. Baste the quarters with the butter and increase the grill's temperature to 375°F (191ºC). Continue to cook until the chicken's internal temperature reaches 170ºF (77ºC).
5. Remove the quarters from the grill and let them rest for 10 minute before serving.

Mandarin Glazed Whole Duck

Prep time: 20 minute | Cook time: 4 hours | Serves 4
1 quart buttermilk
1 (5-pound / 2.3-kg) whole duck
¾ cup soy sauce
½ cup hoisin sauce
½ cup rice wine vinegar
2 tablespoons sesame oil
1 tablespoon freshly ground black pepper
1 tablespoon minced garlic
Mandarin Glaze, for drizzling
1. With a very sharp knife, remove as much fat from the duck as you can. Refrigerate or freeze the fat for later use.
2. Pour the buttermilk into a large container with a lid and submerge the whole duck in it. Cover and let brine in the refrigerator for 4 to 6 hours.
3. Supply your smoker with wood pellets and follow the manufacturer's specific start-up procedure. Preheat, with the lid closed, to 250ºF (121ºC).
4. Remove the duck from the buttermilk brine, then rinse it and pat dry with paper towels.
5. In a bowl, combine the soy sauce, hoisin sauce, vinegar, sesame oil, pepper, and garlic to form a paste. Reserve ¼ cup for basting.
6. Poke holes in the skin of the duck and rub the remaining paste all over and inside the cavity.
7. Place the duck on the grill breast-side down, close the lid, and smoke for about 4 hours, basting every hour with the reserved paste, until a meat thermometer inserted in the thickest part of the meat reads 165ºF (74ºC) Use aluminum foil to tent the duck in the last 30 minute or so if it starts to brown too quickly.
8. To finish, drizzle with glaze.

Roast Whole Chicken

Prep time: 10 minute | Cook time: 1 to 2 hours | Serves 4
1 (4-pound / 1.8-kg) whole chicken, giblets removed
Extra-virgin olive oil, for rubbing
3 tablespoons Greek seasoning
Juice of 1 lemon
Butcher's string
1. Supply your smoker with wood pellets and follow the manufacturer's specific start-up procedure. Preheat, with the lid closed, to 450ºF (232ºC).
2. Rub the bird generously all over with oil, including inside the cavity.
3. Sprinkle the Greek seasoning all over and under the skin of the bird, and squeeze the lemon juice over the breast.

4.	Tuck the chicken wings behind the back and tie the legs together with butcher's string or cooking twine.

5.	Put the chicken directly on the grill, breast-side up, close the lid, and roast for 1 hour to 1 hour 30 minute, or until a meat thermometer inserted in the thigh reads 165ºF (74ºC).

6.	Let the meat rest for 10 minute before carving.

Cheesy Chicken Enchiladas

Prep time: 15 minutes | Cook time: 45 minutes | Serves 6

6 cups diced cooked chicken
3 cups grated Monterey Jack cheese, divided
1 cup sour cream
1 (4-ounce / 113-g) can chopped green chiles
2 (10-ounce / 283-g) cans red or green enchilada sauce, divided
12 (8-inch) flour tortillas
½ cup chopped scallions
¼ cup chopped fresh cilantro

1.	Supply your smoker with wood pellets and follow the manufacturer's specific start-up procedure. Preheat, with the lid closed, to 350ºF (177ºC).

2.	In a large bowl, combine the cooked chicken, 2 cups of cheese, the sour cream, and green chiles to make the filling.

3.	Pour one can of enchilada sauce in the bottom of a 9-by-13-inch baking dish or aluminum pan.

4.	Spoon ⅓ cup of the filling on each tortilla and roll up securely.

5.	Transfer the tortillas seam-side down to the baking dish, then pour the remaining can of enchilada sauce over them, coating all exposed surfaces of the tortillas.

6.	Sprinkle the remaining 1 cup of cheese over the enchiladas and cover tightly with aluminum foil.

7.	Bake on the grill, with the lid closed, for 30 minute, then remove the foil.

8.	Continue baking with the lid closed for 15 minutes, or until bubbly.

9.	Garnish the enchiladas with the chopped scallions and cilantro and serve immediately.

Cajun Turducken Roulade

Prep time: 20 minute | Cook time: 2 hours | Serves 6

1 (16-ounce / 454-g) boneless turkey breast
1 (8-to 10-ounce / 227-to 283-g) boneless duck breast
1 (8-ounce / 227-g) boneless, skinless chicken breast
Salt, to taste

Freshly ground black pepper, to taste
2 cups Italian dressing
2 tablespoons Cajun seasoning
1 cup prepared seasoned stuffing mix
8 slices bacon
Butcher's string

1.	Butterfly the turkey, duck, and chicken breasts, cover with plastic wrap and, using a mallet, flatten each ½ inch thick.

2.	Season all the meat on both sides with a little salt and pepper.

3.	In a medium bowl, combine the Italian dressing and Cajun seasoning. Spread one-fourth of the mixture on top of the flattened turkey breast.

4.	Place the duck breast on top of the turkey, spread it with one-fourth of the dressing mixture, and top with the stuffing mix.

5.	Place the chicken breast on top of the duck and spread with one-fourth of the dressing mixture.

6.	Supply your smoker with wood pellets and follow the manufacturer's specific start-up procedure. Preheat, with the lid closed, to 275ºF (135ºC).

7.	Tightly roll up the stack, tie with butcher's string, and slather the whole thing with the remaining dressing mixture.

8.	Wrap the bacon slices around the turducken and secure with toothpicks, or try making a bacon weave (see the technique for this in the Jalapeño-Bacon Pork Tenderloin recipe).

9.	Place the turducken roulade in a roasting pan. Transfer to the grill, close the lid, and roast for 2 hours, or until a meat thermometer inserted in the turducken reads 165ºF (74ºC). Tent with aluminum foil in the last 30 minute, if necessary, to keep from overbrowning.

10.	Let the turducken rest for 15 to 20 minute before carving. Serve warm.

Roasted Chicken Thighs

Prep time: 5 minutes | Cook time: 1 to 2 hours | Serves 12 to 15

3 pounds (1.4kg) chicken thighs
2 teaspoons salt
2 teaspoons freshly ground black pepper
2 teaspoons garlic powder
2 teaspoons onion powder
2 cups prepared Italian dressing

1.	Place the chicken thighs in a shallow dish and sprinkle with the salt, pepper, garlic powder, and onion powder, being sure to get under the skin.

2.	Cover with the Italian dressing, coating all sides, and refrigerate for 1 hour.

3.   Supply your smoker with wood pellets and follow the manufacturer's specific start-up procedure. Preheat, with the lid closed, to 250ºF (121ºC).
4.   Remove the chicken thighs from the marinade and place directly on the grill, skin-side down. Discard the marinade.
5.   Close the lid and roast the chicken for 1 hour 30 minute to 2 hours, or until a meat thermometer inserted in the thickest part of the thighs reads 165ºF (74ºC). Do not turn the thighs during the smoking process.

Mandarin Glazed Smoked Turkey Legs

Prep time: 15 minutes | Cook time: 4 to 5 hours | Serves 4

1 gallon hot water
1 cup curing salt (such as Morton Tender Quick)
¼ cup packed light brown sugar
1 teaspoon freshly ground black pepper
1 teaspoon ground cloves
1 bay leaf
2 teaspoons liquid smoke
4 turkey legs
Mandarin Glaze, for serving

1.   In a large container with a lid, stir together the water, curing salt, brown sugar, pepper, cloves, bay leaf, and liquid smoke until the salt and sugar are dissolved; let come to room temperature.
2.   Submerge the turkey legs in the seasoned brine, cover, and refrigerate overnight.
3.   When ready to smoke, remove the turkey legs from the brine and rinse them; discard the brine.
4.   Supply your smoker with wood pellets and follow the manufacturer's specific start-up procedure. Preheat, with the lid closed, to 225ºF (107ºC).
5.   Arrange the turkey legs on the grill, close the lid, and smoke for 4 to 5 hours, or until dark brown and a meat thermometer inserted in the thickest part of the meat reads 165ºF (74ºC).
6.   Serve with Mandarin Glaze on the side or drizzled over the turkey legs.

Jamaican Jerk Chicken Leg Quarters

Prep time: 15 minutes | Cook time: 1 to 2 hours | Serves 4

4 chicken leg quarters, scored
¼ cup canola oil
½ cup Jamaican Jerk Paste
1 tablespoon whole allspice (pimento) berries

1.   Supply your smoker with wood pellets and follow the manufacturer's specific start-up procedure. Preheat, with the lid closed, to 275ºF (135ºC).
2.   Brush the chicken with canola oil, then brush 6 tablespoons of the Jerk paste on and under

the skin. Reserve the remaining 2 tablespoons of paste for basting.
3.   Throw the whole allspice berries in with the wood pellets for added smoke flavor.
4.   Arrange the chicken on the grill, close the lid, and smoke for 1 hour to 1 hour 30 minute, or until a meat thermometer inserted in the thickest part of the thigh reads 165ºF (74ºC).
5.   Let the meat rest for 5 minutes and baste with the reserved jerk paste prior to serving.

Smo-Fried Spiced Chicken

Prep time: 30 minute | Cook time: 55 minutes | Serves 4 to 6

1 egg, beaten
½ cup milk
1 cup all-purpose flour
2 tablespoons salt
1 tablespoon freshly ground black pepper
2 teaspoons freshly ground white pepper
2 teaspoons cayenne pepper
2 teaspoons garlic powder
2 teaspoons onion powder
1 teaspoon smoked paprika
8 tablespoons (1 stick) unsalted butter, melted
1 whole chicken, cut up into pieces

1.   Supply your smoker with wood pellets and follow the manufacturer's specific start-up procedure. Preheat, with the lid closed, to 375°F (191ºC).
2.   In a medium bowl, combine the beaten egg with the milk and set aside.
3.   In a separate medium bowl, stir together the flour, salt, black pepper, white pepper, cayenne, garlic powder, onion powder, and smoked paprika.
4.   Line the bottom and sides of a high-sided metal baking pan with aluminum foil to ease cleanup.
5.   Pour the melted butter into the prepared pan.
6.   Dip the chicken pieces one at a time in the egg mixture, and then coat well with the seasoned flour. Transfer to the baking pan.
7.   Smoke the chicken in the pan of butter("smo-fry") on the grill, with the lid closed, for 25 minutes, then reduce the heat to 325°F and turn the chicken pieces over.
8.   Continue smoking with the lid closed for about 30 minute, or until a meat thermometer inserted in the thickest part of each chicken piece reads 165ºF (74ºC).
9.   Serve immediately.

Grilled AppleTurkey

Prep time: 10 minute | Cook time: 5 to 6 hours | Serves 6 to 8

- 1 (10- to 12-pound / 4.5- to 5.4-kg) turkey, giblets removed

Extra-virgin olive oil, for rubbing

¼ cup poultry seasoning

8 tablespoons (1 stick) unsalted butter, melted

½ cup apple juice

2 teaspoons dried sage

2 teaspoons dried thyme

1.	Supply your smoker with wood pellets and follow the manufacturer's specific start-up procedure. Preheat, with the lid closed, to 250ºF (121ºC).

2.	Rub the turkey with oil and season with the poultry seasoning inside and out, getting under the skin.

3.	In a bowl, combine the melted butter, apple juice, sage, and thyme to use for basting.

4.	Put the turkey in a roasting pan, place on the grill, close the lid, and grill for 5 to 6 hours, basting every hour, until the skin is brown and crispy, or until a meat thermometer inserted in the thickest part of the thigh reads 165ºF (74ºC).

5.	Let the bird rest for 15 to 20 minute before carving.

Teriyaki Chicken Breast

Prep time: 20 minute | Cook time: 1 to 2 hours | Serves 4

- 2 boneless chicken breasts with drumettes attached

½ cup soy sauce

½ cup teriyaki sauce

¼ cup canola oil

¼ cup white vinegar

1 tablespoon minced garlic

¼ cup chopped scallions

2 teaspoons freshly ground black pepper

1 teaspoon ground mustard

1.	Place the chicken in a baking dish.

2.	In a bowl, whisk together the soy sauce, teriyaki sauce, canola oil, vinegar, garlic, scallions, pepper and ground mustard, then pour this marinade over the chicken, coating both sides.

3.	Refrigerate the chicken in marinade for 4 hours, turning over every hour.

4.	When ready to smoke the chicken, supply your smoker with wood pellets and follow the manufacturer's specific start-up procedure. Preheat, with the lid closed, to 250ºF (121ºC).

5.	Remove the chicken from the marinade but do not rinse. Discard the marinade.

6.	Arrange the chicken directly on the grill, close the lid, and smoke for 1 hour 30 minute to 2

hours, or until a meat thermometer inserted in the thickest part of the meat reads 165ºF (74ºC).

7.	Let the meat rest for 3 minutes before serving.

Barbecue Chicken Breast

Prep time: 10 minute | Cook time: 1 to 2 hours | Serves 8

8 boneless, skinless chicken breasts

2 teaspoons salt

2 teaspoons freshly ground black pepper

2 teaspoons garlic powder

2 cups the ultimate BBQ sauce or your preferred barbecue sauce, divided

1.	Supply your smoker with wood pellets and follow the manufacturer's specific start-up procedure. Preheat, with the lid closed, to 250ºF (121ºC).

2.	Place the chicken breasts in a large pan and sprinkle both sides with the salt, pepper, and garlic powder, being sure to rub under the skin.

3.	Place the roasting pan on the grill, close the lid, and smoke for 1 hour 30 minute to 2 hours, or until a meat thermometer inserted in the thickest part of each breast reads 165ºF (74ºC). During the last 15 minutes of cooking, cover the chicken with 1 cup of barbecue sauce.

4.	Serve the chicken warm with the remaining 1 cup of barbecue sauce.

Wild West Chicken Wings

Prep time: 10 minute | Cook time: 1 hour | Serves 4

2 pounds (907 g) chicken wings

2 tablespoons extra-virgin olive oil

2 packages ranch dressing mix (such as Hidden Valley brand)

¼ cup prepared ranch dressing (optional)

1.	Supply your smoker with wood pellets and follow the manufacturer's specific start-up procedure. Preheat, with the lid closed, to 350ºF (177ºC).

2.	Place the chicken wings in a large bowl and toss with the olive oil and ranch dressing mix.

3.	Arrange the wings directly on the grill, or line the grill with aluminum foil for easy cleanup, close the lid, and smoke for 25 minutes.

4.	Flip and smoke for 20 to 35 minutes more, or until a meat thermometer inserted in the thickest part of the wings reads 165ºF (74ºC) and the wings are crispy. (Note: The wings will likely be done after 45 minutes, but an extra 10 to 15 minutes makes them crispy without drying the meat.)

5.	Serve warm with ranch dressing (if using)

Classic Thanksgiving Turkey

Prep time: 25 minutes | Cook time: 5 to 6 hours | Serves 12 to 14

•

1 whole turkey (make sure the turkey is not pre-brined)
2 batches Garlic Butter Injectable
3 tablespoons olive oil
1 batch Chicken Rub
2 tablespoons butter

1.   Supply your smoker with wood pellets and follow the manufacturer's specific start-up procedure. Preheat the grill, with the lid closed, to 180ºF (82ºC).
2.   Inject the turkey throughout with the garlic butter injectable. Coat the turkey with olive oil and season it with the rub. Using your hands, work the rub into the meat and skin.
3.   Place the turkey directly on the grill grate and smoke for 3 or 4 hours (for an 8- to 12-pound turkey, cook for 3 hours; for a turkey over 12 pounds, cook for 4 hours), basting it with butter every hour.
4.   Increase the grill's temperature to 375°F (191ºC) and continue to cook until the turkey's internal temperature reaches 170ºF (77ºC).
5.   Remove the turkey from the grill and let it rest for 10 minute, before carving and serving.

Somked Spatchcocked Turkey

Prep time: 25 minutes | Cook time: 2 hours | Serves 10 to 14

1 whole turkey
2 tablespoons olive oil
1 batch Chicken Rub

1.   Supply your smoker with wood pellets and follow the manufacturer's specific start-up procedure. Preheat the grill, with the lid closed, to 350ºF (177ºC).
2.   To remove the turkey's backbone, place the turkey on a work surface, on its breast. Using kitchen shears, cut along one side of the turkey's backbone and then the other. Pull out the bone.
3.   Once the backbone is removed, turn the turkey breast-side up and flatten it.
4.   Coat the turkey with olive oil and season it on both sides with the rub. Using your hands, work the rub into the meat and skin.
5.   Place the turkey directly on the grill grate, breast-side up, and cook until its internal temperature reaches 170ºF (77ºC).
6.   Remove the turkey from the grill and let it rest for 10 minute, before carving and serving.

Homemade Turkey Breast

Prep time: 15 minutes | Cook time: 1 to 2 hours | Serves 2 to 4

1 (3-pound /1.4-kg) turkey breast
Salt, to taste
Freshly ground black pepper, to taste
1 teaspoon garlic powder

1.   Supply your smoker with wood pellets and follow the manufacturer's specific start-up procedure. Preheat the grill, with the lid closed, to 180ºF (82ºC).
2.   Season the turkey breast all over with salt, pepper, and garlic powder.
3.   Place the breast directly on the grill grate and smoke for 1 hour.
4.   Increase the grill's temperature to 350ºF (177ºC) and continue to cook until the turkey's internal temperature reaches 170ºF (77ºC). Remove the breast from the grill and serve immediately.

Smoked Cornish Game Hen

Prep time: 10 minute | Cook time: 2 to 3 hours | Serves 4

4 Cornish game hens
Extra-virgin olive oil, for rubbing
2 teaspoons salt
1 teaspoon freshly ground black pepper
1 teaspoon celery seeds

1.   Supply your smoker with wood pellets and follow the manufacturer's specific start-up procedure. Preheat, with the lid closed, to 275ºF (135ºC).
2.   Rub the game hens over and under the skin with olive oil and season all over with the salt, pepper, and celery seeds.
3.   Place the birds directly on the grill grate, close the lid, and smoke for 2 to 3 hours, or until a meat thermometer inserted in each bird reads 170ºF (77ºC).
4.   Serve the Cornish game hens hot.

Sweet- Spicy Cinnamon Turkey Wings

Prep time: 15 minutes | Cook time: 1 hour | Serves 2

4 turkey wings
1 batch sweet and spicy cinnamon rub

1.   Supply your smoker with wood pellets and follow the manufacturer's specific start-up procedure. Preheat the grill, with the lid closed, to 180ºF (82ºC).
2.   Using your hands, work the rub into the turkey wings, coating them completely.
3.   Place the wings directly on the grill grate and cook for 30 minute.
4.   Increase the grill's temperature to 325ºF (163ºC) and continue to cook until the turkey's internal temperature reaches 170ºF (77ºC). Remove the wings from the grill and serve immediately.

Sweet Spiced Pheasant

Prep time: 25 minutes | Cook time: 3 to 4 hours | Serves 4 to 6

1 gallon hot water
1 cup salt
1 cup packed brown sugar
2 (2- to 3-pound / 907- to 1360-g) whole pheasants, cleaned and plucked
¼ cup extra-virgin olive oil
2 tablespoons onion powder
2 tablespoons freshly ground black pepper
2 tablespoons cayenne pepper
1 tablespoon minced garlic
2 teaspoons smoked paprika
1 cup molasses

1.　In a large container with a lid, combine the hot water, salt, and brown sugar, stirring to dissolve the salt and sugar. Let cool to room temperature, then submerge the pheasants in the brine, cover, and refrigerate for 8 to 12 hours.
2.　Remove the pheasants from the brine, then rinse them and pat dry. Discard the brine.
3.　Supply your smoker with wood pellets and follow the manufacturer's specific start-up procedure. Preheat, with the lid closed, to 250ºF (121ºC).
4.　In a small bowl, combine the olive oil, black pepper, cayenne pepper, onion powder, garlic, and paprika to form a paste.
5.　Rub the pheasants with the paste and place breast-side up on the grill grate. Close the lid and smoke for 1 hour.
6.　Open the smoker and baste the pheasants with some of the molasses. Close the lid and continue smoking for 2 to 3 hours, basting with the molasses every 30 minute, until a meat thermometer inserted into the thigh reads 160ºF (71ºC).
7.　Remove the pheasants from the grill and let rest for 20 minute before serving warm or cold.

Quail with Smoked Peaches

Prep time: 20 minute | Cook time: 1 hour | Serves 4

4 quail, spatchcocked
2 teaspoons salt
2 teaspoons freshly ground black pepper
2 teaspoons garlic powder
4 ripe peaches or pears
4 tablespoons (½ stick) salted butter, softened
1 tablespoon sugar
1 teaspoon ground cinnamon

1.　Supply your smoker with wood pellets and follow the manufacturer's specific start-up procedure. Preheat, with the lid closed, to 225ºF (107ºC).
2.　Season the quail all over with the salt, pepper, and garlic powder.

3.　Cut the peaches (or pears) in half and remove the pits (or the cores).
4.　In a small bowl, combine the butter, sugar, and cinnamon; set aside.
5.　Arrange the quail on the grill grate, close the lid, and smoke for about 1 hour, or until a meat thermometer inserted in the thickest part reads 145ºF (63ºC).
6.　After the quail has been cooking for about 15 minutes, add the peaches (or pears) to the grill, flesh-side down, and smoke for 30 to 40 minute.
7.　Top the cooked peaches (or pears) with the cinnamon butter and serve alongside the quail.

Grilled Whole Chicken

Prep time: 5 minutes | Cook time: 1 hour 10 minutes | Serves 4

1 (4 pounds) whole chicken, giblets removed
Traeger Chicken Rub, as needed

1.　When ready to cook, set Traeger temperature to 375ºF (191ºC) and preheat, lid closed for 15 minutes.
2.　Rinse and pat dry the chicken. Season the whole chicken lightly, including the cavity, with Traeger Chicken Rub.
3.　Arrange the chicken on the grill and cook for about 1 hour and 10 minutes, or until the internal temperature of the chicken registers 160ºF (71ºC).
4.　Remove the chicken from the grill and set aside to rest for 15 to 20 minutes, or until it has an internal temperature of 165ºF (74ºC). Serve warm.

Brine Smoked Chicken

Prep time: 10 minutes | Cook time: 3 hours | Serves 6

1 cup brown sugar
½ cup kosher salt
1 (3- to 3½-pounds / 1.4- to 1.6-kg) whole chicken
1 teaspoon minced garlic
Traeger Big Game Rub, as needed
1 medium yellow onion, quartered
1 lemon, halved
3 whole garlic clove
5 thyme sprigs

1.　Make the Brine: Dissolve the kosher salt and brown sugar in 1 gallon of water. Once dissolved, put the chicken into the brine, ensuring the chicken is completely submerged, then place in the refrigerator overnight.
2.　When ready to cook, set Traeger temperature to 225ºF (107ºC) and preheat, lid closed for 15 minutes. For optimal flavor, use Super Smoke if available.

3. Remove the chicken from the brine and pat dry with paper towels. Rub the minced garlic and Traeger Big Game Rub over the chicken. Stuff the cavity with the onion, lemon, garlic clove, and thyme sprigs. Tie the legs together.

4. Arrange the chicken on the grill and smoke for 2½ to 3 hours, or until an instant-read thermometer reads 160ºF (71ºC) when inserted into the thickest part of the chicken.

5. Remove the chicken from the grill and let rest for 15 minutes before serving (the internal temperature will rise to 165ºF (74ºC) as the chicken rests).

Roasted Christmas Goose

Prep time: 30 minutes | Cook time: 2 hours | Serves 8

5½ pounds (2.5 kg) goose
2 limes, zested and cut into wedges
2 lemons, zested and cut into wedges
2 teaspoons salt, plus more as needed
2 thyme sprigs
2 sage sprigs
1 medium green apple, cut into wedges
3 tablespoons honey

1. When ready to cook, set Traeger temperature to High and preheat, lid closed for 15 minutes.

2. Using the tip of a sharp knife, lightly score the breast and leg skin in a criss-cross pattern. Combine the citrus zest with the salt in a bowl. Generously season the cavity of the goose with salt, then rub the citrus mix well into the skin and sprinkle some inside the cavity. Stuff the goose with thyme, sage, lime, lemon and apple wedges.

3. Arrange the stuffed goose on the grill cook for 40 minutes.

4. Brush the honey on top of the goose and reduce the temperature to 325ºF (163ºC). Continue to cook for 1½ to 2 hours, or until an instant-read thermometer inserted in the thickest part of the goose registers 160ºF (71ºC).

5. Remove the goose from the grill and lightly tent with foil. Let rest in the foil for 30 minutes before serving.

Pimentón Roast Chickens with Potatoes

Prep time: 15 minutes | Cook time: 1 hour 10 minutes | Serves 9

2 whole chicken, giblets removed
6 clove garlic, minced
2 tablespoons salt
3 tablespoons pimentón, plus additional for sprinkling
6 tablespoons extra-virgin olive oil, divided
2 bunch fresh thyme
3 pounds (1.4 kg) Yukon gold potatoes, scrubbed
Salt and ground black pepper, to taste
2 lemon, halved
½ cup chopped flat-leaf parsley

1. Rinse the chickens, inside and out, under cold running water. Pat them dry with paper towels. Tie the legs together with butcher's string and tuck the wings behind the backs.

2. Stir together the minced garlic, pimentón, and salt in a small bowl. Whisk in 3 tablespoons of olive oil. Slather the mixture all over the outside of the chickens. Tuck one bunch of thyme inside the main cavity of each chicken. Arrange the chickens on a rimmed baking sheet and transfer to the refrigerator, uncovered, for at least 6 hours or overnight.

3. In a large bowl, toss the potatoes with the salt, pepper, and the remaining 3 tablespoons of olive oil. Spread the potatoes in a large roasting pan.

4. Place the chickens side by side on top of the potatoes. Squeeze the lemons over the chickens and add the rinds to the potatoes.

5. When ready to cook, set Traeger temperature to 400ºF (204ºC) and preheat, lid closed for 10 to 15 minutes.

6. Place the roasting pan with the chickens and potatoes on the grill and roast for 30 minutes. Stir the potatoes.

7. Reduce the temperature to 350ºF (177ºC) and continue to roast for about 40 minutes, or until an instant-read meat thermometer inserted into the thickest part of the thighs registers 165ºF (74ºC).

8. Transfer the potatoes and lemons to a large platter. Lightly sprinkle additional pimentón on top and garnish with the parsley. Place the chickens on top and serve.

Cajun Wings

Prep time: 15 minutes | Cook time: 30 minutes | Serves 4

2 pounds (907 g) chicken wings
Traeger Cajun Shake, as needed
Traeger Pork & Poultry Rub, as needed

1. In a large bowl, toss the chicken wings with Traeger Cajun Shake and Traeger Pork & Poultry Rub.

2. When ready to cook, set the Traeger to 350ºF (177ºC) and preheat, lid closed for 15 minutes.

3. Lay the chicken wings on the grill and cook for 30 minutes, or until the skin is browned and center is juicy and an instant-read thermometer reaches at least 165ºF (74ºC).

4. Let rest for 5 minutes before serving.

Spicy Chicken Skewers

Prep time: 3 hours | Cook time: 20 minutes | Serves 6

16 ounces (454 g) chicken breast, cubed
½ cup ranch
2 tablespoons chile sauce
½ teaspoon dried oregano
½ teaspoon garlic powder
1 whole red onion, sliced
1 whole green bell peppers, sliced
8 strips bacon, sliced

1.   Toss the chicken breast with the ranch, chile sauce, oregano, and garlic powder in a large bowl until evenly coated. Marinate for 1 to 3 hours in the refrigerator.
2.   When ready to cook, set Traeger temperature to High and preheat, lid closed for 15 minutes.
3.   Assemble the Traeger skewers: Slide on a slice of onion, a slice of bell pepper, a slice of bacon, and chicken. Continue to alternate the bacon and chicken, so the bacon weaves around the chicken pieces. Finish off each skewer with a slice of bell pepper and onion. Be sure to not overcrowd skewer and repeat with all skewers.
4.   Arrange the skewers on the grill, keeping a piece of foil under the end of the skewers to prevent them from burning and to make turning them easier. Grill each side for approximately 5 minutes, doing a quarter-turn each time, for a total of 20 minutes, or until the chicken reads an internal temperature of 165ºF (74ºC).
5.   Remove the skewers from the grill and serve hot.

Tandoori Chicken Wings

Prep time: 30 minutes | Cook time: 50 minutes | Serves 4

Marinade:
¼ cup yogurt
1 tablespoon minced cilantro leaves
1 whole scallions, minced
2 teaspoons ginger, minced
1 teaspoon garam masala
1 teaspoon ground black pepper
1 teaspoon salt

Wings:
1½ pounds (680 g) chicken wings
Cooking spray

Sauce:
¼ cup yogurt
2 tablespoons cucumber
2 tablespoons mayonnaise
2 teaspoons lemon juice

½ teaspoon salt
½ teaspoon cumin
⅛ teaspoon cayenne pepper

1.   Place the yogurt, cilantro, scallions, ginger, garam masala, pepper, and salt in a blender and pulse until smooth.
2.   Place the chicken wings in a large resealable plastic bag and pour the yogurt mixture over the chicken wings, massaging the bag to coat all the wings. Let marinate for 4 to 8 hours in the refrigerator.
3.   Drain the chicken wings of excess marinade, discarding the marinade.
4.   When ready to cook, set Traeger temperature to 350ºF (177ºC) and preheat, lid closed for 10 to 15 minutes. Oil the grill grates with cooking spray.
5.   Lay the chicken wings on the grill and cook for 45 to 50 minutes until the skin is crispy, flipping the wings once or twice during cooking.
6.   Meanwhile, whisk all the sauce ingredients to combine in a bowl and refrigerate until ready to use.
7.   When the wings are done, transfer them to a platter and serve alongside the prepared sauce.

Pan-Roasted Game Birds

Prep time: 10 minutes | Cook time: 1 hour | Serves 6

4 pounds (1.8 kg) game birds
4 tablespoons melted butter, divided
Salt and black pepper, to taste
2 whole lemon, halved
1 bunch fresh thyme
1 bunch fresh parsley
1 bunch fresh rosemary

1.   When ready to cook, set Traeger temperature to high and preheat, lid closed for 15 minutes. Put a large cast iron skillet on the grill while preheating.
2.   Rub 2 tablespoons of butter all over the game birds and season the inside and outside with salt and pepper.
3.   Stuff the cavity of each bird of half a lemon, a sprig of parsley, thyme, and rosemary. Truss the birds by simply tying the legs together with string.
4.   Add the remaining 2 tablespoons of butter to the cast iron skillet on the grill. Place the birds in the hot cast iron skillet and roast for 45 to 60 minutes, or until the internal temperature reaches 165ºF (74ºC).
5.   Rest for 10 minutes before serving.

Glazed Chicken Breasts

Prep time: 20 minutes | Cook time: 30 minutes | Serves 4

¼ cup olive oil
1 tablespoon Worcestershire sauce
1 teaspoon freshly pressed garlic
Traeger Fin & Feather Rub, as needed
4 whole chicken breasts
½ cup Traeger 'Que BBQ sauce
½ cup Traeger Sweet & Heat BBQ Sauce

1. Whisk together the olive oil, Worcestershire sauce, garlic, and Traeger Fin & Feather rub in a small bowl. Rub the mixture all over the chicken breasts. Combine the both sauces in another bowl and set aside.
2. When ready to cook, set Traeger temperature to 500ºF (260ºC) and preheat, lid closed for 15 minutes.
3. Arrange the chicken breasts on the grill and cook for 20 to 30 minutes, or until the internal temperature reaches 160ºF (71ºC) when inserted into the thickest part of the breasts. Glaze the chicken breasts with the sauce mixture during the last 5 minutes of cooking.
4. Remove the chicken breasts from the grill and cool for 5 minutes before serving.

Traeger BBQ Half Chickens

Prep time: 15 minutes | Cook time: 1 hour 30 minutes | Serves 2

1 (3- to 3½-pounds / 1.4- to 1.6-kg) fresh young chicken
Traeger Leinenkugel's Summer Shandy Rub
Traeger Apricot BBQ Sauce, as needed

1. Put the chicken, breast-side down, on a cutting board with the neck pointing away from you. Cut along one side of the backbone, staying as close to the bone as possible, from the neck to the tail. Repeat on the other side of the backbone and then remove it.
2. Open the chicken and slice through the white cartilage at the tip of the breastbone to pop it open. Cut down either side of the breast bone then use your fingers to pull it out. Flip the chicken over so it is skin side up and cut down the center splitting the chicken in half. Tuck the wings back on each chicken half.
3. Season the chicken with Traeger Leinenkugel's Summer Shandy Rub on both sides.
4. When ready to cook, set Traeger temperature to 375ºF (191ºC) and preheat, lid closed for 15 minutes.
5. Arrange the chicken, skin-side up, on the grill and cook for about 60 to 90 minutes, or until the

chicken reaches an internal temperature of 160ºF (71ºC).
6. Brush all over the chicken skin with Traeger Apricot BBQ Sauce and grill for 10 minutes more.
7. Remove the chicken from the grill and cool for 5 minutes before serving.

Classic Chicken Pot Pie

Prep time: 20 minutes | Cook time: 50 minutes | Serves 4

2 tablespoons butter
1 stalk celery, diced
1 small yellow onion, diced
2 tablespoons flour
2 cup chicken or turkey stock
½ cup milk
2 teaspoons dry sherry (optional)
½ teaspoon Traeger Pork & Poultry Rub
¼ teaspoon dried thyme leaves
1½ cups frozen peas and carrots, thawed
4 cups cooked skinless chicken or turkey, diced
Salt and pepper, to taste
Cooking spray
1 sheet frozen puff pastry
1 egg, beaten with 1 tablespoon water

1. When ready to cook, set Traeger temperature to 400ºF (204ºC) and preheat, lid closed for 15 minutes.
2. In a saucepan over medium heat, melt the butter. Add the celery and onion and sauté for 3 to 5 minutes, or until the onion is translucent. Scatter with the flour and stir to coat.
3. Slowly stream in the chicken stock, whisking out any lumps. Add the milk and bring the mixture to a boil. Allow to simmer for a few minutes until slightly thickened. Whisk in the dry sherry, if desired.
4. Add the Traeger Pork & Poultry Rub, thyme, chicken, and peas and carrots, stirring well. Let simmer for 5 to 10 minutes. Season with salt and pepper to taste.
5. Spritz a cast iron skillet with cooking spray and fill with the pot pie filling.
6. On a lightly floured surface, unroll the puff pastry sheet and let thaw slightly.
7. Cover the top of the cast iron skillet with the puff pastry crimping any overhang. Make several small slits in the center to let the steam escape and lightly brush with the egg wash.
8. Bake for 30 minutes, or until the puff pastry is nicely browned and the filling is bubbling.
9. Let rest for 5 to 10 minutes before serving.

Smoked Turkey with Fig BBQ Sauce

Prep time: 4 hours | Cook time: 2 hours | Serves 2
Brine:
1 gallon water
½ cup sugar
½ cup salt
Meat:
6 turkey thighs
½ cup ras el hanout
6 tablespoons extra-virgin olive oil
Fig BBQ Sauce:
4 fresh figs, stems removed and cut into quarters
1 cup Traeger Apricot BBQ Sauce
3 tablespoons water, plus more as needed
1. In a large pot, bring the brine ingredients to a boil over high heat, stirring until the sugar and salt are dissolved. Remove from the heat and let cool.
2. Place the turkey thighs in the brine for at least 4 hours or overnight.
3. Remove the turkey thighs from the brine, rinse and pat dry with paper towels.
4. When ready to cook, set Traeger temperature to 250ºF (121ºC) and preheat, lid closed for 15 minutes. For optimal flavor, use Super Smoke if available.
5. Rub the ras el hanout all over the turkey thighs, then rub each thigh with a tablespoon of olive oil.
6. Place the thighs on the grill and smoke for 2 hours.
7. Meanwhile, make the fig BBQ sauce: In a small saucepan over medium-heat, combine the figs and BBQ sauce. Add the water and cook for 20 minutes, or until the figs are softened, adding more water as needed. Remove what remains of the figs and discard.
8. Remove the thighs from the grill and set aside to rest.
9. Set the temperature to High and preheat, lid closed for 15 minutes.
10. Place the thighs back on the grill and continue to cook, basting occasionally with the fig BBQ sauce, or until the thighs are caramelized and the internal temperature registers 165ºF (74ºC).
11. Remove the thighs from the grill and baste with the remaining fig BBQ sauce. Serve immediately.

Grilled Lemon Chicken Breasts

Prep time: 5 minutes | Cook time: 15 minutes | Serves 6
Marinade:
½ cup olive oil or vegetable oil
2 teaspoons honey
2 teaspoons kosher salt
2 sprig fresh thyme leaves
1 lemon, zested and juiced
1 clove garlic, coarsely chopped
1 teaspoon freshly ground black pepper
Chicken:
6 (6-ounce / 170-g) boneless, skinless chicken breasts
1 lemon, cut into wedges, for serving
1. In a small mixing bowl, whisk together all the marinade ingredients until well incorporated.
2. Put the chicken breasts in a large resealable plastic bag and pour the marinade over them, massaging the bag to coat the chicken evenly. Marinate for 4 hours in the refrigerator.
3. When ready to cook, set Traeger temperature to 400ºF (204ºC) and preheat, lid closed for 15 minutes.
4. Remove the chicken breasts from the marinade and drain, discarding the marinade.
5. Place the chicken breasts on the grill and cook until the internal temperature registers 165ºF (74ºC).
6. If desired, grill the reserved lemon wedges alongside the chicken, cut sides down, about 15 minutes.
7. Transfer the chicken breasts to a platter and serve with the lemon wedges.

Teriyaki Wings

Prep time: 4 hours | Cook time: 1 hour | Serves 6
Chicken:
2½ pounds (1.1 kg) large chicken wings
1 tablespoon lightly toasted sesame seeds, for serving
Marinade:
½ cup soy sauce
¼ cup brown sugar
¼ cup water
2 scallions
2 tablespoons rice wine vinegar
2 teaspoons sesame oil
2 tablespoons smashed fresh ginger
1 clove garlic, minced
1. On your cutting board, cut the wings into three pieces through the joints. Discard the wing tips or reserve for chicken stock.
2. Transfer the remaining chicken drumettes and flats to a large resealable plastic bag.
3. In a small saucepan, stir together all the marinade ingredients and bring to a boil. Reduce the heat and allow to simmer for 10 minutes. Let cool to room temperature, then pour the marinade over the chicken wings. Seal the bag and refrigerate for 4 hours or overnight.

4. Remove the wings from the marinade and drain, discarding the marinade.

5. When ready to cook, set Traeger temperature to 350ºF (177ºC) and preheat, lid closed for 15 minutes.

6. Lay the chicken wings on the grill and cook for 45 to 50 minutes, or until the skin is brown and crisp, flipping the wings once during cooking.

7. Remove the wings from the grill. Serve sprinkled with the sesame seeds.

CHAPTER 7 SEAFOOD

Pacific Northwest Salmon Fillet

Prep time: 15 minutes | Cook time: 1¼ hours | Serves 4

1 (2-pound / 907-g) half salmon fillet
1 batch dill seafood rub
2 tablespoons butter, cut into 3 or 4 slices
1.   Supply your smoker with wood pellets and follow the manufacturer's specific start-up procedure. Preheat the grill, with the lid closed, to 180ºF (82ºC).
2.   Season the salmon all over with the rub. Using your hands, work the rub into the flesh.
3.   Place the salmon directly on the grill grate, skin-side down, and smoke for 1 hour.
4.   Place the butter slices on the salmon, equally spaced. Increase the grill's temperature to 300ºF (149ºC) and continue to cook until the salmon's internal temperature reaches 145°F (63ºC). Remove the salmon from the grill and serve immediately.

Grilled Salmon Fillet

Prep time: 25 minutes | Cook time: 25 minutes | Serves 4

1 (2-pound / 907-g) half salmon fillet
3 tablespoons mayonnaise
1 batch dill seafood rub
1.   Supply your smoker with wood pellets and follow the manufacturer's specific start-up procedure. Preheat the grill, with the lid closed, to 325ºF (163ºC).
2.   Using your hands, rub the salmon fillet all over with the mayonnaise and sprinkle it with the rub.
3.   Place the salmon directly on the grill grate, skin-side down, and grill until its internal temperature reaches 145°F (63ºC). Remove the salmon from the grill and serve immediately.

Hot-Smoked Salmon Fillet

Prep time: 15 minutes | Cook time: 4 to 6 hours | Serves 4

1 (2-pound / 907-g) half salmon fillet
1 batch dill seafood rub
1.   Supply your smoker with wood pellets and follow the manufacturer's specific start-up procedure. Preheat the grill, with the lid closed, to 180ºF (82ºC).
2.   Season the salmon all over with the rub. Using your hands, work the rub into the flesh.
3.   Place the salmon directly on the grill grate, skin-side down, and smoke until its internal

temperature reaches 145°F (63ºC). Remove the salmon from the grill and serve immediately.

Wood-Fired Halibut Fillet

Prep time: 5 minutes | Cook time: 20 minutes | Serves 4

1 pound (454 g) halibut fillet
1 batch dill seafood rub
1.   Supply your smoker with wood pellets and follow the manufacturer's specific start-up procedure. Preheat the grill, with the lid closed, to 325ºF (163ºC).
2.   Sprinkle the halibut fillet on all sides with the rub. Using your hands, work the rub into the meat.
3.   Place the halibut directly on the grill grate and grill until its internal temperature reaches 145°F (63ºC). Remove the halibut from the grill and serve immediately.

Grilled Tuna Steaks

Prep time: 10 minutes | Cook time: 10 minutes | Serves 2

2 (1½- to 2-inch-thick) tuna steaks
2 tablespoons olive oil
Salt, to taste
Freshly ground black pepper, to taste
1.   Supply your smoker with wood pellets and follow the manufacturer's specific start-up procedure. Preheat the grill, with the lid closed, to 500ºF (260ºC).
2.   Rub the tuna steaks all over with olive oil and season both sides with salt and pepper.
3.   Place the tuna steaks directly on the grill grate and grill for 3 to 5 minutes per side, leaving a pink center. Remove the tuna steaks from the grill and serve immediately.

BBQ Shrimp

Prep time: 15 minutes | Cook time: 10 minutes | Serves 4

1 pound (454 g) peeled and deveined shrimp, with tails on
2 tablespoons olive oil
1 batch dill seafood rub
1.   Soak wooden skewers in water for 30 minutes.
2.   Supply your smoker with wood pellets and follow the manufacturer's specific start-up procedure. Preheat the grill, with the lid closed, to 375°F (191ºC).
3.   Thread 4 or 5 shrimp per skewer.

4.   Coat the shrimp all over with olive oil and season each side of the skewers with the rub.
5.   Place the skewers directly on the grill grate and grill the shrimp for 5 minutes per side. Remove the skewers from the grill and serve immediately.

Buttered Cajun Shrimp

Prep time: 10 minutes | Cook time: 20 minutes | Serves 4

1 pound (454 g) peeled and deveined shrimp, with tails on
1 batch Cajun rub
8 tablespoons (1 stick) butter
¼ cup Worcestershire sauce

1.   Supply your smoker with wood pellets and follow the manufacturer's specific start-up procedure. Preheat the grill, with the lid closed, to 450ºF (232ºC) and place a cast-iron skillet on the grill grate. Wait about 10 minutes after your grill has reached temperature, allowing the skillet to get hot.
2.   Meanwhile, season the shrimp all over with the rub.
3.   When the skillet is hot, place the butter in it to melt. Once the butter melts, stir in the Worcestershire sauce.
4.   Add the shrimp and gently stir to coat. Smoke-braise the shrimp for about 10 minutes per side, until opaque and cooked through. Remove the shrimp from the grill and serve immediately.

Lemon Buttered Oysters

Prep time: 5 minutes | Cook time: 20 minutes | Serves 4

8 medium oysters, unopened, in the shell, rinsed and scrubbed
1 batch lemon butter mop for seafood

1.   Supply your smoker with wood pellets and follow the manufacturer's specific start-up procedure. Preheat the grill, with the lid closed, to 375°F (191ºC).
2.   Place the unopened oysters directly on the grill grate and grill for about 20 minutes, or until the oysters are done and their shells open.
3.   Discard any oysters that do not open. Shuck the remaining oysters, transfer them to a bowl, and add the mop. Serve immediately.

Cajun Catfish Fillet

Prep time: 15 minutes | Cook time: 15 minutes | Serves 6

2½ pounds catfish fillets
2 tablespoons olive oil
1 batch Cajun Rub

1.   Supply your smoker with wood pellets and follow the manufacturer's specific start-up procedure. Preheat the grill, with the lid closed, to 300ºF (149ºC).
2.   Coat the catfish fillets all over with olive oil and season with the rub. Using your hands, work the rub into the flesh.
3.   Place the fillets directly on the grill grate and smoke until their internal temperature reaches 145°F (63ºC). Remove the catfish from the grill and serve immediately.

King Crab Legs

Prep time: 5 minutes | Cook time: 10 minutes | Serves 4

8 King crab legs
A dipping sauce of your choice

1.   Supply your smoker with wood pellets and follow the manufacturer's specific start-up procedure. Preheat the grill, with the lid closed, to 325ºF (163ºC).
2.   Place the crab legs directly on the grill grate and grill for 10 minutes, flipping once after 5 minutes. Serve the crab with the mop on the side for dipping.

Grilled Lobster Tail

Prep time: 25 minutes | Cook time: 25 minutes | Serves 2

2 lobster tails
Salt, to taste
Freshly ground black pepper, to taste
1 batch lemon butter mop for seafood

1.   Supply your smoker with wood pellets and follow the manufacturer's specific start-up procedure. Preheat the grill, with the lid closed, to 375°F (191ºC).
2.   Using kitchen shears, slit the top of the lobster shells, through the center, nearly to the tail. Once cut, expose as much meat as you can through the cut shell.
3.   Season the lobster tails all over with salt and pepper.
4.   Place the tails directly on the grill grate and grill until their internal temperature reaches 145°F (63ºC). Remove the lobster from the grill and serve with the mop on the side for dipping.

BBQ Scallops

Prep time: 10 minutes | Cook time: 10 minutes | Serves 4

1 pound (454 g) large scallops
2 tablespoons olive oil
1 batch dill seafood rub

1. Supply your smoker with wood pellets and follow the manufacturer's specific start-up procedure. Preheat the grill, with the lid closed, to 375°F (191ºC).
2. Coat the scallops all over with olive oil and season all sides with the rub.
3. Place the scallops directly on the grill grate and grill for 5 minutes per side. Remove the scallops from the grill and serve immediately.

Charleston Crab Cakes

Prep time: 30 minutes | Cook time: 45 minutes | Serves 4

1¼ cups mayonnaise
¼ cup yellow mustard
2 tablespoons sweet pickle relish, with its juices
1 tablespoon smoked paprika
2 teaspoons Cajun seasoning
2 teaspoons prepared horseradish
1 teaspoon hot sauce
1 garlic clove, finely minced
2 pounds (907 g) fresh lump crabmeat, picked clean
20 butter crackers (such as Ritz brand), crushed
2 tablespoons Dijon mustard
1 cup mayonnaise
2 tablespoons freshly squeezed lemon juice
1 tablespoon salted butter, melted
1 tablespoon Worcestershire sauce
1 tablespoon Old Bay seasoning
2 teaspoons chopped fresh parsley
1 teaspoon ground mustard
2 eggs, beaten
¼ cup extra-virgin olive oil, divided
For the Remoulade
1. In a small bowl, combine the mayonnaise, mustard, pickle relish, paprika, Cajun seasoning, horseradish, hot sauce, and garlic.
2. Refrigerate until ready to serve.
For the Crab Cakes
1. Supply your smoker with wood pellets and follow the manufacturer's specific start-up procedure. Preheat, with the lid closed, to 375°F (191ºC).
2. Spread the crabmeat on a foil-lined baking sheet and place over indirect heat on the grill, with the lid closed, for 30 minutes.
3. Remove from the heat and let cool for 15 minutes.
4. While the crab cools, combine the crushed crackers, Dijon mustard, mayonnaise, lemon juice, melted butter, Worcestershire sauce, Old Bay, parsley, ground mustard, and eggs until well incorporated.
5. Fold in the smoked crabmeat, then shape the mixture into 8 (1-inch-thick) crab cakes.

6. In a large skillet or cast-iron pan on the grill, heat 2 tablespoons of olive oil. Add half of the crab cakes, close the lid, and smoke for 4 to 5 minutes on each side, or until crispy and golden brown.
7. Remove the crab cakes from the pan and transfer to a wire rack to drain. Pat them to remove any excess oil.
8. Repeat steps 6 and 7 with the remaining oil and crab cakes.
9. Serve the crab cakes with the remoulade.

Tangy Rainbow Trout

Prep time: 10 minutes | Cook time: 1 to 2 hours | Serves 6

6 to 8 skin-on rainbow trout, cleaned and scaled
1 gallon orange juice
½ cup packed light brown sugar
¼ cup salt
1 tablespoon freshly ground black pepper
Nonstick spray, oil, or butter, for greasing
1 tablespoon chopped fresh parsley
1 lemon, sliced
1. Fillet the fish and pat dry with paper towels.
2. Pour the orange juice into a large container with a lid and stir in the brown sugar, salt, and pepper.
3. Place the trout in the brine, cover, and refrigerate for 1 hour.
4. Cover the grill grate with heavy-duty aluminum foil. Poke holes in the foil and spray with cooking spray (see Tip).
5. Supply your smoker with wood pellets and follow the manufacturer's specific start-up procedure. Preheat, with the lid closed, to 225ºF (107ºC).
6. Remove the trout from the brine and pat dry. Arrange the fish on the foil-covered grill grate, close the lid, and smoke for 1 hour 30 minutes to 2 hours, or until flaky.
7. Remove the fish from the heat. Serve garnished with the fresh parsley and lemon slices.

Dijon-Smoked Halibut Steak

Prep time: 25 minutes | Cook time: 2 hours | Serves 6

4 (6-ounce / 170-g) halibut steaks
¼ cup extra-virgin olive oil
2 teaspoons kosher salt
1 teaspoon freshly ground black pepper
½ cup mayonnaise
½ cup sweet pickle relish
¼ cup finely chopped sweet onion
¼ cup chopped roasted red pepper
¼ cup finely chopped tomato
¼ cup finely chopped cucumber

2 tablespoons Dijon mustard
1 teaspoon minced garlic

1.   Rub the halibut steaks with the olive oil and season on both sides with the salt and pepper. Transfer to a plate, cover with plastic wrap, and refrigerate for 4 hours.

2.   Supply your smoker with wood pellets and follow the manufacturer's specific start-up procedure. Preheat, with the lid closed, to 200°F (93ºC).

3.   Remove the halibut from the refrigerator and rub with the mayonnaise.

4.   Put the fish directly on the grill grate, close the lid, and smoke for 2 hours, or until opaque and an instant-read thermometer inserted in the fish reads 140ºF (60ºC).

5.   While the fish is smoking, combine the pickle relish, onion, roasted red pepper, tomato, cucumber, Dijon mustard, and garlic in a medium bowl. Refrigerate the mustard relish until ready to serve.

Salmon with Avocado

Prep time: 20 minutes | Cook time: 6 hours | Serves 6

¼ cup salt
¼ cup sugar
1 tablespoon freshly ground black pepper
1 bunch dill, chopped
1 pound sashimi-grade salmon, skin removed
1 avocado, sliced
8 bagels
4 ounces (113 g) cream cheese
1 bunch alfalfa sprouts
1 (3.5-ounce / 99-g) jar capers

1.   In a small bowl, combine the salt, sugar, pepper, and fresh dill to make the curing mixture. Set aside.

2.   On a smooth surface, lay out a large piece of plastic wrap and spread half of the curing salt mixture in the middle, spreading it out to about the size of the salmon.

3.   Place the salmon on top of the curing salt.

4.   Top the fish with the remaining curing salt, covering it completely. Wrap the salmon, leaving the ends open to drain.

5.   Place the wrapped fish in a rimmed baking pan or dish lined with paper towels to soak up liquid.

6.   Place a weight on the salmon evenly, such as a pan with a couple of heavy jars of pickles on top.

7.   Put the salmon pan with weights in the refrigerator. Place something (a dishtowel, for example) under the back of the pan in order to slightly tip it down so the liquid drains away from the fish.

8.   Leave the salmon to cure in the refrigerator for 24 hours.

9.   Place the wood pellets in the smoker, but do not follow the start-up procedure and do not preheat.

10.   Remove the salmon from the refrigerator, unwrap it, rinse it off, and pat dry.

11.   Put the salmon in the smoker while still cold from the refrigerator to slow down the cooking process. You'll need to use a cold-smoker attachment or enlist the help of a smoker tube to hold the temperature at 80°F and maintain that for 6 hours to absorb smoke and complete the cold-smoking process.

12.   Remove the salmon from the smoker, place it in a sealed plastic bag, and refrigerate for 24 hours. The salmon will be translucent all the way through.

13.   Thinly slice the lox and serve with sliced avocado, bagels, cream cheese, alfalfa sprouts, and capers.

Rizty Summer Paella

Prep time: 1 hour | Cook time: 45 minutes | Serves 6

6 tablespoons extra-virgin olive oil, divided, plus more for drizzling
2 green or red bell peppers, cored, seeded, and diced
2 medium onions, diced
2 garlic cloves, slivered
1 (29-ounce / 822-g) can tomato purée
1½ pounds chicken thighs
Kosher salt, to taste
1½ pounds (680 g) tail-on shrimp, peeled and deveined
1 cup dried thinly sliced chorizo sausage
1 tablespoon smoked paprika
1½ teaspoons saffron threads
2 quarts chicken broth
3½ cups white rice
2 (7½-ounce / 213-g) cans chipotle chiles in adobo sauce
1½ pounds (680 g) fresh clams, soaked in cold water for 15 to 20 minutes2 tablespoons chopped fresh parsley
2 lemons, cut into wedges, for serving

1.   Make the sofrito: On the stove top, in a saucepan over medium-low heat, combine ¼ cup of olive oil, the bell peppers, onions, and garlic, and cook for 5 minutes, or until the onions are translucent.

2.   Stir in the tomato purée, reduce the heat to low, and simmer, stirring frequently, until most of the liquid has evaporated, about 30 minutes. Set aside. (Note: The sofrito can be made in advance and refrigerated.)

3. Supply your smoker with wood pellets and follow the manufacturer's specific start-up procedure. Preheat, with the lid closed, to 450ºF (232ºC).

4. Heat a large paella pan on the smoker and add the remaining 2 tablespoons of olive oil.

5. Add the chicken thighs, season lightly with salt, and brown for 6 to 10 minutes, then push to the outer edge of the pan.

6. Add the shrimp, season with salt, close the lid, and smoke for 3 minutes.

7. Add the sofrito, chorizo, paprika, and saffron, and stir together.

8. In a separate bowl, combine the chicken broth, uncooked rice, and 1 tablespoon of salt, stirring until well combined.

9. Add the broth-rice mixture to the paella pan, spreading it evenly over the other ingredients.

10. Close the lid and smoke for 5 minutes, then add the chipotle chiles and clams on top of the rice.

11. Close the lid and continue to smoke the paella for about 30 minutes, or until all of the liquid is absorbed.

12. Remove the pan from the grill, cover tightly with aluminum foil, and let rest off the heat for 5 minutes.

13. Drizzle with olive oil, sprinkle with the fresh parsley, and serve with the lemon wedges.

Cheesy Potato

Prep time: 20 minutes | Cook time: 1½ hours | Serves 16

8 Idaho, Russet, or Yukon Gold potatoes
1 (12-ounce / 340-g) can evaporated milk, heated
1 cup (2 sticks) butter, melted
½ cup sour cream, at room temperature
1 cup grated Parmesan cheese
½ pound (227 g) bacon, cooked and crumbled
¼ cup chopped scallions
Salt, to taste
Freshly ground black pepper, to taste
1 cup shredded Cheddar cheese

1. Supply your smoker with wood pellets and follow the manufacturer's specific start-up procedure. Preheat, with the lid closed, to 400ºF (204ºC).

2. Poke the potatoes all over with a fork. Arrange them directly on the grill grate, close the lid, and smoke for 1 hour and 15 minutes, or until cooked through and they have some give when pinched.

3. Let the potatoes cool for 10 minutes, then cut in half lengthwise.

4. Into a medium bowl, scoop out the potato flesh, leaving ¼ inch in the shells; place the shells on a baking sheet.

5. Using an electric mixer on medium speed, beat the potatoes, milk, butter, and sour cream until smooth.

6. Stir in the Parmesan cheese, bacon, and scallions, and season with salt and pepper.

7. Generously stuff each shell with the potato mixture and top with Cheddar cheese.

8. Place the baking sheet on the grill grate, close the lid, and smoke for 20 minutes, or until the cheese is melted.

Cauliflower and Broccoli Salad

Prep time: 25 minutes | Cook time: 0 minute | Serves 4

1½ cups mayonnaise
½ cup sour cream
¼ cup sugar
1 bunch broccoli, cut into small pieces
1 head cauliflower, cut into small pieces
1 small red onion, chopped
6 slices bacon, cooked and crumbled (precooked bacon works well)
1 cup shredded Cheddar cheese

1. In a small bowl, whisk together the mayonnaise, sour cream, and sugar to make a dressing.

2. In a large bowl, combine the broccoli, cauliflower, onion, bacon, and Cheddar cheese.

3. Pour the dressing over the vegetable mixture and toss well to coat.

4. Serve the salad chilled.

BBQ Baked Beans

Prep time: 15 minutes | Cook time: 2 to 3 hours | Serves 12 to 15

3 (28-ounce / 794-g) cans baked beans
1 large onion, finely chopped
1 cup The Ultimate BBQ Sauce
½ cup light brown sugar
¼ cup Worcestershire sauce
3 tablespoons yellow mustard
Nonstick cooking spray or butter, for greasing
1 large bell pepper, cut into thin rings
½ pound thick-cut bacon, partially cooked and cut into quarters

1. Supply your smoker with wood pellets and follow the manufacturer's specific start-up procedure. Preheat, with the lid closed, to 300ºF (149ºC).

2. In a large mixing bowl, stir together the beans, onion, barbecue sauce, brown sugar, Worcestershire sauce, and mustard until well combined

3. Coat a 9-by-13-inch aluminum pan with cooking spray or butter.

4. Pour the beans into the pan and top with the bell pepper rings and bacon pieces, pressing them down slightly into the sauce.
5. Place a layer of heavy-duty foil on the grill grate to catch drips, and place the pan on top of the foil. Close the lid and cook for 2 hours 30 minutes to 3 hours, or until the beans are hot, thick, and bubbly.
6. Let the beans rest for 5 minutes before serving.

Homemade Blt Pasta Salad

Prep time: 10 minutes | Cook time: 35 to 45 minutes | Serves 6
1 pound (454 g) thick-cut bacon
16 ounces (454 g)bowtie pasta, cooked according to package directions and drained
2 tomatoes, chopped
½ cup chopped scallions
½ cup Italian dressing
½ cup ranch dressing
1 tablespoon chopped fresh basil
1 teaspoon salt
1 teaspoon freshly ground black pepper
1 teaspoon garlic powder
1 head lettuce, cored and torn
1. Supply your smoker with wood pellets and follow the manufacturer's specific start-up procedure. Preheat, with the lid closed, to 225ºF (107ºC).
2. Arrange the bacon slices on the grill grate, close the lid, and cook for 30 to 45 minutes, flipping after 20 minutes, until crisp.
3. Remove the bacon from the grill and chop.
4. In a large bowl, combine the chopped bacon with the cooked pasta, tomatoes, scallions, Italian dressing, ranch dressing, basil, salt, pepper, and garlic powder. Refrigerate until ready to serve.
5. Toss in the lettuce just before serving to keep it from wilting.

Salad with Smoked Cornbread

Prep time: 25 minutes | Cook time: 35 to 45 minutes | Serves 6
1 cup all-purpose flour
1 cup yellow cornmeal
1 tablespoon sugar
2 teaspoons baking powder
1 teaspoon salt
1 cup milk
1 egg, beaten, at room temperature
4 tablespoons (½ stick) unsalted butter, melted and cooled
Nonstick cooking spray or butter, for greasing
½ cup milk
½ cup sour cream

2 tablespoons dry ranch dressing mix
1 pound (454 g) bacon, cooked and crumbled
3 tomatoes, chopped
1 bell pepper, chopped
1 cucumber, seeded and chopped
2 stalks celery, chopped (about 1 cup)
½ cup chopped scallions
For the Cornbread
1. In a medium bowl, combine the flour, cornmeal, sugar, baking powder, and salt.
2. In a small bowl, whisk together the milk and egg. Pour in the butter, then slowly fold this mixture into the dry ingredients.
3. Supply your smoker with wood pellets and follow the manufacturer's specific start-up procedure. Preheat, with the lid closed, to 375°F (191ºC).
4. Coat a cast iron skillet with cooking spray or butter.
5. Pour the batter into the skillet, place on the grill grate, close the lid, and smoke for 35 to 45 minutes, or until the cornbread is browned and pulls away from the side of the skillet.
6. Remove the cornbread from the grill and let cool, then coarsely crumble.
For the Salad
1. In a small bowl, whisk together the milk, sour cream, and ranch dressing mix.
2. In a medium bowl, combine the crumbled bacon, tomatoes, bell pepper, cucumber, celery, and scallions.
3. In a large serving bowl, layer half of the crumbled cornbread, half of the bacon-veggie mixture, and half of the dressing. Toss lightly.
4. Repeat the layering with the remaining cornbread, bacon-veggie mixture, and dressing. Toss again.
5. Refrigerate the salad for at least 1 hour. Serve cold.

Swordfish Steaks with Corn Salsa

Prep time: 10 minutes | Cook time: 30 to 33 minutes | Serves 4
4 whole ears corn, husked
Olive oil, as needed
Salt and black pepper, to taste
1 pint cherry tomatoes
1 whole serrano chile, chopped
1 whole red onion, diced
1 whole lime, juiced
4 whole swordfish fillets
1. When ready to cook, set the Traeger to High and preheat, lid closed for 15 minutes.
2. Brush the corn with the olive oil and season with salt and pepper. Place the corn on the grill grate

and grill for 12 to 15 minutes, or until cooked through and lightly browned. Set aside to cool.
3. Once corn has cooled, cut the kernels from the corn and transfer to a medium bowl. Stir in the tomatoes, serrano, red onion and lime juice.
4. Brush the swordfish fillets with the olive oil and season with salt and pepper.
5. Arrange the fillets on the grill grate and grill for about 18 minutes, or until the fish is opaque and flakes easily when pressed with a fork.
6. Serve the grilled swordfish topped with the corn salsa.

Grilled Oysters with Veggie Sauce

Prep time: 20 minutes | Cook time: 25 to 27 minutes | Serves 4
5 tablespoons extra-virgin olive oil
2 medium onions, chopped
1 medium red bell pepper, chopped
2 lemons, juiced
3 dried bay leaves
5 tablespoons minced garlic
3 tablespoons Traeger Chicken Rub
3 teaspoons dried thyme
¼ cup white wine
5 tablespoons hot pepper sauce
3 tablespoons Worcestershire Sauce
4 butter sticks
12 whole oysters, cleaned and shucked
Italian cheese blend, as needed
1. When ready to cook, set the Traeger to High and preheat, lid closed for 15 minutes.
2. Heat the olive oil in a cast iron pan over medium heat. Add the onions, bell peppers, lemon juice, bay leaves, garlic, Traeger Chicken Rub and thyme to the pan. Sauté the vegetable mixture for 5 to 7 minutes, or until the onions are translucent and peppers are tender.
3. Add the white wine, hot pepper sauce, Worcestershire Sauce and butter to the pan. Sauté for another 15 minutes.
4. Place the oysters on the grill and top with the sauce. Cook for 5 minutes.
5. Top with Italian cheese and serve hot.

Crispy Fried Halibut Fish Sticks

Prep time: 10 minutes | Cook time: 3 to 4 minutes | Serves 4
Extra-virgin olive oil, as needed
1½ pounds (680 g) halibut, rinsed, patted dry and cut into 1-inch strips
½ cup all-purpose flour
1½ teaspoons salt
1 teaspoon ground black pepper

2 large eggs
1½ cups panko bread crumbs
2 tablespoons dried parsley
1 teaspoon dried dill weed
1. When ready to cook, set Traeger temperature to 500ºF (260ºC) and preheat, lid closed for 15 minutes.
2. Place a dutch oven inside the grill to preheat for about 10 minutes, with enough olive oil to fry the fish.
3. In a bowl, stir together the all-purpose flour, salt and pepper. In a separate bowl, beat the eggs. In a third bowl, combine the panko, parsley and dill.
4. Dredge the fish fillets first in the flour mixture, then the eggs and then the panko mixture.
5. Place the coated fish fillets in the oil and fry for about 3 to 4 minutes, or until they reach an internal temperature of 130ºF (54ºC).
6. Serve warm.

White Fish Steaks with Orange Basil Pesto

Prep time: 10 minutes | Cook time: 12 to 15 minutes | Serves 4
1 orange, juiced
2 cups fresh basil
1 cup chopped flat-leaf parsley
½ cup toasted walnuts
2 teaspoons orange zest
½ cup olive oil
1 cup grated Parmesan cheese
4 white fish steaks, rinsed and patted dry
½ teaspoon coarse sea salt
½ teaspoon black pepper
1. When ready to cook, set the Traeger to High and preheat, lid closed for 15 minutes.
2. Meanwhile, make the pesto: In a food processor, combine the orange juice, basil, parsley, walnuts and orange zest and pulse until finely chopped. With the machine running, slowly drizzle in the olive oil until the mixture is emulsified.
3. Scrape the pesto into a bowl and stir in the Parmesan cheese.
4. Brush the fish steaks with olive oil on both sides and season with salt and pepper.
5. Arrange the fish steaks on the grill grate. Grill for 12 to 15 minutes, turning once with a thin-bladed metal spatula, or until the fish is opaque and breaks into chunks when pressed with a fork.
6. Transfer the steaks to a platter. Drizzle with the prepared pesto and serve immediately.

Lemony Salmon Fillets

Prep time: 10 minutes | Cook time: 15 to 20 minutes | Serves 2

2 tablespoons butter, softened

2 teaspoons fresh chopped dill, plus more for garnish

1 teaspoon lemon juice

½ teaspoon lemon zest

½ teaspoon salt

Black pepper, to taste

4 (8-ounce / 227-g) salmon fillets, skin on

1 lemon, thinly sliced

1. When ready to cook, set Traeger temperature to 350ºF (177ºC) and preheat, lid closed for 15 minutes.

2. Meanwhile, stir together all the ingredients, except for the salmon and lemon, in a bowl.

3. Generously spread the lemon-dill butter over the top of the salmon fillets and top with a slice of lemon.

4. Place the salmon fillets on the grill grate, skin-side facing down. Cook for 15 to 20 minutes, for a medium-rare salmon, or until the salmon is done to your liking.

5. Serve garnished with the fresh dill.

Grilled Salmon Teriyaki Sauce

Prep time: 10 minutes | Cook time: 13 to 15 minutes | Serves 2

1 cup soy sauce

6 tablespoons brown sugar

1 tablespoon minced ginger

4 cloves garlic

Juice and zest of 2 whole oranges

4 (6-ounce / 170-g) pieces salmon fillets

1 tablespoon sesame seeds

Toasted sesame seeds, as needed

Chopped scallions, as needed

1. When ready to cook, set the Traeger to High and preheat, lid closed for 15 minutes.

2. In a saucepan, place the soy sauce, brown sugar, ginger, garlic, orange juice and zest. Bring to a boil and slowly simmer for 1o minutes, or until a syrupy consistency is achieved, about a 50 percent reduction. Let cool completely. Add the salmon and sesame seeds and marinate for 1 hour.

3. Remove the salmon from the marinade and bring the sauce to a boil.

4. Place the salmon fillets directly on the grill grate, skin-side up. Cook for about 3 to 5 minutes per side, or until they are done until your liking and occasionally, brush the salmon with the sauce.

5. Remove the salmon from the grill and serve topped with the toasted sesame seeds and chopped scallions.

Roasted Stuffed Rainbow Trout

Prep time: 10 minutes | Cook time: 15 minutes | Serves 1

4 tablespoons butter

Lemon juice, as needed

1 whole rainbow trout, rinsed

1 tablespoon salt

1 teaspoon chipotle pepper

2 whole oranges, sliced

4 sprigs thyme sprigs

3 whole bay leaves

1 clove garlic, chopped

1. When ready to cook, set Traeger temperature to 400ºF (204ºC) and preheat, lid closed for 15 minutes.

2. Melt the butter in a saucepan over medium high heat. After the butter melts completely, it will begin to foam and the milk solids will begin to brown. After all foam subsides and the butter looks golden brown, remove the pan from the heat and drizzle in a bit of lemon juice to stop the browning process. Set aside.

3. Lay out a piece of foil 3 inches longer on each end than the fish. Drizzle the exterior and cavity of the fish with the brown butter and season with salt and chipotle powder. Stuff the cavity with the remaining ingredients and fold the foil into a packet.

4. Place the packet directly on the grill grate and cook for about 15 minutes, or until the internal temperature has reached 145ºF (63ºC).

5. Remove from the grill and serve hot.

Buttery Crab Legs

Prep time: 10 minutes | Cook time: 20 to 30 minutes | Serves 4

3 pounds (1.4 kg) crab legs, thawed and halved

1 cup butter, melted

2 tablespoons fresh lemon juice

2 cloves garlic, minced

1 tablespoon Traeger Fin & Feather Rub

Chopped Italian parsley, for garnish

1. When ready to cook, set Traeger temperature to 350ºF (177ºC) and preheat, lid closed for 15 minutes.

2. Split the crab shells open lengthwise. Transfer to the roasting pan.

3. In a small bowl, whisk together the butter, lemon juice and garlic.

4. Spread the butter mixture over the crab legs, turning the legs to coat. Sprinkle the Traeger Fin & Feather Rub over the legs.

5. Place the pan on the grill grate. Cook for 20 to 30 minutes, or until warmed through, basting once or twice with the butter sauce from the bottom of the pan.

6. Transfer the crab legs to a large platter and divide the sauce and accumulated juices between 4 dipping bowls. Serve topped with the parsley.

Grilled Buttery BBQ Oysters

Prep time: 10 minutes | Cook time: 6 minutes | Serves 4

1 pound (454 g) unsalted butter, softened
1 bunch green onions, chopped, plus more for garnish
2 cloves garlic, minced
1 tablespoon Meat Church Holy Gospel BBQ Rub
12 oysters, shucked, juice reserved
¼ cup seasoned bread crumbs
8 ounces (227 g) shredded Pepper Jack cheese
Traeger Sweet & Heat BBQ Sauce, as needed

1. When ready to cook, set Traeger temperature to 375ºF (191ºC) and preheat, lid closed for 15 minutes.
2. Make the compound butter: Stir together the butter, green onions, garlic and Meat Church Holy Gospel BBQ Rub in a medium bowl.
3. Lay the butter on parchment paper. Roll it up to form a log and tie each end with cooking twine. Place in the freezer for an hour to solidify.
4. Sprinkle the bread crumbs over the oysters and place directly on the grill. Cook for 5 minutes, or until the edge of the oyster starts to curl slightly.
5. After 5 minutes, place a spoonful of compound butter in the oysters. After the butter melts, add a pinch of Pepper Jack cheese. Cook for 1 more minutes.
6. Remove the oysters from the grill. Top the oysters with a squirt of Traeger Sweet & Heat BBQ Sauce and a few chopped onions. Let cool for 5 minutes before serving.

Smoked Vodka Salmon

Prep time: 5 minutes | Cook time: 1 hour | Serves 4

1 cup brown sugar
1 cup vodka
½ cup coarse salt
1 tablespoon black pepper
1 wild caught salmon (1½ to 2 pounds / 680 to 907 g)
1 lemon, wedged, for serving
Capers, for serving

1. In a small bowl, whisk together the brown sugar, vodka, salt and pepper.
2. Place the salmon in a large resealable bag. Pour in the marinade and massage into the salmon. Refrigerate for 2 to 4 hours.
3. Remove the salmon from the bag, rinse and pat dry with paper towels.

4. When ready to cook, set Traeger temperature to 180ºF (82ºC) and preheat, lid closed for 15 minutes.
5. Place the salmon on the grill, skin-side down, and smoke for 30 minutes.
6. Increase the temperature to 225ºF (107ºC) and continue to cook the salmon for an additional 45 to 60 minutes, or until the fish flakes easily when pressed with a fork.
7. Serve with the lemons and capers.

Easy Grilled Fresh Fish

Prep time: 5 minutes | Cook time: 12 to 15 minutes | Serves 2

1 cup soy sauce
⅓ cup extra-virgin olive oil
1 tablespoon minced garlic
Juice of 2 medium lemons
1 stalk fresh basil
4 pounds (1.8 kg) fresh fish, cut into portion-sized pieces

1. When ready to cook, set the Traeger to High and preheat, lid closed for 15 minutes.
2. In a large bowl, stir together all the ingredients, except for the fish. Add the fish and let marinade for 45 minutes.
3. Remove the fish from the marinade and place on the grill.
4. Grill for 12 to 15 minutes, or until an instant-read thermometer inserted in the thickest part of the meat registers 140ºF (60ºC).
5. Serve immediately.

Sweet Mandarin Glazed Salmon

Prep time: 5 minutes | Cook time: 15 to 20 minutes | Serves 2

1 jar Traeger Mandarin Glaze
Juice of 1 lime
2 tablespoons finely chopped cilantro
1½ tablespoons soy sauce
1 teaspoon sesame oil
Cracked black pepper, to taste
1 whole salmon, cut into 4 fillets

1. When ready to cook, set the Traeger to High and preheat, lid closed for 15 minutes.
2. Meanwhile, make the glaze: In a bowl, stir together all the ingredients, except for the salmon.
3. Brush the salmon fillets with the glaze and place the fillets directly on the grill grate, skin-side down. Cook for 15 to 20 minutes, or an instant-read thermometer inserted in the thickest part of the meat registers 155ºF (68ºC). Brush the salmon again with the glaze halfway through cooking.

4. Remove the salmon from the grill and serve with the remaining glaze if desired.

Grilled Salmon Patties

Prep time: 10 minutes | Cook time: 35 to 44 minutes | Serves 4

2 pounds (907 g) salmon, cut into fillets
Salt and ground black pepper, to taste
2 large eggs
1 red bell pepper, diced
1 stalk celery, diced
½ small onion, diced
1½ tablespoons bread crumbs
1 tablespoon fresh dill
1 teaspoon lemon zest
½ teaspoon black pepper
¼ teaspoon coarse sea salt
3 tablespoons extra-virgin olive oil

1. When ready to cook, set Traeger temperature to 275ºF (135ºC) and preheat, lid closed for 15 minutes.
2. Season the salmon fillets with salt and pepper and place directly on the grill grate. Grill for 15 to 20 minutes, or until the internal temperature reaches 120ºF (49ºC). Remove from grill and set aside to cool.
3. Place the cooled salmon fillets in a large bowl and break up with a fork. Stir in the remaining ingredients, except for the olive oil. Shape the salmon mixture into 6 patties.
4. Increase Traeger temperature to 375ºF (191ºC) and preheat, lid closed for 10 to 15 minutes.
5. Place a cast iron pan in the grill and pour in the olive oil.
6. When the oil is hot, add the patties to the pan and cook in two batches. Cook for 10 to 12 minutes, flipping once halfway through or until the sides are golden brown.
7. Serve hot.

Teriyaki Shrimp Skewers

Prep time: 5 minutes | Cook time: 6 minutes | Serves 4

1½ pounds (680 g) uncooked shrimp, per person
1 cup Teriyaki Sauce
1 cup extra-virgin olive oil
1 cup sweet sherry
1 cup soy sauce
1 teaspoon Traeger Asian BBQ Rub
1 teaspoon grated fresh ginger
1 clove garlic, minced

1. Cut the shrimp along the back of the shell. Remove the black veins and shrimp heads. Wipe the shrimp with a damp paper towel and set aside.

2. Whisk together the remaining ingredients in a shallow pan. Add the shrimp and marinate for 2 to 4 hours in the refrigerator.
3. When ready to cook, set the Traeger to High and preheat, lid closed for 15 minutes.
4. Remove the shrimp from the marinade and thread on metal skewers.
5. Place the skewers on the grill, close the lid and cook for 3 minutes.
6. Turn the shrimp over, close the lid and cook for an additional 3 minutes, or until shrimp are opaque.
7. Remove the shrimp from the grill and serve immediately.

Crispy Bacon Wrapped Jumbo Shrimp

Prep time: 10 minutes | Cook time: 18 to 20 minutes | Serves 6

10 large jumbo shrimp, rinsed and patted dry
¼ cup extra-virgin olive oil
2 tablespoons lemon juice
1 tablespoon lemon zest
1 teaspoon chopped flat-leaf parsley
1 teaspoon minced garlic
1 teaspoon salt
½ teaspoon black pepper
10 strips bacon

1. Place the shrimp in a bowl..
2. Make the marinade: Combine the remaining ingredients, except for the bacon, in an airtight jar and shake vigorously until combined. Pour the marinade over the shrimp and refrigerate for 30 minutes to 1 hour.
3. When ready to cook, set Traeger temperature to 400ºF (204ºC) and preheat, lid closed for 15 minutes.
4. Lay the bacon strips diagonally on the grill grate and grill for 10 to 12 minutes, or until the bacon is partially cooked but still very pliable. Remove the bacon from the grill and cut each strip in half width-wise.
5. Drain the shrimp, discarding the marinade. Wrap a strip of bacon around the body of each shrimp, securing with a toothpick.
6. Place the wrapped bacon on the grill grate. Grill for 4 minutes per side, turning once.
7. Remove from the grill and serving immediately.

Ham-Wrapped Shrimp with Peach Salsa

Prep time: 10 minutes | Cook time: 10 to 12 minutes | Serves 4

2 pounds (907 g) shrimp, peeled and deveined
8 slices prosciutto ham

Peach Salsa:

2 peaches, diced
1 serrano chile, chopped
2 tablespoons chopped fresh basil
2 tablespoons honey
2 tablespoons balsamic vinegar
Salt, to taste
Black pepper, to taste

1.   When ready to cook, set the Traeger to High and preheat, lid closed for 15 minutes.
2.   In a medium bowl, stir together all the ingredients for the peach salsa.
3.   Rinse the shrimp under cold running water and pat dry thoroughly with paper towels. Wrap a piece of prosciutto around each shrimp and secure with a toothpick.
4.   Arrange the prosciutto-wrapped shrimp on the grill grate and grill for 4 to 6 minutes per side, or until the shrimp is opaque.
5.   Serve the shrimp warm topped with the peach salsa.

Citrus Smoked Scallops and Shrimp

Prep time: 20 minutes | Cook time: 50 minutes | Serves 4

1 pound (454 g) sea scallops, shucked
1 pound (454 g) shrimp, peeled and deveined
1 tablespoon canola oil
1 avocado, diced
1 orange, juiced
1 lemon, juiced
1 lime, zested and juiced
½ red onion, diced
1 tablespoon finely chopped cilantro
1 teaspoon onion powder
1 teaspoon garlic powder
2 teaspoons salt
½ teaspoon black pepper
Pinch of red pepper flakes

1.   When ready to cook, set Traeger temperature to 180ºF (82ºC) and preheat, lid closed for 15 minutes.
2.   In a bowl combine the scallops, shrimp and canola oil.
3.   Arrange the scallops and shrimp on the grill and smoke for 45 minutes.
4.   Meanwhile, stir together all the remaining ingredients in a large mixing bowl. Set aside.
5.   When the shrimp and scallops have finished smoking, turn the grill up to 325ºF (163ºC) and cook for an additional 5 minutes, to make sure they are fully cooked.

6.   Let scallops and shrimp cool, then cut in half width-wise, and toss them with the ingredients in the bowl.
7.   Refrigerate the dish for at least 2 to 3 hours to let the flavors combine. Serve chilled.

Traeger Grilled Soft-Shell Crabs

Prep time: 10 minutes | Cook time: 16 to 20 minutes | Serves 8

8 soft-shell crab, rinsed and patted dry
⅓ cup Traeger Cajun Shake, plus more for dusting
3 tablespoons chopped fresh basil
2 tablespoons Worcestershire sauce
1 lemon, juiced
½ cup extra-virgin olive oil
Tartar sauce, as needed

1.   Place the crabs in a large resealable plastic bag.
2.   Make the marinade: In a small bowl, whisk together the Traeger Cajun Shake, basil, Worcestershire sauce and lemon juice. Slowly whisk in the olive oil. Pour the marinade over the crabs and refrigerate for 1 hour.
3.   Drain the crabs and discard the marinade. Lightly dust the crabs with Traeger Cajun Shake.
4.   When ready to cook, set Traeger temperature to 450ºF (232ºC) and preheat, lid closed for 15 minutes.
5.   Arrange the crabs directly on the grill grate and grill for 16 to 20 minutes, turning once, or until the crabs turn orangish-pink and don't seem "squishy" when pressed with a finger.
6.   Transfer to a platter and serve with the tartar sauce.

Roasted Mussels, Clams and Lobsters

Prep time: 15 minutes | Cook time: 1 hour | Serves 6

16 mussels, unshucked
16 clams, in shell
4 mild Italian sausage
4 ears fresh corn
2 yellow onions, quartered
1 red potato
8 small russet potatoes
1 cup white wine
3 cloves garlic, smashed
2 whole lobsters, in shell
½ cup butter, melted
1 lemon, quartered
1 French bread

1.   When ready to cook, set the Traeger to High and preheat, lid closed for 15 minutes.

2.	Arrange the mussels, clams, sausages, corn, onions and potatoes in a baking pan. Drizzle with the wine and sprinkle with the garlic. Place the lobster tails on top, shell-side down.

3.	Pour the butter over the lobster halves and tuck the lemon quarters into the pan. Cover the pan tightly with heavy duty aluminum foil.

4.	Place the pan directly on the grill grate. Roast for 60 to 70 minutes, or until the potatoes are cooked through.

5.	Remove the foil from the pan and transfer the vegetables and seafood to a large platter. Ladle some of the cooking juices over all.

6.	Serve immediately with the French bread.

Grilled Salmon with Italian Dressing

Prep time: 5 minutes | Cook time: 20 to 30 minutes | Serves 4

1 salmon fillets
Zesty Italian dressing, as needed
Traeger Blackened Saskatchewan Rub, as needed
Lemon wedges, as needed

1.	When ready to cook, set Traeger temperature to 325ºF (163ºC) and preheat, lid closed for 15 minutes.

2.	Brush the salmon with the Italian dressing and season with the Traeger Blackened Saskatchewan Rub.

3.	Place the salmon on the grill and cook for 20 to 30 minutes, or until it reaches an internal temperature of 145ºF (63ºC) and flakes easily.

4.	Remove the salmon from the grill. Serve with the lemon wedges.

CHAPTER 8 BURGERS

Smoked Beef Burgers

Prep time: 15 minutes | Cook time: 45 minutes | Serves 4

1 pound (454 g) ground beef
1 egg
Wood-Fired Burger Seasoning

1.   Supply your Traeger with wood pellets and follow the start-up procedure. Preheat the grill, with the lid closed, to 180ºF (82ºC).
2.   In a medium bowl, thoroughly mix together the ground beef and egg. Divide the meat into 4 portions and shape each into a patty. Season the patties with the burger shake.
3.   Place the burgers directly on the grill grate and smoke for 30 minute.
4.   Increase the grill's temperature to 400ºF (204ºC) and continue to cook the burgers until their internal temperature reaches 145°F (63ºC). Remove the burgers from the grill and serve as you like.

Ranch Cheeseburgers

Prep time: 10 minute | Cook time: 30 minute | Serves 4

1 lb (454 g) ground beef (preferably 80% lean 20% fat ground chuck)
½ yellow onion, chopped
1(1-ounce / 28-g) package ranch dressing mix
1 cup cheddar cheese, shredded
1 egg, beaten
4 buns, toasted (optional)
¾ cup bread crumbs
¾ cup mayonnaise
¼cup relish
¼ cup ketchup
2 tablespoon Worcestershire sauce

1.   Mix ground beef, cheese, ranch dressing mix, egg, bread crumbs, and onion in a bowl until evenly combined.
2.   Form burger mixture into ¼ pound circular patties.
3.   Preheat pellet grill to 350ºF (177ºC).
4.   Lightly oil grill grate and place burger patties on the grill.
5.   Cook burgers until they reach an internal temperature of 155°F (68ºC) (typically cooks for about 6 minutes per side).
6.   Remove burgers once done and let rest at room temperature for 15 minutes.
7.   Combine sauce ingredients in a bowl and whisk well.

8.   Place burger patties on buns and top with desired toppings, including homemade sauce.

Spicy Chunk Cheeseburgers

Prep time: 15 minutes | Cook time: 30 minute | Serves 4

1 lb (454 g) ground chuck (80% lean, 20% fat)
4 Monterey Jack cheese slices
¼ cup yellow onion, finely chopped
4 hamburger buns
2 tablespoon hatch chiles, peeled and chopped
6 tablespoon hatch chile salsa
1 teaspoon kosher salt
Mayonnaise, to taste
1 teaspoon ground black pepper

1.   In a bowl, combine beef, diced onion, chopped hatch chiles, salt, and fresh ground pepper. Once evenly mixed, shape into 4 burger patties
2.   Preheat pellet grill to 350ºF (177ºC)
3.   Place burgers on grill, and cook for about 6 minutes per side or until both sides of each burger are slightly crispy
4.   After burger is cooked to desired doneness and both sides have light sear, place cheese slices on each burger. Allow to heat for around 45 seconds or until cheese melts
5.   Remove from grill and allow to rest for about 10 minute6. Spread a little bit of mayonnaise on both sides of each bun. Place burger patty on bottom side of the bun, then top with hatch chile salsa on top to taste

Bison Cheeseburgers

Prep time: 30 minute | Cook time: 17 to 19 minutes | Serves 6

2 pounds (907 g) ground bison
2 tablespoons steak seasoning
4 tablespoons (½ stick) unsalted butter, cut into pieces
1 large onion, finely minced
6 slices Swiss cheese
6 ciabatta buns, split
Sweet and Spicy Jalapeño Relish, for serving
Lettuce and sliced tomatoes, for serving
Supply your smoker with wood pellets and follow the manufacturer's specific start-up procedure. Preheat, with the lid closed, to 425ºF (218ºC).
In a large bowl, combine the ground bison and steak seasoning until well blended.
Shape the meat mixture into 6 patties and make a thumb indentation in the center of each. Set aside.

Place a rimmed baking sheet on the grill and add the butter and onion. Sauté for 5 minutes, or until the onion is translucent. Top with the bison burger patties, indention-side down.

Close the lid and smoke for 6 to 7 minutes, then flip the burgers and smother them in the sautéed onion. Close the lid again and continue smoking for 6 to 7 minutes. During the last few minutes of cooking, top each burger with a slice of Swiss cheese. For safe consumption, the internal temperature should reach between 140ºF (60ºC) (medium) and 160ºF (71ºC) (well-done).

Lightly toast the ciabatta buns, split-side down, on one side of the smoker.

Serve the onion-smothered cheeseburgers on the toasted buns with jalapeño relish, lettuce, and tomato—or whatever toppings you like.

French Beef Burgers

Prep time: 35 minutes | Cook time: 20 to 25 minutes | Serves 4

1 pound (454 g) lean ground beef
1 tablespoon minced garlic
1 teaspoon Better Than Bouillon Beef Base
1 teaspoon dried chives
1 teaspoon freshly ground black pepper
8 slices Gruyère cheese, divided
½ cup soy sauce
1 tablespoon extra-virgin olive oil
1 teaspoon liquid smoke
3 medium onions, cut into thick slices (do not separate the rings)
1 loaf French bread, cut into 8 slices
4 slices provolone cheese

1. In a large bowl, mix together the ground beef, minced garlic, beef base, chives, and pepper until well blended
2. Divide the meat mixture and shape into 8 thin burger patties
3. Top each of 4 patties with one slice of Gruyère, then top with the remaining 4 patties to create 4 stuffed burgers
4. Supply your smoker with wood pellets and follow the manufacturer's specific start-up procedure. Preheat, with the lid closed, to 425ºF (218ºC)
5. Arrange the burgers directly on one side of the grill, close the lid, and smoke for 10 minute. Flip and smoke with the lid closed for 10 to 15 minutes more, or until a meat thermometer inserted in the burgers reads 160ºF (71ºC). Add another Gruyère slice to the burgers during the last 5 minutes of smoking to melt.
6. Meanwhile, in a small bowl, combine the soy sauce, olive oil, and liquid smoke

7. Arrange the onion slices on the grill and baste on both sides with the soy sauce mixture. Smoke with the lid closed for 20 minute, flipping halfway through
8. Lightly toast the French bread slices on the grill. Layer each of 4 slices with a burger patty, a slice of provolone cheese, and some of the smoked onions. Top each with another slice of toasted French bread. Serve immediately.

Fennel Pork Burger

Prep time: 10 minute | Cook time: 30 minute | Serves 4

1 fennel bulb, trimmed and cut into large chunks
3 to 4 garlic cloves
2½ pounds (1.1 kg) boneless pork shoulder, with some of the fat, cut into 1-inch cubes
1 tablespoon fennel seeds
1 teaspoon caraway seeds (optional)
1 teaspoon salt
½ teaspoon pepper, or more to taste
Peeled orange slices to garnish (optional)
Chopped olives to garnish (optional)
Chopped parsley to garnish (optional)
Chopped roasted red pepper to garnish (optional)
Fennel slices, to garnish (optional)

1. Put fennel and garlic into a food processor and pulse until just chopped; remove to a large bowl. Put pork fat in processor and grind until just chopped; add to bowl. Working in batches, process meat with fennel seeds, caraway, if using and salt and pepper, until meat is just chopped (be careful not to over-process). Add to bowl and mix well. Shape mixture into 8 patties.
2. Supply your smoker with wood pellets and follow the manufacturer's specific start-up procedure. Preheat, with the lid closed, to 425ºF (218ºC).
3. Arrange the burgers directly on one side of the grill, close the lid, and smoke for 10 minute. Flip and smoke with the lid closed for 10 to 15 minutes more, or until a meat thermometer inserted in the burgers reads 160ºF (71ºC). Add another Gruyère slice to the burgers during the last 5 minutes of smoking to melt.
4. Garnish with peeled orange slices, chopped olives, chopped parsley, chopped roasted red pepper and fennel slices, to taste.

Pork and Mushroom Burgers

Prep time: 10 minute | Cook time: 30 minute | Serves 4

1 pound (454 g) ground pork
1 tablespoon minced garlic

1 teaspoon minced fresh rosemary, fennel seed or parsley
Salt and ground black pepper, to taste
4 large portobello mushroom caps, stems removed
Olive oil
4 burger buns
Any burger fixings you like

1.   Combine the ground pork, garlic, rosemary and a sprinkle of salt and pepper. Use a spoon to lightly scrape away the gills of the mushrooms and hollow them slightly. Drizzle the mushrooms (inside and out) with olive oil and sprinkle with salt and pepper. Press ¼ of the mixture into each of the hollow sides of the mushrooms; you want the meat to spread all the way across the width of the mushrooms. They should look like burgers.

2.   Grill the burgers, meat side down, until the pork is well browned, 4 to 6 minutes. Flip and cook until the top side of the mushrooms are browned and the mushrooms are tender, another 6 to 8 minutes. If you like, use an instant-read thermometer to check the interior temperature of the pork, which should be a minimum of 145°F (63ºC).

3.   Serve the burgers on buns (toasted, if you like) with any fixings you like.

CHAPTER 9 VEGETABLES

Balsamic Mexican Street Corn

Prep time: 15 minutes | Cook time: 45 minutes | Serves 6

16 to 20 long toothpicks
1 pound (454 g) Brussels sprouts, trimmed and wilted, leaves removed
½ pound (227 g) bacon, cut in half
1 tablespoon packed brown sugar
1 tablespoon Cajun seasoning
¼ cup balsamic vinegar
¼ cup extra-virgin olive oil
¼ cup chopped fresh cilantro
2 teaspoons minced garlic

1.   Soak the toothpicks in water for 15 minutes.
2.   Supply your smoker with wood pellets and follow the manufacturer's specific start-up procedure. Preheat, with the lid closed, to 300ºF (149ºC).
3.   Wrap each Brussels sprout in a half slice of bacon and secure with a toothpick.
4.   In a small bowl, combine the brown sugar and Cajun seasoning. Dip each wrapped Brussels sprout in this sweet rub and roll around to coat.
5.   Place the sprouts on a Frogmat or parchment paper–lined baking sheet on the grill grate, close the lid, and smoke for 45 minutes to 1 hour, turning as needed, until cooked evenly and the bacon is crisp.
6.   In a small bowl, whisk together the balsamic vinegar, olive oil, cilantro, and garlic.
7.   Remove the toothpicks from the Brussels sprouts, transfer to a plate and serve drizzled with the cilantro-balsamic sauce.

Potato Fries with Chipotle Ketchup

Prep time: 10 minutes | Cook time: 10 to 15 minutes | Serves 4

Chipotle Ketchup:
4 whole chipotle peppers, chopped
1 cup ketchup
1 tablespoon extra-virgin olive oil
1 teaspoon garlic powder
1 teaspoon onion powder
1 tablespoon chili powder
1 tablespoon sugar
1 tablespoon cumin
1 whole limes
Fries:
6 whole Yukon gold potatoes, cut into thick strips
2 tablespoons butter, melted
1 tablespoon Traeger Beef Rub
¼ cup chopped flat-leaf parsley

1.   Stir together all the chipotle ketchup in a mixing bowl until combined. Place in the refrigerator for at least 1 hour to blend the flavors (making it one day ahead of time is even better if you can swing it).
2.   When ready to cook, set Traeger temperature to High and preheat, lid closed for 15 minutes.
3.   Place the potatoes in a bowl, drizzle with melted butter and sprinkle with the Beef rub, tossing to coat.
4.   Lay the potatoes on a Traeger Grilling Basket and bake for 10 to 15 minutes, or until the fries reach your desired level of crispiness
5.   Remove the fries from the grill to a serving bowl, and toss with parsley. Serve with the chipotle ketchup for dipping.

Romaine Salad with Bacon

Prep time: 5 minutes | Cook time: 20 minutes | Serves 2

Salad:
1 romaine lettuce heart, cut in half
1 teaspoon olive oil
Salt and freshly ground black pepper, to taste
2 teaspoons grated Parmesan cheese
6 slices cooked bacon, crumbled
Dressing:
¼ cup milk
2 teaspoons blue cheese
2 teaspoons mayonnaise
Salt and pepper, to taste
Garlic powder, to taste

1.   When ready to cook, set Traeger temperature to 450ºF (232ºC) and preheat, lid closed for 15 minutes.
2.   Drizzle the olive oil over both faces of the romaine. Season lettuce with salt, pepper, and Parmesan cheese.
3.   Lay the romaine lettuce, face-down, on the grill and cook for 2 minutes.
4.   Remove romaine from grill to a salad bowl. Make the dressing by mixing the blue cheese, mayonnaise, and milk in a small bowl. Season to taste with a little salt, pepper, and garlic powder.
5.   Add the bacon to the salad bowl with romaine and pour over the dressing. Toss well and serve immediately.

Bacon-Wrapped Jalapeños

Prep time: 15 minutes | Cook time: 1 hour | Serves 4

12 medium jalapeño

8 ounces (227 g) cream cheese, softened
2 tablespoons Traeger Pork & Poultry Rub
1 cup grated cheese
6 slices bacon, cut in half

1.   When ready to cook, set Traeger temperature to 180ºF (82ºC) and preheat, lid closed for 15 minutes. For optimal flavor, use Super Smoke if available.
2.   Slice the jalapeños in half lengthwise. Scrape out any seeds and ribs with a small spoon or paring knife. In a bowl, stir together softened cream cheese with Traeger Pork & Poultry rub and grated cheese. Spoon the mixture into each jalapeño half. Wrap with bacon and secure with a toothpick.
3.   Place the jalapeños on a rimmed baking sheet. Place on the grill and smoke for 30 minutes.
4.   Increase the grill temperature to 375ºF (191ºC) and cook for an additional 30 minutes, or until bacon is cooked to desired doneness.
5.   Serve warm.

Creamy Mashed Red Potatoes

Prep time: 15 minutes | Cook time: 40 minutes | Serves 4

8 large red potatoes
Salt and black pepper, to taste
½ cup heavy cream
¼ cup butter, softened

1.   When ready to cook, set temperature to 180ºF (82ºC) and preheat, lid closed for 15 minutes.
2.   Slice red potatoes in half lengthwise, then cut in half again to make quarters. Season potatoes with salt and pepper.
3.   Increase the heat to High and preheat. Once the grill is hot, place the potatoes directly on the grill. Every 15 minutes flip the potatoes to ensure all sides get color. Continue to do this until potatoes are fork-tender.
4.   When tender, mash potatoes with heavy cream, butter, salt, and pepper to taste. Serve immediately.

Herb-Infused Riced Potatoes

Prep time: 20 minutes | Cook time: 1 hour | Serves 6

2½ pounds (1.1 kg) russet potatoes, peeled and cut into 1-inch cubes
1½ cups water
1 cup heavy cream
6 sage leaves
3 thyme sprigs
2 rosemary sprigs
2 tablespoons thyme leaves
6 peppercorns

2 garlic cloves
2 butter, sticks
Salt and ground black pepper, to taste

1.   When ready to cook, set Traeger temperature to 350ºF (177ºC) and preheat, lid closed for 15 minutes.
2.   Place the potatoes in a heatproof dish with water, cover and cook for 1 hour or until fork-tender.
3.   Meanwhile, combine the heavy cream with the herbs, peppercorns, and garlic cloves in a small saucepan.
4.   Place on the grill, cover, and allow to steep for 15 minutes. Strain the cream through a sieve to remove the herbs and garlic, place back in the saucepan and keep warm on the stove.
5.   Drain and using a potato ricer, rice the potatoes back into the large stockpot. Slowly pour in two-thirds of the cream, then stir in 1 stick of the butter and 1 tablespoon of salt. Continue to add more cream, butter and salt to reach your desired consistency.
6.   Serve immediately.

Roasted Green Beans and Bacon

Prep time: 15 minutes | Cook time: 20 minutes | Serves 4

1½ pounds (680 g) fresh green beans
4 strips bacon, cut into small pieces
4 tablespoons extra-virgin olive oil
2 clove garlic, minced
1 teaspoon kosher salt

1.   When ready to cook, set Traeger temperature to High and preheat, lid closed for 15 minutes.
2.   Toss all ingredients together and spread out evenly on a sheet tray.
3.   Place the tray directly on the grill and roast until the bacon is crispy and beans are lightly browned, about 20 minutes. Serve hot.

Smoked Olives

Prep time: 10 minutes | Cook time: 20 to 30 minutes | Serves 4

1 pound (454 g) mixed olives
1 quart extra-virgin olive oil
1 whole lemon zest
1 whole orange zest
½ tablespoon red pepper flakes
½ tablespoon dried fennel seed
3 whole dried bay leaves
4 whole thyme sprigs
4 whole rosemary sprigs

1.   When ready to cook, set Traeger temperature to 225ºF (107ºC) and preheat, lid closed

for 15 minutes. For optimal flavor, use Super Smoke if available.

2.   Spread the olives out on a roasting pan and place on the grill. Smoke for 20 to 30 minutes or until the olives have a smoky flavor.

3.   Remove from the grill when olives reach desired smokiness and cool. Once cooled, combine smoked olives, olive oil, orange and lemon zest, red pepper flakes, fennel, bay leaves, thyme, and rosemary. Store in an airtight container, ensuring all the olives are submerged. Serve.

Grilled Peach and Tomato Salsa

Prep time: 5 minutes | Cook time: 8 to 10 minutes | Serves 6

6 peaches, halved
3 tomatoes, halved
2 jalapeños
2 green onions
2 cloves garlic
½ cup cilantro
5 teaspoons apple cider vinegar
1 teaspoon lime juice
½ teaspoon salt
¼ teaspoon black pepper

1.   When ready to cook, set Traeger temperature to 375ºF (191ºC) and preheat, lid closed for 15 minutes.

2.   Place the peaches, tomatoes, and jalapeños on the grill grate. Close the lid and roast for 8 to 10 minutes, or until the skin has split and the tomatoes and jalapeños have blistered.

3.   Remove from the grill and let rest for 5 minutes, or until the fruit can be easily handled.

4.   Remove the skin from the peaches and tomatoes. Remove the skin, stems, and seeds from the jalapeños.

5.   In a food processor, place the peeled peaches, tomatoes, jalapeños along with the green onions and pulse until coarsely chopped.

6.   Add all the remaining ingredients and pulse until it reaches the desired consistency.

7.   Serve immediately or stored in sealed jars in the refrigerator for up to 1 week.

Smoked Macaroni Veggie Salad

Prep time: 10 minutes | Cook time: 28 to 30 minutes | Serves 4

1 pound (454 g) macaroni, uncooked
1 green bell pepper, diced
½ small red onion, diced
½ cup shredded carrot
Dressing:
1 cup mayonnaise

3 tablespoons white wine vinegar
2 tablespoons sugar
Salt, to taste
Black pepper, to taste

1.   Bring a large stockpot of salted water to a boil over medium heat and cook the pasta for 8 to 10 minutes, or until al dente. Drain the pasta and rinse under cold water.

2.   When ready to cook, set Traeger temperature to 180ºF (82ºC) and preheat, lid closed for 15 minutes.

3.   Spread the cooked pasta on a sheet tray and place the sheet tray on the grill grate. Smoke for 20 minutes, remove from the heat and transfer to the refrigerator to cool.

4.   Meanwhile, whisk together all the ingredients for the dressing in a medium bowl.

5.   In a large bowl, stir together the smoked pasta, bell pepper, onion, carrot and dressing. Cover in plastic and set in the refrigerator for 20 minutes before serving.

6.   Serve chilled.

Vinegary Rotini Salad

Prep time: 10 minutes | Cook time: 18 to 20 minutes | Serves 8
Salad:

1 pound (454 g) salami
8 ounces (227 g) Mozzarella cheese
1 red onion, diced
1 jar roasted red peppers, sliced
3 jarred pepperoncini peppers, thinly sliced
3 cups sliced cherry tomatoes
¾ cup black olives
¼ cup chopped flat-leaf parsley
1 pound (454 g) rotini pasta
Vinaigrette:
3 cloves garlic, minced
½ cup extra-virgin olive oil
½ cup red wine vinegar
1 tablespoon Italian seasoning
1 tablespoon honey
Kosher salt, to taste
Black pepper, to taste

1.   When ready to cook, set Traeger temperature to 180ºF (82ºC) and preheat, lid closed for 15 minutes.

2.   Put all the salad ingredients, except for the pasta, on a sheet tray. Place the tray on the grill and smoke for 10 minutes. Remove from the grill and set aside.

3.   Bring a large pot of salted water to a boil over high heat and cook the pasta for 8 to 10 minutes, or until al dente.

4.   Meanwhile, stir together all the ingredients for the vinaigrette in a small bowl and set aside.

5.   Drain the pasta and rinse under cold water. Transfer the pasta to a large mixing bowl.

6.   Chop all the salad ingredients and transfer to the mixing bowl with the pasta. Spread the vinaigrette over the top and toss to coat well.

7.   Cover in plastic and set in the refrigerator for 30 minutes before serving.

8.   Serve chilled.

Mini Veggie Quiches

Prep time: 10 minutes | Cook time: 26 to 28 minutes | Serves 8

1 tablespoon extra-virgin olive oil
½ yellow onion, diced
3 cups fresh spinach
10 eggs
4 ounces (113 g) shredded Cheddar cheese
¼ cup fresh basil
1 teaspoon kosher salt
½ teaspoon black pepper
Cooking spray

1.   Spritz a 12-cup muffin tin with cooking spray. Set aside.

2.   Heat the oil in a skillet over medium heat. Add the onion and cook for about 7 minutes, or until tender, stirring frequently. Add the spinach and cook for 1 more minute, or until wilted.

3.   Transfer the cooked veggies to a clean work surface to cool, then chop the veggies.

4.   When ready to cook, set Traeger temperature to 350ºF (177ºC) and preheat, lid closed for 15 minutes.

5.   In a large bowl, whisk the eggs until frothy. Stir in the cooled veggies along with the remaining ingredients. Divide the egg mixture evenly among the muffin cups.

6.   Place the muffin tin on the grill and bake for 18 to 20 minutes, or until the eggs have puffed up, are set, and are beginning to brown.

7.   Serve immediately, or let cool on a wire rack, then refrigerate in a sealed container for up to 4 days.

Smoked Chickpeas with Roasted Veggies

Prep time: 15 minutes | Cook time: 30 to 40 minutes | Serves 4

1½ cups chickpeas, drained and rinsed
$^1/_3$ cup tahini
4 tablespoons lemon juice
2 tablespoons extra-virgin olive oil
1 tablespoon minced garlic,
1 teaspoon salt
2 cups cauliflower, cut into florets
2 cups butternut squash
2 cups fresh Brussels sprouts
2 whole portobello mushrooms
1 red onion, sliced
4 tablespoons extra-virgin olive oil

1.   When ready to cook, set Traeger temperature to 180ºF (82ºC) and preheat, lid closed for 15 minutes.

2.   Spread the chickpeas on a sheet tray. Place the tray on the grill grate and smoke for 15 to 20 minutes.

3.   In a food processor, combine the smoked chickpeas, tahini, lemon juice, olive oil, garlic and salt. Pulse until mixed well but not completely smooth. Transfer to a bowl and set aside.

4.   Increase Traeger temperature to High and preheat, lid closed for 15 minutes.

5.   Toss the veggies with the olive oil to coat and spread on a sheet tray. Place the sheet tray on the grill and roast for 15 to 20 minutes, or until lightly browned and cooked through.

6.   Transfer the mashed chickpeas to a serving platter and top with the roasted veggies.

7.   Serve immediately.

Sweet Potatoes with Marshmallow Sauce

Prep time: 5 minutes | Cook time: 1 hour 5 minutes | Serves 4

4 large sweet potatoes
8 tablespoons sliced butter
½ cup brown sugar
¼ teaspoon ground nutmeg
Salt, to taste

Marshmallow Sauce:

1 cup mini marshmallows
1 tablespoon melted butter

1.   When ready to cook, set the Traeger to High and preheat, lid closed for 15 minutes.

2.   Place a sweet potato on a clean work surface horizontally between the handles of 2 wooden spoons. Slice the potato into thin slices, leaving ¼ inch at the bottom unsliced. The spoon handles will prevent slicing the potato all the way through. Repeat with the remaining potatoes.

3.   Insert a thin slice of butter between the potato slices. Sprinkle with the brown sugar, nutmeg and salt.

4.   Arrange the potatoes on a sheet tray. Place the tray on the grill and bake for 1 hour, or until cooked through and crispy on top.

5.   Meanwhile, make the marshmallow sauce: Combine the mini marshmallows and melted butter

in a saucepan over medium heat, until the mallows are melted and creamy.

6.   When the potatoes are baked, add a dollop of marshmallow sauce to the top of each potato.

7.   Return the tray to the grill and bake for an additional 5 minutes, or until the marshmallows have melted.

8.   Remove from the oven. Let cool for 5 minutes before serving.

Crispy Sweet Potato Fries

Prep time: 5 minutes | Cook time: 20 to 30 minutes | Serves 4

4 sweet potatoes, peeled and cut into sticks
3 tablespoons extra-virgin olive oil
1 tablespoon salt
1 teaspoon black pepper
1 cup mayonnaise
2 chipotle peppers in adobe sauce
2 limes, juiced

1.   When ready to cook, set the Traeger to High and preheat, lid closed for 15 minutes.

2.   In a medium bowl, toss together the sweet potatoes, olive oil, salt and pepper to coat. Transfer to a sheet pan.

3.   Place the sheet pan on the grill grate and roast for 20 to 30 minutes, or until the potatoes are brown and crispy, stirring occasionally.

4.   Meanwhile, combine the mayonnaise, chipotle peppers and lime juice in a blender and pulse until smooth.

5.   Serve the sweet potato fries with the mayonnaise sauce.

Grilled Corn Salad

Prep time: 10 minutes | Cook time: 15 minutes | Serves 6

4 large corn husks
4 tomatoes, chopped
1 red onion, diced
1 jalapeño pepper, grilled, deseeded and diced
1 lime, juiced
½ cup finely chopped cilantro
1 teaspoon onion powder
1 teaspoon garlic powder
Salt, to taste
Black pepper, to taste

1.   When ready to cook, set the Traeger to High and preheat, lid closed for 15 minutes.

2.   Place the corn on the grill and cook for 15 minutes, or until thoroughly charred. Remove the husk and cut the kernels from the cob.

3.   Toss the corn with the remaining ingredients in a large bowl. Cover in plastic and refrigerate until ready to eat.

4.   Serve chilled.

Red Pepper and White Bean Mashup

Prep time: 5 minutes | Cook time: 40 minutes | Serves 4

4 whole garlic
2 tablespoons extra-virgin olive oil
2 red bell peppers, washed and dried
2 cans cannellini beans, drained, rinsed and mashed
3 tablespoons chopped flat-leaf parsley
3 tablespoons fresh dill weed
2 tablespoons extra-virgin olive oil
4 teaspoons lemon juice
1½ teaspoons salt

1.   When ready to cook, set Traeger temperature to 400ºF (204ºC) and preheat, lid closed for 15 minutes.

2.   Peel away the outside layers of the garlic husk. Cut off the top of the garlic bulb, exposing each of the individual cloves. Drizzle the olive oil over the top of the head of garlic and rub it in. Wrap the garlic in foil. Put the garlic and red bell peppers on the grill.

3.   Roast the garlic for 25 to 30 minutes and the peppers for about 40 minutes. Rotate the peppers a quarter-turn every 10 minutes until the exterior is blistered and blackened.

4.   Transfer the peppers to a bowl. Cover in plastic and let rest for 15 minutes. The steam will loosen the skins so that they can slip off easily.

5.   Peel the skin off the peppers. Cut off the stems and scrape out the seeds.

6.   Transfer the garlic to another bowl. Let cool and then pull out the individual cloves.

7.   In a blender, combine the roasted red peppers, 4 cloves of the roasted garlic along with the remaining ingredients. Blend until smooth and creamy.

8.   Serve immediately.

Baked Creamy Spinach

Prep time: 15 minutes | Cook time: 30 to 35 minutes | Serves 4

2 tablespoons butter
2 cloves garlic
1 shallot, finely chopped
1 teaspoon red pepper flakes
1½ cups heavy cream
1 teaspoon ground nutmeg
Salt, to taste
Black pepper, to taste
2 packages frozen spinach, thawed and drained

¾ cup sour cream
½ cup Romano cheese
½ cup Parmesan cheese
½ cup panko bread crumbs

1.   In a saucepan over medium heat, melt the butter. Add the garlic and shallot to the saucepan and sauté for 3 minutes. Add the red pepper flakes and cook for 2 more minutes.
2.   Add the heavy cream and nutmeg and bring to a boil. Season with salt and pepper. Stir in the spinach and sour cream. Remove from the heat and stir in cheeses.
3.   Pour the mixture into a baking dish and sprinkle the panko on top.
4.   When ready to cook, set Traeger temperature to 375ºF (191ºC) and preheat, lid closed for 15 minutes.
5.   Place the baking dish on the grill grate and bake for 25 to 30 minutes, or until the top is browned and bubbly.
6.   Serve immediately.

Roasted Carrots with Pomegranate Relish

Prep time: 15 minutes | Cook time: 30 minutes | Serves 6

2 bunches slender rainbow carrots, rinsed
2 teaspoons dried fennel seed
2 teaspoons kosher salt
1 teaspoon ground coriander
1 teaspoon sugar
½ teaspoon cumin
3 tablespoons extra-virgin olive oil
2 cloves garlic, thinly sliced
1 lime, zested and juiced

Pomegranate Relish:
½ cup chopped pistachios
½ cup pomegranate seeds
¼ cup chopped flat-leaf parsley
¼ cup fresh mint leaves
Salt, to taste

1.   When ready to cook, set the Traeger to High and preheat, lid closed for 15 minutes.
2.   In a small bowl, whisk together the fennel seed, salt, coriander, sugar and cumin.
3.   Toss the carrots with 2 tablespoons of the olive oil to coat evenly. Stir in the spice mixture and garlic. Toss to coat.
4.   Place the coated carrots on a sheet tray. Place the sheet tray on the grill and roast for 30 minutes, or until the carrots can be pierced with a fork, turning once. Remove from the grill. Sprinkle with the lime zest.
5.   Make the pomegranate relish: Stir together the remaining 1 tablespoon of the olive oil, lime juice, pistachios, pomegranate seeds, parsley, mint and a generous pinch of salt in a medium bowl.
6.   Transfer the carrots to a serving platter. Spread the pomegranate relish generously over the carrots and serve.

CHAPTER 10 VEGETARIAN AND VEGAN

Mexican Street Corn

Prep time: 10 minutes | Cook time: 12 to 14 minutes | Serves 4

•

4 ears corn
½ cup sour cream
½ cup mayonnaise
¼ cup chopped fresh cilantro, plus more for garnish
Chipotle Butter, for topping
1 cup grated Parmesan cheese

1.	Supply your smoker with wood pellets and follow the manufacturer's specific start-up procedure. Preheat, with the lid closed, to 450ºF (232ºC).
2.	Shuck the corn, removing the silks and cutting off the cores.
3.	Tear four squares of aluminum foil large enough to completely cover an ear of corn.
4.	In a medium bowl, combine the sour cream, mayonnaise, and cilantro. Slather the mixture all over the ears of corn.
5.	Wrap each ear of corn in a piece of foil, sealing tightly. Place on the grill, close the lid, and smoke for 12 to 14 minutes.
6.	Remove the corn from the foil and place in a shallow baking dish. Top with chipotle butter, the Parmesan cheese, and more chopped cilantro.
7.	Serve immediately.

Smoked Okra

Prep time: 10 minutes | Cook time: 30 minutes | Serves 4

Nonstick cooking spray or butter, for greasing
1 pound (454 g) whole okra
2 tablespoons extra-virgin olive oil
2 teaspoons seasoned salt
2 teaspoons freshly ground black pepper

1.	Supply your smoker with wood pellets and follow the manufacturer's specific start-up procedure. Preheat, with the lid closed, to 400ºF (204ºC). Alternatively, preheat your oven to 400ºF (204ºC).
2.	Line a shallow rimmed baking pan with aluminum foil and coat with cooking spray.
3.	Arrange the okra on the pan in a single layer. Drizzle with the olive oil, turning to coat. Season on all sides with the salt and pepper.
4.	Place the baking pan on the grill grate, close the lid, and smoke for 30 minutes, or until crisp and slightly charred. Alternatively, roast in the oven for 30 minutes.
5.	Serve hot.

Garlic-Wine Buttered Spaghetti Squash

Prep time: 20 minutes | Cook time: 40 minutes | Serves 4

1 spaghetti squash
2 tablespoons extra-virgin olive oil
1 teaspoon salt
1 teaspoon freshly ground black pepper
2 teaspoons garlic powder
4 tablespoons (½ stick) unsalted butter
½ cup white wine
1 tablespoon minced garlic
2 teaspoons chopped fresh parsley
1 teaspoon red pepper flakes
½ teaspoon salt
½ teaspoon freshly ground black pepper

For the Squash

1.	Supply your smoker with wood pellets and follow the manufacturer's specific start-up procedure. Preheat, with the lid closed, to 375°F (191ºC).
2.	Cut off both ends of the squash, then cut it in half lengthwise. Scoop out and discard the seeds.
3.	Rub the squash flesh well with the olive oil and sprinkle on the salt, pepper, and garlic powder.
4.	Place the squash cut-side up on the grill grate, close the lid, and smoke for 40 minutes, or until tender

For the Sauce

1.	On the stove top, in a medium saucepan over medium heat, combine the butter, white wine, minced garlic, parsley, red pepper flakes, salt, and pepper, and cook for about 5 minutes, or until heated through. Reduce the heat to low and keep the sauce warm.
2.	Remove the squash from the grill and let cool slightly before shredding the flesh with a fork; discard the skin.
3.	Stir the shredded squash into the garlic-wine butter sauce and serve immediately.

Georgia Parmesan Sweet Onion

Prep time: 25 minutes | Cook time: 1 hour | Serves 6

Nonstick cooking spray or butter, for greasing
4 large Vidalia or other sweet onions
8 tablespoons (1 stick) unsalted butter, melted
4 chicken bouillon cubes
1 cup grated Parmesan cheese

1.	Supply your smoker with wood pellets and follow the manufacturer's specific start-up procedure. Preheat, with the lid closed, to 350ºF (177ºC).

2. Coat a high-sided baking pan with cooking spray or butter.

3. Peel the onions and cut into quarters, separating into individual petals.

4. Spread the onions out in the prepared pan and pour the melted butter over them.

5. Crush the bouillon cubes and sprinkle over the buttery onion pieces, then top with the cheese.

6. Transfer the pan to the grill, close the lid, and smoke for 30 minutes.

7. Remove the pan from the grill, cover tightly with aluminum foil, and poke several holes all over to vent.

8. Place the pan back on the grill, close the lid, and smoke for an additional 30 to 45 minutes.

9. Uncover the onions, stir, and serve hot.

Crispy Sweet Potato Chips

Prep time: 40 minutes | Cook time: 35 to 45 minutes | Serves 3

2 sweet potatoes
1 quart warm water
1 tablespoon cornstarch, plus 2 teaspoons
¼ cup extra-virgin olive oil
1 tablespoon salt
1 tablespoon packed brown sugar
1 teaspoon ground cinnamon
1 teaspoon freshly ground black pepper
½ teaspoon cayenne pepper

1. Using a mandolin, thinly slice the sweet potatoes.

2. Pour the warm water into a large bowl and add 1 tablespoon of cornstarch and the potato slices. Let soak for 15 to 20 minutes.

3. Supply your smoker with wood pellets and follow the manufacturer's specific start-up procedure. Preheat, with the lid closed, to 375°F (191ºC).

4. Drain the potato slices, then arrange in a single layer on a perforated pizza pan or a baking sheet lined with aluminum foil. Brush the potato slices on both sides with the olive oil.

5. In a small bowl, whisk together the salt, brown sugar, cinnamon, black pepper, cayenne pepper, and the remaining 2 teaspoons of cornstarch. Sprinkle this seasoning blend on both sides of the potatoes.

6. Place the pan or baking sheet on the grill grate, close the lid, and smoke for 35 to 45 minutes, flipping after 20 minutes, until the chips curl up and become crispy.

7. Store in an airtight container.

Classic Southern Slaw

Prep time: 5 minutes | Cook time: 0 minute | Serves 10

1 head cabbage, shredded
¼ cup white vinegar
¼ cup sugar
1 teaspoon paprika
½ teaspoon salt
½ teaspoon freshly ground black pepper
1 cup heavy (whipping) cream

1. Place the shredded cabbage in a large bowl.

2. In a small bowl, combine the vinegar, sugar, paprika, salt, and pepper.

3. Pour the vinegar mixture over the cabbage and mix well.

4. Fold in the heavy cream and refrigerate for at least 1 hour before serving.

Bunny Dogs with Carrot Relish

Prep time: 20 minutes | Cook time: 35 to 40 minutes | Serves 8

8 hot dog-size carrots, peeled
¼ cup honey
¼ cup yellow mustard
Nonstick cooking spray or butter, for greasing
Salt, to taste
Freshly ground black pepper, to taste
8 hot dog buns
Sweet and Spicy Jalapeño Relish

1. Prepare the carrots by removing the stems and slicing in half lengthwise.

2. In a small bowl, whisk together the honey and mustard.

3. Supply your smoker with wood pellets and follow the manufacturer's specific start-up procedure. Preheat, with the lid closed, to 375°F (191ºC).

4. Line a baking sheet with aluminum foil and coat with cooking spray.

5. Brush the carrots on both sides with the honey mustard and season with salt and pepper; put on the baking sheet.

6. Place the baking sheet on the grill grate, close the lid, and smoke for 35 to 40 minutes, or until tender and starting to brown.

7. To serve, lightly toast the hot dog buns on the grill and top each with two slices of carrot and some relish.

Ratatouille Salad

Prep time: 15 minutes | Cook time: 25 minutes | Serves 6

1 whole sweet potatoes
1 whole red onion, diced
1 whole zucchini
1 whole squash

1 large tomato, diced
As needed vegetable oil
As needed salt and pepper

1. Preheat grill to high setting with the lid closed for 10-15 minutes.
2. Slice all vegetables to a ¼ inch thickness.
3. Lightly brush each vegetable with oil and season with Traeger's Veggie Shake or salt and pepper.
4. Place sweet potato, onion, zucchini, and squash on grill grate and grill for 20 minutes or until tender, turn halfway through.
5. Add tomato slices to the grill during the last 5 minutes of cooking time.
6. For presentation, alternate vegetables while layering them vertically. Enjoy!

Rainbow Carrots and Fennel

Prep time: 10 minutes | Cook time: 45 minutes | Serves 8 to 12

1 pound (454 g) slender rainbow carrots
2 whole fennel, bulb
2 tablespoon extra-virgin olive oil
1 teaspoon salt
Salt, to taste
1 tablespoon fresh thyme

1. When ready to cook, set temperature to High and preheat, lid closed for 15 minutes. For optimal results, set to 500ºF (260ºC) if available.
2. Trim the carrot tops to 1". Peel the carrots and halve any larger ones so they are all about 1/2" thick. Cut the fennel bulbs lengthwise into 1/2" thick slices.
3. Place the fennel and potato slices in a large mixing bowl. Drizzle with 2 tablespoon of the olive oil and a teaspoon of salt.
4. Toss to coat the vegetables evenly with the oil.
5. Place the carrots on a sheet pan. Drizzle with the additional 2 tablespoon of olive oil and a generous pinch of salt. Brush the olive oil over the carrots to distribute evenly.
6. Add the potatoes and fennel slices to the sheet pan. Nestle a few sprigs of herbs into the vegetables as well.
7. Place the pan directly on the grill grate and cook, stirring occasionally until the vegetables are browned and softened, about 35-45 minutes.
8. Allow to cool and serve with the smoked romesco sauce. Enjoy!

CHAPTER 11 APPETIZERS AND SNACKS

Smoked Salted Cashews

Prep time: 5 minutes | Cook time: 1 hour | Serves 6

1 pound (454 g) roasted, salted cashews

1.   Supply your smoker with wood pellets and follow the manufacturer's specific start-up procedure. Preheat the grill, with the lid closed, to 120ºF (49ºC).
2.   Pour the cashews onto a rimmed baking sheet and smoke for 1 hour, stirring once about halfway through the smoking time.
3.   Remove the cashews from the grill, let cool, and store in an airtight container for as long as you can resist.

Smoked Cheddar Cheese

Prep time: minutes | Cook time: 2½ hours | Serves 4

1 (2-pound / 907-g) block medium Cheddar cheese, or your favorite cheese, quartered lengthwise

1.   Supply your smoker with wood pellets and follow the manufacturer's specific start-up procedure. Preheat the grill, with the lid closed, to 90ºF (32ºC).
2.   Place the cheese directly on the grill grate and smoke for 2 hours, 30 minutes, checking frequently to be sure it's not melting. If the cheese begins to melt, try flipping it. If that doesn't help, remove it from the grill and refrigerate for about 1 hour and then return it to the cold smoker.
3.   Remove the cheese, place it in a zip-top bag, and refrigerate overnight.
4.   Slice the cheese and serve with crackers, or grate it and use for making a smoked mac and cheese.

Cheesy Bacon-Wrapped Jalapeño

Prep time: 20 minutes | Cook time: 30 minutes | Serves 12

8 ounces (227 g) cream cheese, softened
½ cup shredded Cheddar cheese
¼ cup chopped scallions
1 teaspoon chipotle chile powder or regular chili powder
1 teaspoon garlic powder
1 teaspoon salt
18 large jalapeño peppers, stemmed, seeded, and halved lengthwise
1 pound (454 g) bacon (precooked works well)

1.   Supply your smoker with wood pellets and follow the manufacturer's specific start-up procedure. Preheat, with the lid closed, to 350ºF (177ºC). Line a baking sheet with aluminum foil.
2.   In a small bowl, combine the cream cheese, Cheddar cheese, scallions, chipotle powder, garlic powder, and salt.
3.   Stuff the jalapeño halves with the cheese mixture.
4.   Cut the bacon into pieces big enough to wrap around the stuffed pepper halves.
5.   Wrap the bacon around the peppers and place on the prepared baking sheet.
6.   Put the baking sheet on the grill grate, close the lid, and smoke the peppers for 30 minutes, or until the cheese is melted and the bacon is cooked through and crisp.
7.   Let the jalapeño poppers cool for 3 to 5 minutes. Serve warm.

Pulled Pork Nachos with Avocado

Prep time: 15 minutes | Cook time: 10 minutes | Serves 4

2 cups leftover smoked pulled pork
1 small sweet onion, diced
1 medium tomato, diced
1 jalapeño pepper, seeded and diced
1 garlic clove, minced
1 teaspoon salt
1 teaspoon freshly ground black pepper
1 bag tortilla chips
1 cup shredded Cheddar cheese
½ cup The Ultimate BBQ Sauce, divided
½ cup shredded jalapeño Monterey Jack cheese
Juice of ½ lime
1 avocado, halved, pitted, and sliced
2 tablespoons sour cream
1 tablespoon chopped fresh cilantro

1.   Supply your smoker with wood pellets and follow the manufacturer's specific start-up procedure. Preheat, with the lid closed, to 375ºF (191ºC).
2.   Heat the pulled pork in the microwave.
3.   In a medium bowl, combine the onion, tomato, jalapeño, garlic, salt, and pepper, and set aside.
4.   Arrange half of the tortilla chips in a large cast iron skillet. Spread half of the warmed pork on top and cover with the Cheddar cheese. Top with half of the onion-jalapeño mixture, then drizzle with ¼ cup of barbecue sauce.
5.   Layer on the remaining tortilla chips, then the remaining pork and the Monterey Jack cheese. Top with the remaining onion-jalapeño mixture and drizzle with the remaining ¼ cup of barbecue sauce.
6.   Place the skillet on the grill, close the lid, and smoke for about 10 minutes, or until the cheese

is melted and bubbly. (Watch to make sure your chips don't burn!)

7.   Squeeze the lime juice over the nachos, top with the avocado slices and sour cream, and garnish with the cilantro before serving hot.

Pig Pops

Prep time: 15 minutes | Cook time: 25 to 30 minutes | Serves 24

Nonstick cooking spray, oil, or butter, for greasing
2 pounds (907 g) thick-cut bacon (24 slices)
24 metal skewers
1 cup packed light brown sugar
2 to 3 teaspoons cayenne pepper
½ cup maple syrup, divided

1.   Supply your smoker with wood pellets and follow the manufacturer's specific start-up procedure. Preheat, with the lid closed, to 350ºF (177ºC).
2.   Coat a disposable aluminum foil baking sheet with cooking spray, oil, or butter.
3.   Thread each bacon slice onto a metal skewer and place on the prepared baking sheet.
4.   In a medium bowl, stir together the brown sugar and cayenne.
5.   Baste the top sides of the bacon with ¼ cup of maple syrup.
6.   Sprinkle half of the brown sugar mixture over the bacon.
7.   Place the baking sheet on the grill, close the lid, and smoke for 15 to 30 minutes.
8.   Using tongs, flip the bacon skewers. Baste with the remaining ¼ cup of maple syrup and top with the remaining brown sugar mixture.
9.   Continue smoking with the lid closed for 10 to 15 minutes, or until crispy. You can eyeball the bacon and smoke to your desired doneness, but the actual ideal internal temperature for bacon is 155°F (68ºC).
10.   Using tongs, carefully remove the bacon skewers from the grill. Let cool completely before handling.

Chorizo Queso Fundido with Tortilla Chips

Prep time: 40 minutes | Cook time: 20 minutes | Serves 4 to 6

1 poblano chile
1 cup chopped queso quesadilla or queso Oaxaca
1 cup shredded Monterey Jack cheese
¼ cup milk
1 tablespoon all-purpose flour
2 (4-ounce / 113-g) links Mexican chorizo sausage, casings removed
⅓ cup beer
1 tablespoon unsalted butter

1 small red onion, chopped
½ cup whole kernel corn
2 serrano chiles or jalapeño peppers, stemmed, seeded, and coarsely chopped
1 tablespoon minced garlic
1 tablespoon freshly squeezed lime juice
1 teaspoon ground cumin
1 teaspoon salt
1 teaspoon freshly ground black pepper
1 tablespoon chopped fresh cilantro
1 tablespoon chopped scallions
Tortilla chips, for serving

1.   Supply your smoker with wood pellets and follow the manufacturer's specific start-up procedure. Preheat, with the lid closed, to 350ºF (177ºC).
2.   On the smoker or over medium-high heat on the stove top, place the poblano directly on the grate (or burner) to char for 1 to 2 minutes, turning as needed. Remove from heat and place in a closed-up lunch-size paper bag for 2 minutes to sweat and further loosen the skin.
3.   Remove the skin and coarsely chop the poblano, removing the seeds; set aside.
4.   In a bowl, combine the queso quesadilla, Monterey Jack, milk, and flour; set aside.
5.   On the stove top, in a cast iron skillet over medium heat, cook and crumble the chorizo for about 2 minutes.
6.   Transfer the cooked chorizo to a small, grill-safe pan and place over indirect heat on the smoker.
7.   Place the cast iron skillet on the preheated grill grate. Pour in the beer and simmer for a few minutes, loosening and stirring in any remaining sausage bits from the pan.
8.   Add the butter to the pan, then add the cheese mixture a little at a time, stirring constantly.
9.   When the cheese is smooth, stir in the onion, corn, serrano chiles, garlic, lime juice, cuvmin, salt, and pepper. Stir in the reserved chopped charred poblano.
10.   Close the lid and smoke for 15 to 20 minutes to infuse the queso with smoke flavor and further cook the vegetables.
11.   When the cheese is bubbly, top with the chorizo mixture and garnish with the cilantro and scallions.
12.   Serve the chorizo queso fundido hot with tortilla chips.

Cream Cheese Hot Sausage Balls

Prep time: 15 minutes | Cook time: 30 minutes | Serves 4 to 5

1 pound (454 g) ground hot sausage, uncooked
8 ounces (227 g) cream cheese, softened

1 package mini filo dough shells

1. Supply your smoker with wood pellets and follow the manufacturer's specific start-up procedure. Preheat, with the lid closed, to 350ºF (177ºC).

2. In a large bowl, using your hands, thoroughly mix together the sausage and cream cheese until well blended.

3. Place the filo dough shells on a rimmed perforated pizza pan or into a mini muffin tin.

4. Roll the sausage and cheese mixture into 1-inch balls and place into the filo shells.

5. Place the pizza pan or mini muffin tin on the grill, close the lid, and smoke the sausage balls for 30 minutes, or until cooked through and the sausage is no longer pink.

6. Plate and serve warm.

Dijon Pigs in a Blanket

Prep time: 20 minutes | Cook time: 15 minutes | Serves 4 to 6

2 tablespoon poppy seeds
1 tablespoon dried minced onion
2 teaspoon garlic, minced
2 tablespoon sesame seeds
1 teaspoon salt
8 ounce (227 g) original crescent dough
¼ cup Dijon mustard
1 large egg, beaten

1. When ready to cook, start your Traeger at 350ºF (177ºC), and preheat with lid closed, 10 to 15 minutes.

2. Mix together poppy seeds, dried minced onion, dried minced garlic, salt and sesame seeds. Set aside.

3. Cut each triangle of crescent roll dough into thirds lengthwise, making 3 small strips from each roll.

4. Brush the dough strips lightly with Dijon mustard. Put the mini hot dogs on 1 end of the dough and roll up.

5. Arrange them, seam side down, on a greased baking pan. Brush with egg wash and sprinkle with seasoning mixture.

6. Bake in Traeger until golden brown, about 12 to 15 minutes.

7. Serve with mustard or dipping sauce of your choice. Enjoy!

Bacon Pork Pinwheels

Prep time: 10 minutes | Cook time: 20 minutes | Serves 4 to 6

1 whole pork loin, boneless
Salt and pepper, to taste
Greek seasoning, to taste

4 slices bacon
The ultimate BBQ sauce, to taste

1. When ready to cook, start the Traeger and set temperature to 500ºF (260ºC). Preheat, lid closed, for 10 to 15 minutes.

2. Trim pork loin of any unwanted silver skin or fat. Using a sharp knife, cut pork loin length wise, into 4 long strips.

3. Lay pork flat, then season with salt, pepper and Cavender's Greek Seasoning.

4. Flip the pork strips over and layer bacon on unseasoned side. Begin tightly rolling the pork strips, with bacon being rolled up on the inside.

5. Secure a skewer all the way through each pork roll to secure it in place. Set the pork rolls down on grill and cook for 15 minutes.

6. Brush BBQ Sauce over the pork. Turn each skewer over, then coat the other side. Let pork cook for another 5-10 minutes, depending on thickness of your pork. Enjoy!

Deviled Crab Appetizer

Prep time: 25 minutes | Cook time: 10 minutes | Makes 30 mini crab cakes

Nonstick cooking spray, oil, or butter, for greasing
1 cup panko breadcrumbs, divided
1 cup canned corn, drained
½ cup chopped scallions, divided
½ red bell pepper, finely chopped
16 ounces (454 g) jumbo lump crabmeat
¾ cup mayonnaise, divided
1 egg, beaten
1 teaspoon salt
1 teaspoon freshly ground black pepper
2 teaspoons cayenne pepper, divided
Juice of 1 lemon

1. Supply your smoker with wood pellets and follow the manufacturer's specific start-up procedure. Preheat, with the lid closed, to 425ºF (218ºC).

2. Spray three 12-cup mini muffin pans with cooking spray and divide ½ cup of the panko between 30 of the muffin cups, pressing into the bottoms and up the sides. (Work in batches, if necessary, depending on the number of pans you have.)

3. In a medium bowl, combine the corn, ¼ cup of scallions, the bell pepper, crabmeat, half of the mayonnaise, the egg, salt, pepper, and 1 teaspoon of cayenne pepper.

4. Gently fold in the remaining ½ cup of breadcrumbs and divide the mixture between the prepared mini muffin cups.

5. Place the pans on the grill grate, close the lid, and smoke for 10 minutes, or until golden brown.

6.	In a small bowl, combine the lemon juice and the remaining mayonnaise, scallions, and cayenne pepper to make a sauce.

7.	Brush the tops of the mini crab cakes with the sauce and serve hot.

Cheesy Smoked Turkey Sandwich

Prep time: 15 minutes | Cook time:15 minutes | Serves 1

2 slices sourdough bread
2 tablespoons butter, at room temperature
2 (1-ounce / 28-g) slices Swiss cheese
4 ounces (113 g) leftover smoked turkey
1 teaspoon garlic salt

1.	Supply your smoker with wood pellets and follow the manufacturer's specific start-up procedure. Preheat the grill, with the lid closed, to 375°F (191ºC).

2.	Coat one side of each bread slice with 1 tablespoon of butter and sprinkle the buttered sides with garlic salt.

3.	Place 1 slice of cheese on each unbuttered side of the bread, and then put the turkey on the cheese.

4.	Close the sandwich, buttered sides out, and place it directly on the grill grate. Cook for 5 minutes. Flip the sandwich and cook for 5 minutes more. Remove the sandwich from the grill, cut it in half, and serve.

CHAPTER 12 DESSERTS

Bacon and Chocolate Cookies

Prep time: 20 minutes | Cook time: 10 to 12 minutes | Makes 2 douncesen cookies

2¾ cups all-purpose flour
1½ teaspoons baking soda
½ teaspoon salt
12 tablespoons (1½ sticks) unsalted butter, softened
1 cup light brown sugar
1 cup granulated sugar
2 eggs, at room temperature
2½ teaspoons apple cider vinegar
1 teaspoon vanilla extract
2 cups semisweet chocolate chips
8 slices bacon, cooked and crumbled

1.   In a large bowl, combine the flour, baking soda, and salt, and mix well.
2.   In a separate large bowl, using an electric mixer on medium speed, cream the butter and sugars. Reduce the speed to low and mix in the eggs, vinegar, and vanilla.
3.   With the mixer speed still on low, slowly incorporate the dry ingredients, chocolate chips, and bacon pieces.
4.   Supply your smoker with wood pellets and follow the manufacturer's specific start-up procedure. Preheat, with the lid closed, to 375°F (191ºC).
5.   Line a large baking sheet with parchment paper.
6.   Drop rounded teaspoonfuls of cookie batter onto the prepared baking sheet and place on the grill grate. Close the lid and smoke for 10 to 12 minutes, or until the cookies are browned around the edges.

Fast S'Mores Dip Skillet

Prep time: 5 minutes | Cook time: 6 to 8 minutes | Serves 4 to 6

2 tablespoons salted butter, melted
¼ cup milk
12 ounces (340 g) semisweet chocolate chips
16 ounces (454 g) Jet-Puffed marshmallows
Graham crackers and apple wedges, for serving

1.   Supply your smoker with wood pellets and follow the manufacturer's specific start-up procedure. Preheat, with the lid closed, to 450ºF (232ºC).
2.   Place a cast iron skillet on the preheated grill grate and pour in the melted butter and milk, stirring for about 1 minute.
3.   Once the mixture starts to heat, top with the chocolate chips in an even layer and arrange the marshmallows standing up to cover all of the chocolate.
4.   Close the lid and smoke for 5 to 7 minutes, or until the marshmallows are lightly toasted.
5.   Remove from the heat and serve immediately with graham crackers and apple wedges for dipping.

Blackberry Pie

Prep time: 15 minutes | Cook time: 20 to 25 minutes | Serves 4 to 6

Nonstick cooking spray or butter, for greasing
1 box (2 sheets) refrigerated piecrusts
8 tablespoons (1 stick) unsalted butter, melted, plus 8 tablespoons (1 stick) cut into pieces
½ cup all-purpose flour
2 cups sugar, divided
2 pints blackberries
½ cup milk
Vanilla ice cream, for serving

1.   Supply your smoker with wood pellets and follow the manufacturer's specific start-up procedure. Preheat, with the lid closed, to 375°F (191ºC).
2.   Coat a cast iron skillet with cooking spray.
3.   Unroll 1 refrigerated piecrust and place in the bottom and up the side of the skillet. Using a fork, poke holes in the crust in several places.
4.   Set the skillet on the grill grate, close the lid, and smoke for 5 minutes, or until lightly browned. Remove from the grill and set aside.
5.   In a large bowl, combine the stick of melted butter with the flour and 1½ cups of sugar.
6.   Add the blackberries to the flour-sugar mixture and toss until well coated.
7.   Spread the berry mixture evenly in the skillet and sprinkle the milk on top. Scatter half of the cut pieces of butter randomly over the mixture.
8.   Unroll the remaining piecrust and place it over the top of skillet or slice the dough into even strips and weave it into a lattice. Scatter the remaining pieces of butter along the top of the crust.
9.   Sprinkle the remaining ½ cup of sugar on top of the crust and return the skillet to the smoker.
10.   Close the lid and smoke for 15 to 20 minutes, or until bubbly and brown on top. It may be necessary to use some aluminum foil around the edges near the end of the cooking time to prevent the crust from burning.
11.   Serve the pie hot with vanilla ice cream.

Frosted Carrot Cake

Prep time: 20 minutes | Cook time: 1 hour | Serves 4 to 6

8 carrots, peeled and grated

4 eggs, at room temperature
1 cup vegetable oil
½ cup milk
1 teaspoon vanilla extract
2 cups sugar
2 cups self-rising or cake flour
2 teaspoons baking soda
1 teaspoon salt
1 cup finely chopped pecans
Nonstick cooking spray or butter, for greasing
8 ounces (227 g) cream cheese
1 cup confectioners' sugar
8 tablespoons (1 stick) unsalted butter, at room temperature
1 teaspoon vanilla extract
½ teaspoon salt
2 tablespoons to ¼ cup milk
For the Cake
1.	Supply your smoker with wood pellets and follow the manufacturer's specific start-up procedure. Preheat, with the lid closed, to 350ºF (177ºC).
2.	In a food processor or blender, combine the grated carrots, eggs, oil, milk, vanilla, and process until the carrots are finely minced.
3.	In a large mixing bowl, combine the sugar, flour, baking soda, and salt.
4.	Add the carrot mixture to the flour mixture and stir until well incorporated. Fold in the chopped pecans.
5.	Coat a 9-by-13-inch baking pan with cooking spray.
6.	Pour the batter into prepared pan and place on the grill grate. Close the lid and smoke for about 1 hour, or until a toothpick inserted in the center comes out clean.
7.	Remove the cake from the grill and let cool completely.
For the Frosting
1.	Using an electric mixer on low speed, beat the cream cheese, confectioners' sugar, butter, vanilla, and salt, adding two tablespoons to ¼ cup of milk to thin the frosting as needed.
2.	Frost the cooled cake and slice to serve.

Lemony Smokin' Bars

Prep time: 30 minutes | Cook time: 1 hour | Serves 8 to 12
¾ cup lemon juice
1½ cup sugar
2 eggs
3 egg yolk
1½ teaspoon cornstarch
Pinch sea salt
4 tablespoon unsalted butter

¼ cup olive oil
½ tablespoon lemon zest
1¼ cup flour
¼ cup granulated sugar
3 tablespoon confectioner's sugar
1 teaspoon lemon zest
¼ teaspoon sea salt, fine
10 tablespoon unsalted butter, cut into cubes
1.	When ready to cook, set grill temperature to 180ºF (82ºC) and preheat, lid closed for 15 minutes.
2.	In a small mixing bowl, whisk together lemon juice, sugar, eggs and yolks, cornstarch and fine sea salt. Pour into a sheet tray or cake pan and place on grill. Smoke for 30 minutes whisking mixture halfway through smoking. Remove from grill and set aside.
3.	Pour mixture into a small saucepan. Place on stove top set to medium heat until boiling. Once boiling, boil for 60 seconds. Remove from heat and strain through a mesh strainer into a bowl. Whisk in cold butter, olive oil, and lemon zest.
4.	To make a crust, pulse together the flour, granulated sugar, confectioners' sugar, lemon zest and salt in a food processor. Add butter and pulse until just mixed into a crumbly dough. Press dough into a prepared 9" by 9" baking dish lined with parchment paper that is long enough to hang over 2 of the sides.
5.	When ready to cook, set the Traeger to 350ºF (177ºC) and preheat, lid closed for 15 minutes.
6.	Bake until crust is very lightly golden brown, about 30 to 35 minutes.
7.	Remove from grill and pour the lemon filling over the crust. Return to grill and continue to bake until filling is just set about 15 to 20 minutes.
8.	Allow to cool at room temperature, then refrigerate until chilled before slicing into bars. Sprinkle with confectioners' sugar and flaky sea salt right before serving. Enjoy!

Chocolate Chip Brownie Pie

Prep time: 20 minutes | Cook time: 45 minutes | Serves 8 to 12
¾ cup lemon juice
1½ cup sugar
2 eggs
3 egg yolk
1½ teaspoon cornstarch
Pinch sea salt
4 tablespoon unsalted butter
¼ cup olive oil
½ tablespoon lemon zest
1¼ cup flour

¼ cup granulated sugar

3 tablespoon confectioner's sugar

1 teaspoon lemon zest

¼ teaspoon sea salt, fine

10 tablespoon unsalted butter, cut into cubes

1.   When ready to cook, set grill temperature to 180ºF (82ºC) and preheat, lid closed for 15 minutes.

2.   In a small mixing bowl, whisk together lemon juice, sugar, eggs and yolks, cornstarch and fine sea salt. Pour into a sheet tray or cake pan and place on grill. Smoke for 30 minutes whisking mixture halfway through smoking. Remove from grill and set aside.

3.   Pour mixture into a small saucepan. Place on stove top set to medium heat until boiling. Once boiling, boil for 60 seconds. Remove from heat and strain through a mesh strainer into a bowl. Whisk in cold butter, olive oil, and lemon zest.

4.   To make a crust, pulse together the flour, granulated sugar, confectioners' sugar, lemon zest and salt in a food processor. Add butter and pulse until just mixed into a crumbly dough. Press dough into a prepared 9" by 9" baking dish lined with parchment paper that is long enough to hang over 2 of the sides.

5.   When ready to cook, set the Traeger to 350ºF (177ºC) and preheat, lid closed for 15 minutes.

6.   Bake until crust is very lightly golden brown, about 30 to 35 minutes.

7.   Remove from grill and pour the lemon filling over the crust. Return to grill and continue to bake until filling is just set about 15 to 20 minutes.

8.   Allow to cool at room temperature, then refrigerate until chilled before slicing into bars. Sprinkle with confectioners' sugar and flaky sea salt right before serving. Enjoy!

Bourbon Maple Pumpkin Pie

Prep time: 20 minutes | Cook time: 45 minutes | Serves 8 to 12

•

½ cup semisweet chocolate chips

1 cup butter

1 cup brown sugar

1 cup sugar

4 whole eggs

2 teaspoon vanilla extract

2 cup all-purpose flour

⅔ cup cocoa powder, unsweetened

1 teaspoon baking soda

1 teaspoon salt

1 cup semisweet chocolate chips

¾ cup white chocolate chips

¾ cup nuts (optional)

1 (8-ounce / 227-g) whole hot fudge sauce

2 tablespoon guinness beer

1.   Coat the inside of a 10-inch pie plate with non-stick cooking spray.

2.   When ready to cook, set the grill temperature to 350ºF (177ºC) and preheat, lid closed for 15 minutes.

3.   Melt ½ cup (100 g) of the semi sweet chocolate chips in the microwave. Cream together butter, brown sugar and granulated sugar. Beat in the eggs, adding one at a time and mixing after each egg, and the vanilla. Add in the melted chocolate chips.

4.   On a large piece of wax paper, sift together the cocoa powder, flour, baking soda and salt. Lift up the corners of the paper and pour slowly into the butter mixture.

5.   Beat until the dry ingredients are just incorporated. Stir in the remaining semi sweet chocolate chips, white chocolate chips, and the nuts. Press the dough into the prepared pie pan.

6.   Place the brownie pie on the grill and bake for 45-50 minutes or until the pie is set in the middle. Rotate the pan halfway through cooking. If the top or edges begin to brown, cover the top with a piece of aluminum foil.

7.   In a microwave-safe measuring cup, heat the fudge sauce in the microwave. Stir in the Guinness.

8.   Once the brownie pie is done, allow to sit for 20 minutes. Slice into wedges and top with the fudge sauce. Enjoy.

CHAPTER 13 BAKED GOODS

Egg White Glazed Pretzel Rolls

Prep time: 1 hour | Cook time: 20 minutes | Serves 6

2¾ cup bread flour
1 quick-rising yeast, envelope
1 teaspoon salt
1 teaspoon sugar
½ teaspoon celery seed
½ teaspoon caraway seeds
1 cup hot water
As needed cornmeal
8 cup water
¼ cup baking soda
2 tablespoon sugar
1 whole egg white
Coarse salt, to taste

1. Combine bread flour, 1 envelope yeast, salt, 1 teaspoon sugar, caraway seeds and celery seeds in food processor or standing mixer with dough hook and blend.
2. With machine running, gradually pour hot water, adding enough water to form smooth elastic dough. Process 1 minute to knead. (You could also knead it by hand for a few minutes.)
3. Grease medium bowl. Add dough to bowl, turning to coat. Cover bowl with plastic wrap, then towel; let dough rise in warm draft-free area until doubled in volume, about 35 minutes.
4. Flour a large baking sheet. Punch dough down and knead on lightly floured surface until smooth. Divide into 8 pieces. Form each dough piece into a ball.
5. Place dough balls on prepared sheet, flattening each slightly. Using serrated knife, cut X in top center of each dough ball. Cover with towel and let dough balls rise until almost doubled in volume, about 20 minutes.
6. When ready to cook, start the Traeger on Smoke with the lid open until a fire is established (4-5 minutes). Turn temperature to 375°F (191ºC) and preheat, lid closed, for 10 to 15 minutes.
7. Grease another baking sheet and sprinkle with cornmeal. Bring water to boil in large saucepan. Add baking soda and sugar (water will foam up). Add 3 rolls (or however many will fit comfortably in the pot) and cook 30 seconds per side.
8. Using slotted spoon, transfer rolls to prepared sheet, arranging X side up. Repeat with remaining rolls. Brush rolls with egg white glaze. Sprinkle rolls generously with coarse salt.
9. Bake rolls until brown, about 20 to 25 minutes. Transfer to racks and cool 10 minutes. Serve rolls warm or at room temperature. Enjoy!

Italian Focaccia

Prep time: 25 minutes | Cook time: 40 minutes | Serves 6

1 cup warm water (110- to 115-ºF / 43- to 46-ºC)
½ ounce (14 g) yeast, active
1 teaspoon sugar
2½ cup flour
1 teaspoon salt
¼ cup extra-virgin olive oil
1½ teaspoon italian herbs, dried
⅛ teaspoon red pepper flakes
As needed coarse sea salt

1. Measure the water in a glass-measuring cup. Stir in the yeast and sugar. Let rest for in a warm place. After 5 to 10 minutes, the mixture should be foamy, indicating the yeast is "alive." If it does not foam, discard it and start again.
2. Pour the water/yeast mixture in the bowl of a food processor. Add 1 cup of the flour as well as the salt and ¼ cup of olive oil. Pulse several times to blend. Add the remaining flour, Italian herbs, and hot pepper flakes.
3. Process the dough until it's smooth and elastic and pulls away from the sides of the bowl, adding small amounts of flour or water through the feed tube if the dough is respectively too wet or too dry.
4. Let the dough rise in the covered food processor bowl in a warm place until doubled in bulk, about 1 hour.
5. Remove the dough from the food processor (it will deflate) and turn onto a lightly floured surface.
6. Oil two 8- to 9-inch round cake pans generously with olive oil. (Just pour a couple of glugs in and tilt the pan to spread the oil.) Divide the dough into two equal pieces, shape into disks, and put one in each prepared cake pan.
7. Oil the top of each disk with olive oil and dimple the dough with your fingertips. Sprinkle lightly with coarse salt, and if desired, additional dried Italian herbs.
8. Cover the focaccia dough with plastic wrap and let the dough rise in a warm place, about 45 minutes to an hour.
9. When ready to cook, start the Traeger grill and set the temperature to 400F and preheat, lid closed, for 10 to 15 minutes.

10. Put the pans with the focaccia dough directly on the grill grate. Bake until the focaccia breads are light golden in color and baked through, 35 to 40 minutes, rotating the pans halfway through the baking time.

11. Let cool slightly before removing from the pans. Cut into wedges for serving.

Wheat Bread

Prep time: 30 minutes | Cook time: 1 hour | Serves 6

As needed extra-virgin olive oil
2 cup all-purpose flour
1 cup whole wheat flour
1¼ ounce (35 g) packet, active dry yeast
1¼ teaspoon salt
1½ cup water
As needed cornmeal

1. Oil a large mixing bowl and set aside. In a second mixing bowl, combine the flours, yeast, and salt.

2. Push your sleeve up to your elbow and form your fingers into a claw. Mix the dry ingredients until well-combined.

3. Add the water and mix until blended. The dough will be wet, shaggy, and somewhat stringy.

4. Tip the dough into the oiled mixing bowl and cover with plastic wrap.

5. Allow the dough to rise at room temperature-- about 70ºF (21ºC)-- for 2 hours, or until the surface is bubbled.

6. Turn the dough out onto a lightly floured work surface and lightly flour the top. With floured hands, fold the dough over on itself twice. Cover loosely with plastic wrap and allow the dough to rest for 15 minutes.

7. Dust a clean lint-free cotton towel with cornmeal, wheat bran, or flour. With floured hands, gently form the dough into a ball and place it, seam side down, on the towel.

8. Dust the top of the ball with cornmeal, wheat bran, or flour, and cover the dough with a second towel. Let the dough rise until doubled in size; the dough will not spring back when poked with a finger.

9. In the meantime, start the Traeger grill and set temperature to 450ºF (232ºC). Preheat, lid closed, for 10-15 minutes.

10. Put a lidded 6- to 8-quart cast iron Dutch oven - preferably one coated with enamel, on the grill grate.

11. When the dough has risen, remove the top towel, slide your hand under the bottom towel to support the dough, then carefully tip the dough, seam side up, into the preheated pot.

12. Remove the towel. Shake the pot a couple of times if the dough looks lopsided: It will straighten out as it bakes.

13. Cover the pot with the lid and bake the bread for 30 minutes. Remove the lid and continue to bake the bread for 15 to 30 minutes more, or until it is nicely browned and sounds hollow when rapped with your knuckles.

14. Turn onto a wire rack to cool. Slice with a serrated knife. Enjoy!

Pepperoni Pizza Bites

Prep time: 1 day | Cook time: 20 minutes | Serves 6

4½ cup bread flour
1½ tablespoon sugar
2 teaspoon instant yeast
2 teaspoon kosher salt
3 tablespoon extra-virgin olive oil
15 fluid ounce (435 g) water, lukewarm
8 ounce (227 g)pepperoni, sliced
1 cup pizza sauce
1 cup Mounceszarella cheese
1 whole egg, for egg wash
As needed salt

1. For the Pizza Dough: Combine flour, sugar, salt, and yeast in food processor. Pulse 3 to 4 times until incorporated evenly. Add olive oil and water. Run food processor until mixture forms ball that rides around the bowl above the blade, about 15 seconds. Continue processing 15 seconds longer.

2. Transfer dough ball to lightly floured surface and knead once or twice by hand until smooth ball is formed. Divide dough into three even parts and place each into a 1 gallon zip top bag. Place in refrigerator and allow to rise at least one day.

3. At least two hours before baking, remove dough from refrigerator and shape into balls by gathering dough towards bottom and pinching shut. Flour well and place each one in a separate medium mixing bowl. Cover tightly with plastic wrap and allow to rise at warm room temperature until roughly doubled in volume.

4. When ready to cook, set the grill temperature to 350ºF (177ºC) and preheat, lid closed for 15 minutes.

5. After the first rise remove the dough from the fridge and let come to room temperature. Roll dough on a flat surface. Cut dough into long strips 3" wide by 18" long.

6. Slice pepperoni into strips.

7.	In a medium bowl combine the pizza sauce, mounceszarella and pepperoni.

8.	Spoon 1 tablespoon of the pizza filling onto the pizza dough every two inches, about halfway down the length of the dough. Dip a pastry brush into the egg wash and brush around pizza filling. Fold the half side of the dough (without the pizza filling) over the other the half that contains the pizza filling.

9.	Press down between each pizza bite slightly with your fingers. With a ravioli or pizza cutter, cut around each filling- creating a rectangle shape and sealing the crust in.

10.	Transfer each pizza bite onto a parchment lined cookie sheet. Cover with a kitchen towel and let them rise for 30 minutes.

11.	When ready to cook, preheat the grill to 350ºF (177ºC) with the lid closed for 10 to15 minutes.

12.	Brush the bites with remaining egg wash, sprinkle with salt and place directly on the sheet tray. Bake 10 to 15 minutes until the exterior is golden brown.

13.	Remove from grill and transfer to a serving dish. Serve with extra pizza sauce for dipping and enjoy!

Irish Bread

Prep time: 15 minutes | Cook time: 45 minutes | Serves 8 to 12

As needed cornmeal
3½ cup all-purpose flour
1½ teaspoon sugar
1¼ teaspoon baking soda
1 teaspoon salt
1 cup buttermilk
Butter, to taste

1.	When ready to cook, set the temperature to 400ºF (204ºC) and preheat, lid closed, for 10 to 15 minutes.

2.	Lightly dust the bottom of an 8-inch round cake pan with cornmeal and set aside.

3.	Tear off a large sheet of wax paper and lay it on your work surface.

4.	Combine the flour, sugar, soda, and salt in a large sifter and sift onto the wax paper. Carefully lift up the sides of the wax paper and tip the flour mixture back into the sifter. Re-sift into a large mixing bowl.

5.	Lightly flour your work surface. Make a well in the middle of the flour mixture in the bowl and pour in 1 cup (240 mL) of buttermilk. Stir with a wooden spoon. Work quickly and gently as the carbon dioxide bubbles formed when the buttermilk hits the dry ingredients will deflate, the dough will

look somewhat shaggy. If the dough seems dryish, add a little more buttermilk.

6.	Turn out onto the floured surface, and with floured hands, knead gently for 10 to 20 seconds - just long enough to bring the dough bits together. (It will look more like biscuit dough than bread dough.)

7.	Form into a flattish round and transfer to the prepared pan. Flour a sharp knife, and deeply cut a cross in the top of the loaf all the way to the edge of the bread. Quickly get it in to bake, if it sits too long, it will deflate.

8.	Bake the bread for 45 to 50 minutes, or until it is browned and the bottom of the loaf sounds hollow when rapped with your knuckles.

9.	Remove the bread from the baking pan and cool on a cooling rack. Just be-fore serving, cut the loaf in half and then slice each half into thin slices.

10.	Serve with butter. Wrap leftovers tightly in plastic wrap or foil. This bread makes great toast. Enjoy!

Dinner Rolls

Prep time: 1 day | Cook time: 20 minutes | Serves 6

1 cup water, lukewarm
2 tablespoon yeast, quick rise
1 teaspoon salt
¼ cup sugar
3⅓ cup flour
¼ cup unsalted butter, softened
1 egg
As needed cooking spray
1 egg, for egg wash

1.	For the Pizza Dough: Combine flour, sugar, salt, and yeast in food processor. Pulse 3 to 4 times until incorporated evenly. Add olive oil and water. Run food processor until mixture forms ball that rides around the bowl above the blade, about 15 seconds. Continue processing 15 seconds longer.

2.	Transfer dough ball to lightly floured surface and knead once or twice by hand until smooth ball is formed. Divide dough into three even parts and place each into a 1 gallon zip top bag. Place in refrigerator and allow to rise at least one day.

3.	At least two hours before baking, remove dough from refrigerator and shape into balls by gathering dough towards bottom and pinching shut. Flour well and place each one in a separate medium mixing bowl. Cover tightly with plastic wrap and allow to rise at warm room temperature until roughly doubled in volume.

4.	When ready to cook, set the grill temperature to 350ºF (177ºC) and preheat, lid closed for 15 minutes.

5. After the first rise remove the dough from the fridge and let come to room temperature. Roll dough on a flat surface. Cut dough into long strips 3" wide by 18" long.

6. Slice pepperoni into strips.

7. In a medium bowl combine the pizza sauce, mounceszarella and pepperoni.

8. Spoon 1 tablespoon of the pizza filling onto the pizza dough every two inches, about halfway down the length of the dough. Dip a pastry brush into the egg wash and brush around pizza filling. Fold the half side of the dough (without the pizza filling) over the other the half that contains the pizza filling.

9. Press down between each pizza bite slightly with your fingers. With a ravioli or pizza cutter, cut around each filling- creating a rectangle shape and sealing the crust in.

10. Transfer each pizza bite onto a parchment lined cookie sheet. Cover with a kitchen towel and let them rise for 30 minutes.

11. When ready to cook, preheat the grill to 350ºF (177ºC) with the lid closed for 10-15 minutes.

12. Brush the bites with remaining egg wash, sprinkle with salt and place directly on the sheet tray. Bake 10-15 minutes until the exterior is golden brown.

13. Remove from grill and transfer to a serving dish. Serve with extra pizza sauce for dipping and enjoy!

Rizty Pizza

Prep time: 20 minutes | Cook time: 12 minutes | Serves 6

⅔ cup warm water (10- to 115-ºF / 43- to 46-ºC)
2½ teaspoon active dry yeast
½ teaspoon granulated sugar
1 teaspoon kosher salt
1 tablespoon oil
2 cup all-purpose flour
¼ cup fine cornmeal
1 large grilled Portobello mushroom, sliced
1 jar pickled artichoke hearts, drained and chopped
1 cup shredded fontina cheese
½ cup shaved Parmigiano-Reggiano cheese, divided
To taste roasted garlic, minced
¼ cup extra-virgin olive oil
To taste banana peppers

1. In a glass bowl, stir together the warm water, yeast and sugar. Let stand until the mixture starts to foam, about 10 minutes. In a mixer, combine 1¾ cup flour, sugar and salt. Stir oil into the yeast mixture. Slowly add the liquid to the dry ingredients while slowly increasing the mixers speed until fully combined. The dough should be smooth and not sticky.

2. Knead the dough on a floured surface, gradually adding the remaining flour as needed to prevent the dough from sticking, until smooth, about 5 to 10 minutes.

3. Form the dough into a ball. Apply a thin layer of olive oil to a large bowl. Place the dough into the bowl and coat the dough ball with a small amount of olive oil. Cover and let rise in a warm place for about 1 hour or until doubled in size.

4. When ready to cook, set Traeger temperature to 450ºF (232ºC) and preheat, lid closed for 15 minutes.

5. Place a pizza stone in the grill while it preheats.

6. Punch the dough down and roll it out into a 12-inch circle on a floured surface.

7. Spread the cornmeal evenly on the pizza peel. Place the dough on the pizza peel and assemble the toppings evenly in the following order: olive oil, roasted garlic, fontina, portobello, artichoke hearts, Parmigiano-Reggiano and banana peppers.

8. Carefully slide the assembled pizza from the pizza peel to the preheated pizza stone and bake until the crust is golden brown, about 10 to 12 minutes. Enjoy!

Baked Pumpkin Bread

Prep time: 15 minutes | Cook time: 1 hour | Serves 6

1 cup pumpkin, canned
2 eggs
⅔ cup vegetable oil
½ cup sour cream
1 teaspoon vanilla extract
2½ cup flour
1½ teaspoon baking soda
1 teaspoon salt
½ teaspoon ground cinnamon
¼ teaspoon ground nutmeg
¼ teaspoon ground cloves
¼ teaspoon ground ginger
As needed butter

1. In a large mixing bowl, combine the pumpkin, eggs, vegetable oil, sour cream, and vanilla and whisk to blend.

2. In a separate bowl, combine the flour, baking soda, salt, cinnamon, nutmeg, cloves, and ginger. Add the dry ingredients to the wet ingredients and stir to combine. Do not overmix.

3. If desired, stir in one or more of the optional ingredients (walnuts, dried cranberries,

raisins, or chocolate chips). Butter the interiors of two loaf pans.

4.   Sprinkle with flour to coat the buttered surfaces, and tap out any excess. Divide the batter evenly between the two pans.

5.   When ready to cook, set the Traeger to 350ºF (177ºC) and preheat, lid closed for 15 minutes.

6.   Arrange the loaf pans directly on the grill grate. Bake for 45 to 50 minutes, or until a skewer or toothpick inserted in the center comes out clean. Also, the top of the loaf should spring back when pressed gently with a finger.

7.   Transfer the loaf pans to a cooling rack and let cool for 10 minutes before carefully turning out the pumpkin bread. Let the loaves cool thoroughly before slicing. Wrap in aluminum foil or plastic wrap if not eating right away. Serve and enjoy!

Beer Loaf

Prep time: 20 minutes | Cook time: 1 hour | Serves 6

400 g all-purpose flour
2 tablespoon sugar
1 tablespoon baking powder
1 teaspoon salt
12 ounce (340 g) beer
2 tablespoon honey
6 tablespoon butter, melted

1.   Start the Traeger grill on set the temperature to 350ºF (177ºC) and preheat, lid closed, for 10 to 15 minutes.

2.   Spray a loaf pan (9x5x3 inches) (55x12x20 cm) with nonstick cooking spray and set aside.

3.   Put the flour, sugar, baking powder, and salt in a large mixing bowl. Whisk with a wire whisk to combine and aerate. Add the beer and honey and stir with a wooden spoon until the batter is just mixed. (Do not overmix.) If desired, gently stir in one or more of the optional add-ins.

4.   Pour half of the melted butter in the prepared loaf pan and spoon in the batter. Pour the remainder of the butter over the top of the loaf.

5.   Put the loaf pan directly on the grill grate and bake until a wooden skewer or toothpick inserted in the center of the loaf comes out clean, 50 to 60 minutes, and the bread is golden-brown. (Note: If using a glass loaf pan, the baking time might be shorter.)

6.   Let the loaf cool slightly in the pan before removing from the pan. Leftovers make great toast.

7.   Optional Add-ins: bacon, cooked and crumbled, 1 cup (100 g) grated cheese, red bell pepper and onion, diced and sauted in butter (¼ cup each), green onions, minced, dried herbs such as dill,

rosemary, mixed italian herbs, etc,.cracked black pepper, your favorite barbecue rub, such as traeger's pork and poultry shake, ground cinnamon, dry ranch dressing mix, coarse-grained mustard.

Walnuts and Zucchini Bread

Prep time: 10 minutes | Cook time: 50 minutes | Serves 6

1 cup walnuts, chopped
2 large zucchini
1 teaspoon salt
1 teaspoon ground cinnamon
¼ teaspoon ground cloves
¼ teaspoon baking powder
3 cup all-purpose flour
1 eggs
2 cup sugar
½ cup vegetable oil
½ cup yogurt
1½ teaspoon vanilla extract

1.   Grease and flour two 9- by 5-inch bread pans, preferably nonstick.

2.   When ready to cook, set the temperature to 350ºF (177ºC) and preheat, lid closed for 15 minutes.

3.   Spread the walnuts on a pie plate and toast for 10 minutes, stirring once. Let cool, then coarsely chop. Set aside.

4.   Trim the ends off the zucchini, then coarsely grate into a colander set over the sink on a box grater (or use the shredding disk on a food processor). You'll need 2 cups.

5.   Sprinkle with the salt and let drain for 30 minutes. Press on the zucchini with paper towels to expel excess water.

6.   Sift the flour, baking powder, cinnamon, and cloves in a mixing bowl or on a large sheet of parchment or wax paper.

7.   Combine the eggs, sugar, oil, yogurt, and vanilla in a large mixing bowl and mix on medium speed. (You can mix the batter by hand, if desired.) Add half the dry ingredients and mix on low speed; add the remaining dry ingredients and mix until just combined.

8.   Stir in the walnuts and zucchini by hand.

9.   Divide the batter between the prepared baking pans.

10.   Arrange the pans directly on the grill grate and bake for 50 minutes, or until a bamboo skewer inserted in the center of the breads comes out clean.

11.   Transfer to a wire rack and let cool for 10 minutes, then remove the breads from the pans. For best results, let the breads cool completely before slicing.

Cheesy Brown Sugar Muffins

Prep time: 15 minutes | Cook time: 12 to 15 minutes | Makes 3 douncesens mini muffins

1 package butter cake mix
1 package Jiffy Corn Muffin Mix
1 cup self-rising or cake flour
12 tablespoons (1½ sticks) unsalted butter, softened, plus 8 tablespoons (1 stick) melted
3½ cups shredded Cheddar cheese
2 eggs, beaten, at room temperature
2¼ cups buttermilk
Nonstick cooking spray or butter, for greasing
¼ cup packed brown sugar

1. Supply your smoker with wood pellets and follow the manufacturer's specific start-up procedure. Preheat, with the lid closed, to 375°F (191°C).
2. In a large mixing bowl, combine the cake mix, corn muffin mix, and flour.
3. Slice the 1½ sticks of softened butter into pieces and cut into the dry ingredients. Add the cheese and mix thoroughly.
4. In a medium bowl, combine the eggs and buttermilk, then add to the dry ingredients, stirring until well blended.
5. Coat three 12-cup mini muffin pans with cooking spray and spoon ¼ cup of batter into each cup.
6. Transfer the pans to the grill, close the lid, and smoke, monitoring closely, for 12 to 15 minutes, or until the muffins are lightly browned.
7. While the muffins are cooking, make the topping: In a small bowl, stir together the remaining 1 stick of melted butter and the brown sugar until well combined.
8. Remove the muffins from the grill. Brush the tops with the sweet butter and serve warm.

Quick Yeast Dinner Rolls

Prep time: 5 minutes | Cook time: 30 minutes | Serves 8

2 tablespoons yeast, quick rise
1 cup water, lukewarm
3 cups flour
¼ cup sugar
1 teaspoon salt
¼ cup unsalted butter, softened
1 egg
Cooking spray, as needed
1 egg, for egg wash

1. Combine the yeast and warm water in a small bowl to activate the yeast. Let sit for about 5 to 10 minutes, or until foamy.
2. Combine the flour, sugar and salt in the bowl of a stand mixer fitted with the dough hook.

Pour the water and yeast into the dry ingredients with the machine running on low speed.
3. Add the butter and egg and mix for 10 minutes, gradually increasing the speed from low to high.
4. Form the dough into a ball and place in a buttered bowl. Cover with a cloth and let the dough rise for approximately 40 minutes.
5. Transfer the risen dough to a lightly floured work surface and divide into 8 pieces, forming a ball with each.
6. Lightly spritz a cast iron pan with cooking spray and arrange the balls in the pan. Cover with a cloth and let rise for 20 minutes.
7. When ready to cook, set Traeger temperature to 375°F (191°C) and preheat, lid closed for 15 minutes.
8. Brush the rolls with the egg wash. Place the pan on the grill and bake for 30 minutes, or until lightly browned.
9. Remove from the grill. Serve hot.

Baked Cornbread with Honey Butter

Prep time: 10 minutes | Cook time: 35 to 45 minutes | Serves 6

4 ears whole corn
1 cup all-purpose flour
1 cup cornmeal
$^2/_3$ cup white sugar
1½ teaspoons baking powder
½ teaspoon baking soda
½ teaspoon salt
1 cup buttermilk
½ cup butter, softened
2 eggs
½ cup butter, softened
¼ cup honey

1. When ready to cook, set Traeger temperature to High and preheat, lid closed for 15 minutes.
2. Peel back the outer layer of the corn husk, keeping it attached to the cob. Remove the silk from the corn and place the husk back into place. Soak the corn in cold water for 10 minutes.
3. Place the corn directly on the grill grate and cook for 15 to 20 minutes, or until the kernels are tender, stirring occasionally. Remove from the grill and set aside.
4. In a large bowl, stir together the flour, cornmeal, sugar, baking powder, baking soda and salt.
5. In a separate bowl, whisk together the buttermilk, butter and eggs. Pour the wet mixture into the cornmeal mixture and fold together until

there are no dry spots. Pour the batter into a greased baking dish.

6.   Cut the kernels from the corn and sprinkle over the top of the batter, pressing the kernels down with a spoon to submerge.

7.   Turn Traeger temperature down to 350ºF (177ºC). Place the baking dish on the grill. Bake for about 20 to 25 minutes, or until the top is golden brown and a toothpick inserted into the middle of the cornbread comes out clean.

8.   Remove the cornbread from the grill and let cool for 10 minutes before serving.

9.   To make the honey butter, mix the butter and honey until combined. Serve the cornbread with the honey butter.

S'Mores Dip with Candied Pecans

Prep time: 10 minutes | Cook time: 37 to 45 minutes | Serves 4
Candied Smoked Pecans:
½ cup sugar
½ cup brown sugar
1 tablespoon ground cinnamon
1 teaspoon salt
¼ teaspoon cayenne pepper
1 egg white
1 teaspoon water
1 pound (454 g) pecans
S'mores Dip:
1 tablespoon butter
2 cups milk chocolate chips
10 large marshmallows, cut in half
Graham crackers, for serving

1.   When ready to cook, set Traeger temperature to 300ºF (149ºC) and preheat, lid closed for 15 minutes.

2.   In a small bowl, stir together the sugars, cinnamon, salt and cayenne pepper. In a medium bowl, whisk together the egg white and water until frothy.

3.   Pour the pecans into a large bowl. Pour in the egg white mixture and sugar mixture and toss to coat well.

4.   Spread the coated pecans on a sheet tray lined with parchment paper. Place the tray directly on the grill grate. Smoke for 30 to 35 minutes, stirring often.

5.   Remove from the grill and let cool. Break apart and roughly chop. Set aside.

6.   When ready to cook, set Traeger temperature to 400ºF (204ºC) and preheat, lid closed for 15 minutes.

7.   Place a cast iron skillet directly on the grill grate while the grill heats up.

8.   When the cast iron skillet is hot, melt the butter in the skillet and swirl around the skillet to coat.

9.   Add the chocolate chips to the skillet, then top with the marshmallows. Cook for 7 to 10 minutes, or until the chocolate is melted and marshmallows are lightly browned. Remove from the grill.

10.   Spread a handful of the candied pecans over the top and serve with the dip with the graham crackers.

Brown Sugared Bacon Cinnamon Rolls

Prep time: 5 minutes | Cook time: 25 to 35 minutes | Serves 6
12 slices bacon, sliced
⅓ cup brown sugar
8 cinnamon rolls, store-brought
2 ounces (57 g) cream cheese, softened

1.   When ready to cook, set Traeger temperature to 350ºF (177ºC) and preheat, lid closed for 15 minutes.

2.   Dredge 8 slices of the bacon in the brown sugar, making sure to cover both sides of the bacon.

3.   Place the coated bacon slices along with the other bacon slices on a cooling rack placed on top of a large baking sheet.

4.   Place the sheet on the grill and cook for 15 to 20 minutes, or until the fat is rendered, but the bacon is still pliable.

5.   Open and unroll the cinnamon rolls. While bacon is still warm, place 1 slice of the brown sugared bacon on top of 1 of the unrolled rolls and roll back up. Repeat with the remaining rolls.

6.   Turn Traeger temperature down to 325ºF (163ºC). Place the cinnamon rolls in a greased baking dish and cook for 10 to 15 minutes, or until golden. Rotate the pan a half turn halfway through cooking time.

7.   Meanwhile, crumble the cooked 4 bacon slices and add into the cream cheese.

8.   Spread the cream cheese frosting over the warm cinnamon rolls. Serve warm.

Traeger Soft Gingerbread Cookie

Prep time: 10 minutes | Cook time: 10 minutes | Serves 8
1¾ cups all-purpose flour
1½ teaspoons ground ginger
½ teaspoon ground cinnamon
½ teaspoon baking soda
¼ teaspoon ground cloves
¼ teaspoon kosher salt
⅓ cup brown sugar
¾ cup butter

½ cup plus 4 tablespoons granulated sugar, divided

¼ cup molasses

1 egg

1.   When ready to cook, set Traeger temperature to 325ºF (163ºC) and preheat, lid closed for 15 minutes.

2.   In a medium bowl, stir together the flour, ginger, cinnamon, baking soda, cloves and salt. Set aside.

3.   In the bowl of a stand mixer, cream together the brown sugar, butter and ½ cup of the granulated sugar until light and fluffy. Stir in the molasses and egg and mix on medium speed until combined, scraping down the sides of the bowl.

4.   Add the flour mixture to the bowl and mix on low speed until combined. Scrape the sides again and mix for 30 seconds longer.

5.   Roll the dough into balls, 1 tablespoon at a time, and then roll the balls in the remaining 4 tablespoons of the sugar.

6.   Place the dough balls on a baking sheet lined with parchment paper, leaving a couple inches between each cookie.

7.   Place the sheet directly on the grill grate and cook for about 10 minutes, or until lightly browned but still soft in the center.

8.   Remove from the grill and let cool on a wire rack. Serve.

Sweet Pull-Apart Rolls

Prep time: 5 minutes | Cook time: 10 to 12 minutes | Serves 8

⅓ cup vegetable oil

¼ cup warm water

¼ cup sugar

2 tablespoons active dry yeast

1 egg

3½ cups all-purpose flour, divided

½ teaspoon salt

Cooking spray, as needed

1.   When ready to cook, set Traeger temperature to 400ºF (204ºC) and preheat, lid closed for 15 minutes.

2.   Spritz a cast iron pan with cooking spray and set aside.

3.   In the bowl of a stand mixer, combine the oil, warm water, sugar and yeast. Let sit for 5 to 10 minutes, or until frothy and bubbly.

4.   With a dough hook, mix in the egg, 2 cups of the flour and salt until combined. Add the remaining flour, ½ cup at a time.

5.   Spritz your hands with cooking spray and shape the dough into 12 balls.

6.   Arrange the balls in the prepared cast iron pan and let rest for 10 minutes. Place the pan in the grill and bake for about 10 to 12 minutes, or until the tops are lightly golden.

7.   Serve immediately.

Baked Pulled Pork Stuffed Potatoes

Prep time: 10 minutes | Cook time: 50 minutes | Serves 6

4 russet potatoes

Canola oil, as needed

Salt, to taste

2 tablespoons butter, melted

3 cups pulled pork

1 cup Cheddar cheese

1 cup Mozzarella cheese

4 tablespoons Traeger Sweet & Heat BBQ Sauce

Topping:

Sour cream

Chopped bacon

Chopped green onion

1.   When ready to cook, set Traeger temperature to 450ºF (232ºC) and preheat, lid closed for 15 minutes.

2.   Rub the potatoes with canola oil and sprinkle evenly with salt. Place the potatoes directly on the grill grate and cook for 45 minutes, or until fork tender.

3.   Cut the potatoes in half and scoop the flesh out, leaving ¼ inch of the potato on the skin. Brush the inside of the skins with the melted butter and place on a baking tray. Place the tray on the grill and cook for 5 minutes, or until golden brown.

4.   In a bowl, stir together the pulled pork, cheeses and Traeger Sweet & Heat BBQ Sauce.

5.   Fill the potato skins with the mixture and return to the grill. Cook for 30 seconds, lid closed, or until the cheese is melted.

6.   Serve topped with the sour cream, bacon and green onion.

APPENDIX : RECIPES INDEX

Pepperoni Pizza Bites 105
Pig Pops 98
Pimentón Roast Chickens with Potatoes 68
Polish Kielbasa with Smoked Cabbage 59
Porchetta with Italian Salsa Verde 49
Pork and Mushroom Burgers 86
Pork, Pineapple, and Sweet Pepper Kebabs 47
Porterhouse Steaks with Creamed Greens 38
Potato Fries with Chipotle Ketchup 88
Prok-Rub Injected Pork Shoulder 45
Pulled Pork Nachos with Avocado 97

Q

Quail with Smoked Peaches 67
Quick Yeast Dinner Rolls 109

R

Rainbow Carrots and Fennel 96
Ranch Cheeseburgers 85
Ratatouille Salad 95
Red Pepper and White Bean Mashup 92
Reverse-Seared Sirlion Steaks 33
Reverse-Seared Tri-Tip Roast 30
Rizty Pizza 107
Rizty Summer Paella 76
Roast Whole Chicken 62
Roasted Breaded Rack of Lamb 57
Roasted Carrots with Pomegranate Relish 93
Roasted Chicken Thighs 63
Roasted Christmas Goose 68
Roasted Green Beans and Bacon 89
Roasted Lip-Smackin' Pork Loin 47
Roasted Mussels, Clams and Lobsters 83
Roasted Prime Rib 32
Roasted Stuffed Rainbow Trout 80
Romaine Salad with Bacon 88
Rosemary Lamb Chops 55
Rosemary Lamb Seasoning 26
Rosemary-Garlic Rack of Lamb 55
Rosemary-Garlic Smoked Ham 46

S

S'Mores Dip with Candied Pecans 110
Salad with Smoked Cornbread 78
Salmon with Avocado 76
Santa Maria Tri-Tip Bottom Sirloin 31
Seared Rib-Eye Steaks 43
Seared Strip Steak with Butter 42
Simple Espresso Brisket Rub 24
Simple Jerk Seasoning 25

Smo-Fried Spiced Chicken 64
Smoked Beef Brisket with Mop Sauce 42
Smoked Beef Burgers 85
Smoked Brats with Buds 57
Smoked Burnt Ends 30
Smoked Cheddar Cheese 97
Smoked Chicken Breast 61
Smoked Chicken Drumsticks 62
Smoked Chicken Quarters 62
Smoked Chickpeas with Roasted Veggies 91
Smoked Cornish Game Hen 66
Smoked Macaroni Veggie Salad 90
Smoked Marinated Pork Tenderloins 22
Smoked Mustard Baby Back Rids 44
Smoked Mustard Beef Ribs 32
Smoked Mustard Spare Ribs 44
Smoked Okra 94
Smoked Olives 89
Smoked Pastrami 32
Smoked Pork Chops 45
Smoked Pork Tenderloin 45
Smoked Rib-Eye Caps 41
Smoked Salt 29
Smoked Salted Cashews 97
Smoked Skinless Chicken Breast 61
Smoked Tomahawk Steak 40
Smoked Top Round Roast Beef 32
Smoked Traeger Brisket 23
Smoked Tri-Tip Roast 31
Smoked Turkey with Fig BBQ Sauce 71
Smoked Venison Steaks 55
Smoked Vodka Salmon 81
Smoked Wagyu Tri-Tip 37
Smoked Whole Chicken 60
Somked Cheeseburger Hand Pies 35
Somked Spatchcocked Turkey 66
Soy-Sugar Dipping Sauce 29
Spiced Breakfast Grits 47
Spiced Brisket 36
Spiced Tomahawk Steaks 41
Spicy Beef Tenderloin 34
Spicy Braised Lamb Shoulder 56
Spicy Chicken Skewers 69
Spicy Chunk Cheeseburgers 85
Spicy Coffee Rub 25
Spicy Smoked St. Louis Ribs 52
Sriracha Lamb Chops 54

Steak Skewers with Cherry BBQ Sauce 42
Stuffed Pork Loin wwith Bacon 49
Stuffed Pork Ribs 48
Sweet Mandarin Glazed Salmon 81
Sweet Potatoes with Marshmallow Sauce 91
Sweet Pull-Apart Rolls 111
Sweet Spiced Pheasant 66
Sweet- Spicy Cinnamon Turkey Wings 66
Sweet-Spicy Cinnamon Rub 25
Swiss Cheese Beef Meatloaf 35
Swordfish Steaks with Corn Salsa 78

T

Tandoori Chicken Wings 69
Tangy Coconut Dipping Sauce 29
Tangy Rainbow Trout 75
T-Bones Steak 33
Tea Injectable Chicken 61
Teriyaki Chicken Breast 65
Teriyaki Marinade 26
Teriyaki Shrimp Skewers 82
Teriyaki Wings 71
Texas Beef Shoulder Clod 35
Texas Smoked Brisket 38
Thai Tangy Dipping Sauce 28

Tomahawk Ribeye Steak 33
Traeger BBQ Half Chickens 70
Traeger Braised BBQ Ribs 53
Traeger Brisket 22
Traeger Grilled Pork Chops 52
Traeger Grilled Soft-Shell Crabs 83
Traeger Prime Rib Roast 22
Traeger Smoked Pork Sausage 57
Traeger Smoked Pulled Pork 21
Traeger Smoked Queso 51
Traeger Soft Gingerbread Cookie 110
Turkey Brine 27

V

Vegetarian Pesto 28
Vinegary Rotini Salad 90

W

Walnuts and Zucchini Bread 108
Wheat Bread 105
White Barbecue Sauce 28
White Fish Steaks with Orange Basil Pesto 79
Wild West Chicken Wings 65
Wood-Fired Halibut Fillet 73
Worcestershire Spritz 27

CPSIA information can be obtained
at www.ICGtesting.com
Printed in the USA
LVHW052234110721
692435LV00003B/31

9 781802 441697